ON TAP NEW ENGLAND

The Beer Connoisseur's Guide to Brewpubs, Restaurant Breweries, Craft Breweries, Cottage Breweries, and Brewery Inns

Cover photograph by Richard Lubrant, Atlanta, Georgia (404) 636-2308.

Acknowledgement

The creation of this book would not have been possible without the cooperation of many people, especially the brewery and brew-pub owners, presidents, brewers, managers, chefs, and wait staff, who provided me with the information necessary to create this book. I also want to thank the many subscribers to *On Tap, the Newsletter*, who alerted me to brewery openings and closings.

It would be impossible to mention all those who have provided assistance, but I will attempt to list as many as I can here.

Lynne Andersson, Louis Bregger; Sandra Clipp; Teri and Shawn Dunn; Bridgette and Michael Healy; Maria Johnson; Susan Killheffer; Roger Kirkpatrick; Richard Lubrant, Roger and Chris Levesque; Stephen Gosselin, Brett Peruzzi, and Dann Paquette, of the *Yankee Brew News*; Jim Robertson; and Jamie Spritzer.

ON TAP NEW ENGLAND

The Beer Connoisseur's Guide to Brewpubs,

Restaurant Breweries, Craft Breweries,

Cottage Breweries, and Brewery Inns

by
Steve Johnson

WBR Publications
Clemson, South Carolina

On Tap New England: The Beer Connoisseur's Guide to Brewpubs, Restaurant Breweries, Craft Breweries, Cottage Breweries, and Brewery Inns

ISBN 0-9629368-5-5   (pbk.)

WBR Publications
P.O. Box 71
Clemson, South Carolina 29633

tel. (803) 654-3360

fax. (803) 654-5067

TABLE OF CONTENTS

Foreword

by Donald Stephen Gosselin

I love New England. I couldn't imagine living anywhere else. Quite simply, there is no other place on earth where one can find year-round natural beauty, the lure of antiquity and the promise of classic beer. The first settlers must have felt the same way. Since the first Pilgrim walked down the *Mayflower* gangplank, some three and a half centuries ago, New England has been a place where nature, history, politics, and ale have been forever intertwined.

Great beer and renowned taverns have always been part of our unique way of life. Noble patriots once gathered in our taverns and inns and planned the birth and destiny of our nation. The Sons of Liberty, Ethan Allen and his Green Mountain Boys, soldiers of the Continental Army, and George Washington himself were among those who traveled from Burlington to Boston, from Portland to New Haven, stopping at taverns each night for victuals, shelter, local ale, and news. These New England traditions continue to this day--modern day politicians are sometimes found holding court, pint jars in hand, at our local pubs.

As our region grew, its seaports were thrown open to immigrants from afar. Settlers arrived from nearby Nova Scotia, New Brunswick, and Quebec, as well as from England, Scotland, Ireland, and Western Europe. Along with their distinct culture and way of life, each immigrant brought to New England his own taste for and adaptation of the malt beverage. Our brave mariners, fueled perhaps by seaport tankards of ale, went out to sea in ships and upon return, brought home tastes for novel brews. Each contribution, each adaptation, each style, combined to form a regional patchwork or mosaic of beer styles and offerings. For a great many years, New England beers took their inspiration and name from such places as London, Dublin, Edinburgh, and Munich.

I salute Steve Johnson for successfully completing a daunting task. He has traveled the old "post roads" of our region to locate our forty-odd breweries; he's sampled the offerings of each publican and, having returned to South Carolina, he's fought off the irresistible desire to relocate here. The reader is certain to enjoy the fruit of his labor. I am sure that most of you will be intrigued to the point of planning a beer vacation here.

When you visit us, you will find that, although we are all somewhat different, the beers, pubs, and people of New England all share common traits. We're as robust as the rocky coast of Maine, as enigmatic as an old salt, and as welcoming as a centuries-old inn.

Donald Stephan Gosselin
Winthrop, Massachusetts
Publisher
Yankee Brew News
New England's Beeriodical Since 1989

Introduction

New England is experiencing the flowering of a new age of brewing. Who would have ever thought it? From brewing by the Pilgrims to the closing of the last regional brewery in 1977, brewing had seemingly evaporated from the face of the map. It took seventeen years from the death of the last New England brewery to the opening of the first new age brewery.

The new breweries are not faceless industrial giants producing tasteless, overly-carbonated lagers. These are small enterprises producing flavorful, handcrafted brews, using natural, wholesome ingredients. The movement is revivalist in nature, rediscovering old styles of beer and old ways of making it. It is a grassroots movement--very little money is spent on promotion. Almost all the resources are being put into making flavorful beer. The new breweries have made a good product and the public has beaten paths to their doors.

You can visit the breweries, talk with the brewers, taste the beers, and enjoy the ambiance. Be sure to use all your senses--chew the grain, smell the hops, watch the boil, touch the equipment, listen to the blow off. This is a wonderful thing. Children of the sixties would call it a happening.

Although started on the West Coast, New England caught on to the craft brewing trend quickly, and has even become a leader in one aspect--cottage breweries. Bar Harbor Brewing first opened in the home of Tod and Suzi Foster in 1990. Since then, four other cottage breweries have sprung up around the region, and more have appeared in other parts of the country as well.

By and large, the new brewers are young and enthusiastic, dedicated to the art of brewing, and eager to talk to anyone and everyone who will listen to them. The new people behind the beer are just as important as the beer itself. You are lucky to be alive and to be able to experience what is going on. So, jump in your car and go to your nearest brewery (driving carefully, of course). You will be joining the thousands of other Americans who have already done so.

The New England Brewery Scavanger Hunt

For the more ambitious, those who want to visit as many breweries as possible, I have designed a scavenger hunt. Try to see if you can find as many of the sacred things which are listed below:

The Hull clock at Hartford Brewing, the porcelain Elvis Presley at New Haven Brewing, Boomer at Andrews Brewing, Katie at Lake St. George Brewing, the waterfall at the Sea Dog, the mural at Gritty's, the old bottling line at Geary's, George Bush's autographed picture at Kennebunkport, hospitality log cabin at Bar Harbor Brewing, "autographed" picture of Dwight D. Eisenhower at Lompoc Café, stained glass windows at John Harvard's, yard of ale at Cambridge Brewing, Burton Union casks at Commonwealth, harpoon at Mass. Bay Brewing, breathelizer at Boston Beer Co., Red Sox sign outside of Boston Beer Works, racing shell at the Cape Cod Brew House, light from Grand Central Station at Martha's Exchange, tankard outside of Portsmouth Brewing, the rubber duckie at McNeill's, statue of Athena at the Latchis Theatre, the catamount at Catamount Brewing, beer can collection at Mountain Brewers, back bar that isn't a back-bar at the Vermont Pub, Barley and Jasper Murdock at the Norwich Inn, and the malt smoker at Otter Creek Brewing.

Happy hunting,
Steve Johnson

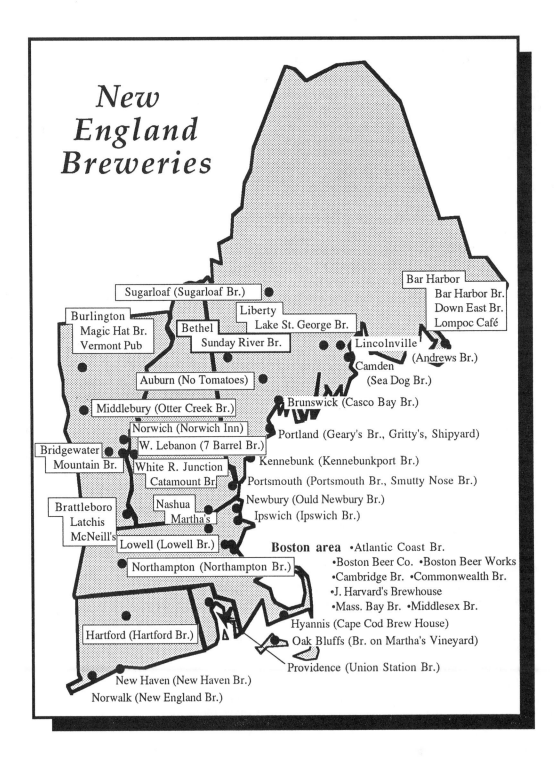

New England Breweries

Sugarloaf (Sugarloaf Br.)

Liberty
Lake St. George Br.

Bar Harbor
Bar Harbor Br.
Down East Br.
Lompoc Café

Burlington
Magic Hat Br.
Vermont Pub

Bethel
Sunday River Br.

Lincolnville

(Andrews Br.)

Camden
(Sea Dog Br.)

Auburn (No Tomatoes)

Middlebury (Otter Creek Br.)

Brunswick (Casco Bay Br.)

Norwich (Norwich Inn)

Portland (Geary's Br., Gritty's, Shipyard)

W. Lebanon (7 Barrel Br.)

Bridgewater
Mountain Br.

White R. Junction
Catamount Br

Kennebunk (Kennebunkport Br.)

Portsmouth (Portsmouth Br., Smutty Nose Br.)

Newbury (Ould Newbury Br.)

Nashua
Martha's

Ipswich (Ipswich Br.)

Brattleboro
Latchis
McNeill's

Lowell (Lowell Br.)

Boston area •Atlantic Coast Br.
•Boston Beer Co. •Boston Beer Works
•Cambridge Br. •Commonwealth Br.
•J. Harvard's Brewhouse
•Mass. Bay Br. •Middlesex Br.

Northampton (Northampton Br.)

Hyannis (Cape Cod Brew House)

Hartford (Hartford Br.)

Oak Bluffs (Br. on Martha's Vineyard)

Providence (Union Station Br.)

New Haven (New Haven Br.)

Norwalk (New England Br.)

What are Brewpubs and Craft Breweries?

The Brewpub

Brewpub is the generic term used to describe establishments which brew and sell beer for consumption on the premises. Beyond this basic definition there is an almost infinite variation on the theme. Some are old and quaint, others, modern; some are open and airy, others, small and cozy; some are primarily restaurants, featuring fine dining; some serve only their own beers, others have fantastic selections of draft and bottled beers from other breweries; some have substantial selections of wines, and still others offer the entire range of alcoholic beverages. However, they all provide a place where you can relax, socialize, and drink fresh beer, brewed on the premises.

Beginning with this book, I have divided brewpubs into three categories: (1) the true brewpub, (2) the restaurant brewery, and (3) the brewery inn (see chart on the following page). Many agree that a true brewpub should have a tavern-like atmosphere and should be primarily a drinking establishment. A restaurant brewery, as the name implies, places at least equal, if not more, emphasis on the dining. In recent years the provision of victuals has received increasing emphasis; so much so, that the true brewpub has almost ceased to grow in numbers. In fact, and this is based on purely subjective judgment on my part, there are only two true brewpubs in New England: **Gritty McDuff's** in Portland and **McNeill's** in Brattleboro. **Federal Jack's** of Kennebunk was originally a brewpub, but with the addition of the kitchen and the new emphasis on food, has changed to a brewery restaurant.

Placing an establishment in one category or the other wasn't always easy, and involved some close calls, as was the case of **Cambridge Brewing**, **Hartford Brewery** and **Boston Beer Works**. Actually, this is one of my favorite subjects of conversation while tasting a beer. So, while others are debating how the Sox will do next season, what's the best investment portfolio, or how many bittering units are in the IPA, I'm busy counting and commenting on the dart boards, bar stools versus chairs, and watching what comes through the kitchen door, versus what comes across the bar.

The brewery inn is the newest and easiest type of brewpub to define. Simply put, if they brew and serve beer on the premises, and provide a bed to sleep in (no, sleeping under a table doesn't count) then it's a brewery inn. Nationwide, brewery inns are among the nicest brewpubs to visit. And New England is no exception, with the lovely and historic **Norwich Inn** in Norwich, Vermont, and the art deco **Latchis Hotel** in Brattleboro. **Bar Harbor Brewing** is a quasi-brewery inn--they provide a room for rent right above the brewery on a weekly basis, but do not serve beer--another close call. So, if you would ever like to spend a pleasant week in Bar Harbor, contact the brewery.

The Craft Brewery

A craft brewery is the generic term used to describe a brewery making beer in small batches. It normally finds its way to the consumer through the normal distribution network, but in some cases, can be sold directly to the customer at the brewery (but not for consumption on the premises).

Again, beginning with this book, I have divided craft breweries into two categories: the industrial craft brewery and the cottage brewery (see chart on the following page). The former is a small brewery located in an industrial park or industrial- or warehouse-like structure, such as **Catamount Brewing** or

New England Breweries
by Category

Brewpubs

Gritty McDuff's	Portland, Maine
McNeill's Brewery	Brattleboro, Vermont

Restaurant Breweries

Boston Beer Works	Boston, Mass.
Cambridge Br.	Cambridge, Mass.
Cape Cod Brew H.	Hyannis, Mass.
Commonwealth Br.	Boston, Mass.
Hartford Brewery	Hartford, Conn.
John Harvard's	Cambridge, Mass.
Kennebunkport Br.	Kennebunk, Maine
Lompoc Café	Bar Harbor, Maine
Lowell Brewing	Lowell, Mass.
Martha's Exchange	Nashua, N.H.
No Tomatoes Br.	Auburn, Maine
Northampton Br.	Northampton, Mass.
Portsmouth Br.	Portsmouth, N.H.
Sea Dog Brewing	Camden, Maine
Seven Barrel Br.	W. Lebanon, N.H.
Sugarloaf Brewing	Sugarloaf, Maine
Sunday River Br.	Bethel, Maine
Union Station Br.	Providence, R.I.
Vermont Pub & Br.	Burlington, Vermont

Cottage Breweries

Andrew's Brewing	Lincolnville, Maine
Bar Harbor Br.	Bar Harbor, Maine
Lake St. George Br.	Liberty, Maine

Middlesex Br.	Burlington, Mass.
Ould Newbury Br.	Newbury, Mass.

Brewery Inns

Latchis Hotel	Brattleboro, Vermont
Norwich Inn	Norwich, Vermont

Industrial Craft Breweries

Atlantic Coast Br.	Boston, Mass.
Boston Beer Co.	Boston, Mass.
Br. on Martha's Vin.	Oak Bluffs, Mass.
Catamount Br.	White R. J., Vermont
Casco Bay Brewing	Brunswick, Maine
Down East Brewing	Bar Harbor, Maine
Geary's Brewing	Portland, Maine
Ipswich Brewing	Ipswich, Mass.
Magic Hat Br.	Burlington, Vermont
Mass. Bay Brewing	Boston, Mass.
Mountain Brewers	Bridgewater, Vermont
New Haven Br.	New Haven, Conn.
New England Br.	Norwalk, Conn.
Otter Creek Br.	Middlebury, Vermont
Shipyard Brewing	Portland, Maine
Smuttynose Br.	Portsmouth, N.H.

Large Industrial Breweries

Anheuser-Busch Br.	Merrimack, N.H.

Ipswich Brewing. The cottage brewery is located in a home. Brewing becomes so all-consuming for the cottage brewer, that the opposite could be said: the home is located in the brewery. New England has been a leader in the field of cottage breweries, beginning with **Bar Harbor Brewing** in 1990. Five cottage breweries now dot the region. It is interesting to note this phenomenon, as it is something that harks back to the roots of New England culture and industry, the cottage industry.

Another term you will hear bandied about is **microbrewery**, or simply "micro." A microbrewery is generally defined as a brewery producing not more than 15,000 barrels of beer annually. Although no New England craft brewery has yet reached this mark, it would seem foolish to eliminate one from the guide once it did.

Now that I have clearly defined what is what, let me muddy the waters just a little. Some breweries are both brewpubs and craft breweries, i.e., they brew and serve beer on the premises, AND they distribute to accounts off the premises. **Kennebunkport Brewing** is a good example of this.

The Contract Brewery

Contract breweries are yet another category. These are not really breweries, they are companies which either pay another brewery to make their beer, or have their own personnel use the equipment of another brewery to make the beer. Contract breweries are primarily involved in marketing and distribution.

While some people turn up their noses at contract breweries, I ask the question: "Is their beer good?" If it is, I have no argument with them. In fact, bottled **Samuel Adams Boston Lager**, brewed under contract in Pittsburgh, Pennsylvania and Portland, Oregon, I regard as one of the best beers made in the world. Any brewer would be envious of a line of beers like the Samuel Adams products (and maybe some of them secretly are). However, this book was designed as a travel guide. My rule is: no brewery, no entry in the book. The four contract breweries in New England are:

Coastal Brewing
106 Access Road
Norwood, MA 02114

Old Harbour Brewing
25 Hayward Street
Ipswich, MA 01938

Old Marlborough Brewing Co.
P.O. Box 1157
Framingham, MA 01701

Olde Time Brewers
402 Rutherford Avenue
Boston, MA 02129

In the Beginning

The Death of New England Breweries

When I lived in Connecticut, the New England brewing industry was on its death bed. In 1977, Hull Brewing of New Haven, the only remnant of a once proud industry, closed its doors for the last time. Although I lived not too far from the brewery, I barely noted its passing. You see, back then I was a Ballantine drinker. Ballantine had two redeeming factors: it was cheap and it had a little more flavor then most other beers I could locate.

The death of Hull Brewing was the final episode of a sad chapter in the decline. There had once been many breweries in New England (80 in 1890). They were household words like Narragansett, Frank Jones, Haffenreffer, and Hull. Then came Prohibition, next the Depression, and finally the move to lighter-tasting beer. Even though ale had been the drink of New England, even they lightened up. Fierce competition between breweries led to the closing of those who could not keep up. Breweries which succeeded brewed a lager, priced it cheap, and spent vast sums of money on advertising. The rest went out of business, including all of the breweries in New England. When it came to beer, Americans would not pay for quality. They just wanted an inexpensive, refreshing, alcoholic drink. True, the Anheuser-Busch plant was built in Merrimack, New Hampshire in 1970. But this was a St. Louis brewery, come to feast on the carcass of the beer industry in New England.

Give Me Liberty or Give Me Death

Then, something wonderful happened. In the 1960s Fritz Maytag bought the Anchor Brewing Co. out in San Francisco, just before it met the fate of almost all other breweries. It took Maytag almost a decade to put the brewery back on its feet.

I trace the beginning of the American beer renaissance to July 4, 1975. That was when Anchor Brewing released Liberty Ale. Liberty was very assertive, very flavorful, and fresh; made with generous portions of whole-leaf Cascade hops, a relatively new variety of hop developed in the United States. Sales of Liberty went far beyond Maytag's expectations. What started out as a beer commemorating the bicentennial of the American Revolution ignited a revolution itself, a revolution in beer flavor. The battle cry from 200 years before, "Give me liberty or give me death," acquired a new meaning.

Two years later, New Albion Brewing, the first modern American craft brewery, was born in Sonoma, California. Although New Albion failed, it served as an inspiration to others. Within a few years craft breweries and brewpubs were appearing up and down the West Coast.

From a Real Ale, to Phoney Beer, and Back Again

Before Liberty Ale, American beer had witnessed a gradual decline, from a flavorful, unfiltered, and natural product, to one which was ultra-filtered, pasteurized, and tasteless. Beer was brewed more for its transportability and shelf life, than for its flavor. The seeds of the downfall of flavorful beer can be traced back to the 1840s, when lager was introduced. Although there are thousands of flavorful brands of lagers, the trend was towards a lighter tasting, clearer beer, served at a colder temperature. Even though the lagers originally had plenty of hops, hops were gradually used to a lesser and lesser degree, until people couldn't see much difference between mass-produced beer and water (an off-color joke has been made about this similarity).

Late twentieth century America has seen a rapid change in tastes in regard to food and beverages. The trend has been toward more natural, fresher, and flavorful products. Coffee, tea, wine, bread, fruits and vegetables--you name it and the revolution in taste has had an influence on it. When the change first appeared in American beer, there were many doubters, including myself. However, my eyes were gradually opened to what was really happening. This was not an overnight fad. The new movement marked the end to the decline in beer flavor which had been going on for over 100 years. At the same time, a rebellion was beginning to shape up against faceless corporations which were turning out mass produced goods. Localism and regionalism were the name of the game. The two forces of flavor and regionalism have combined to create hundreds of local breweries around the country. At one time, in the year 1880, there were 2,272 breweries in the U.S. By the late 1970s the total number of brewing companies had dropped to about 40. At the writing of this book, the number was back up to 500. During the coming years hundreds of new breweries will open and it is likely that we will surpass the 2,272 mark set in 1880.

Go Yeast Young Man

The early eighties was a particularly frustrating period for the few people in the Northeast who appreciated good beer. The beer connoisseurs were typically homebrewers or individuals who had travelled either to Europe or the West Coast, where flavorful beer was available. Looking back now, we can see it only took a few years for the trend to catch on in New England. However, for those waiting for the revolution to take place, the situation seemed rather hopeless.

At this point, things began to ferment in New England. In 1981 came the first glimmer of hope, the Newman Brewing Co. opened in Albany, New York. Bill Newman's traditional style ales began to attract a small following in the Northeast. Rather quickly, a few individuals noticed what was happening on the West Coast and in England and started making plans to lead the way in New England. They came from all walks of life: a balloon salesman, a cello player, homebrewer and beer author, several Harvard MBAs, a fishery biologist, a medical equipment salesman, a high school English teacher, a physical education teacher, and several restaurateurs.

Several individuals and groups were working on projects at the same time. Jim Koch, a Harvard MBA and great-great-great grandson of a German brewmaster saw the trend coming and wanted to be the first to start a new brewery in New England. At this point, David Geary and Stephen Mason were already fairly far advanced in the fund raising and planning of their own breweries. After incorporating the **Boston Beer Co.,** Koch opted to have his beer brewed under contract at another brewery and to construct his own brewery later. With ready access to financial resources, he carried this out quickly. Samuel Adams Boston Lager was brewed at the

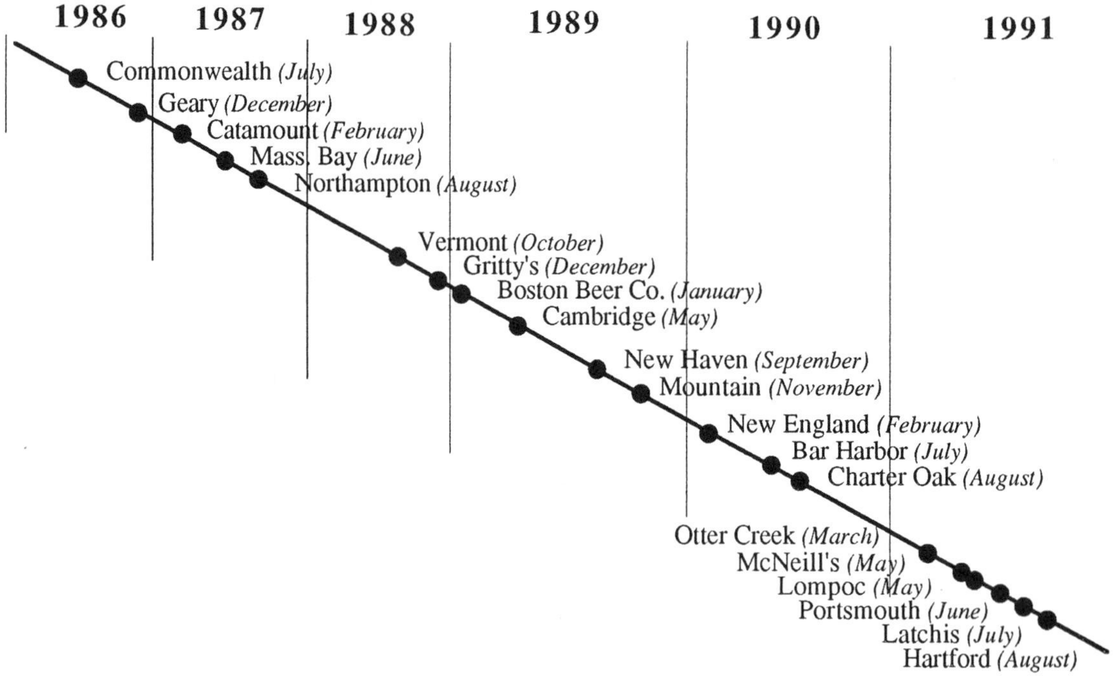

1986   **1987**   **1988**   **1989**   **1990**   **1991**

Commonwealth *(July)*
Geary *(December)*
Catamount *(February)*
Mass. Bay *(June)*
Northampton *(August)*

Vermont *(October)*
Gritty's *(December)*
Boston Beer Co. *(January)*
Cambridge *(May)*

New Haven *(September)*
Mountain *(November)*

New England *(February)*
Bar Harbor *(July)*
Charter Oak *(August)*

Otter Creek *(March)*
McNeill's *(May)*
Lompoc *(May)*
Portsmouth *(June)*
Latchis *(July)*
Hartford *(August)*

Time Line
of New England
Brewery Openings

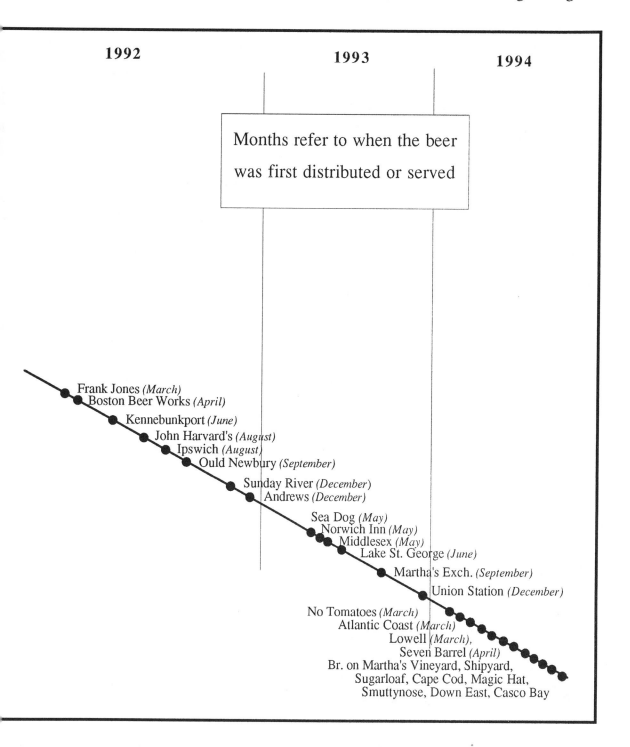

1992

1993

1994

Months refer to when the beer
was first distributed or served

Frank Jones *(March)*
Boston Beer Works *(April)*
Kennebunkport *(June)*
John Harvard's *(August)*
Ipswich *(August)*
Ould Newbury *(September)*
Sunday River *(December)*
Andrews *(December)*
Sea Dog *(May)*
Norwich Inn *(May)*
Middlesex *(May)*
Lake St. George *(June)*
Martha's Exch. *(September)*
Union Station *(December)*
No Tomatoes *(March)*
Atlantic Coast *(March)*
Lowell *(March),*
Seven Barrel *(April)*
Br. on Martha's Vineyard, Shipyard,
Sugarloaf, Cape Cod, Magic Hat,
Smuttynose, Down East, Casco Bay

Pittsburgh Brewing Co. in Pittsburgh, Pennsylvania, and was released in the Boston area on Patriot's Day, April 19, 1985.

The First Breweries

Many were quick to point out that New England still did not have its own brewery. While Geary and Mason were still working on constructing their breweries, an English entrepreneur by the name of Richard Wrigley entered the scene. With two Chinese-American partners, he fairly quickly constructed an authentic English brewery in downtown Boston and in August 1986 captured the prize of having opened the first new brewery in New England--**Commonwealth Brewing**. **Geary Brewing** (a craft brewery in Portland, Maine) followed in December and in February 1987 Mason opened **Catamount Brewing Co.** in White River Junction, Vermont.

While attention was being focused on these earliest of breweries, other groups were working hard on opening their own breweries. Richard Doyle and partners were building their brewery on the banks of Boston Harbor and opened **Mass. Bay Brewing** in June 1987. Peter Egelston and his sister Janet, returned to their native New England and opened their **Northampton Brewery** in Northampton, Massachusetts in August of the same year.

While this was going on, Greg Noonan, celebrated homebrewer and author of *Brewing Lager Beer*, had been making plans to open a brewpub in Burlington, Vermont. Unfortunately, laws regulating beer distribution in the state of Vermont did not allow for brewpubs. It took Noonan more than two years to get the legislation passed. He finally opened his **Vermont Pub and Brewery** on November 5, 1988. A month later Ed Stebbins and Richard Pfeffer opened **Gritty McDuff's** in Portland, Maine, the first brewpub in the state.

After several delays, the **Boston Beer Co.** began brewing test batches in December at the old Haffenreffer Brewery in the Jamaica Plain area of Boston. The first beers made in Boston were distributed in January of 1989.

In May 1989 the first brewery opened in Cambridge, Massachusetts -- **Cambridge Brewing**. By September the first brewery opened in Connecticut--**New Haven Brewing Co.** In November the third brewery had opened in Vermont--**Mountain Brewers**, in Bridgewater.

During 1990 three more breweries opened--**New England Brewing Co.** in Norwalk, Connecticut, in February; **Bar Harbor Brewing** in Bar Harbor, Maine, in July; and **Charter Oak Brewing** in Bristol, Connecticut, in August (Charter Oak closed two years later and was the first New England brewery fatality). By now breweries were opening regularly.

Craft Brewing Gains Momentum

1991 saw the opening of five breweries, including the first one in New Hampshire (**Portsmouth Brewing**). During 1992 eight breweries opened, including three in Maine. Six more opened in 1993, including the first brewpub in Rhode Island, **Union Station Brewing**.

Gazing into the Crystal Ball

1994 will see the opening of at least seven more breweries and perhaps as many as twelve total. Nobody knows what the final picture is going to look like before the dust settles. However, because of the long-term nature of the revolution in beer flavor, the growing demand for flavorful beer, and the minute percentage of the market that craft beer now occupies, I think the trend toward more small breweries will continue for the next 10-20 years.

Brewpeople

This book is about more than just beer. It is about people--people who make the beer, spouses of people who make beer, and owners and founders of companies which make the beer. As you read through the pages you will get to know the individuals who have made things happen; who have taken a dream and made it come true; taken a substantial risk; toiled long, hard hours; and proven to the nay-sayers that good beer is here and now.

David Geary, Greg Noonan, Jim Koch, Alan Pugsley, Marc Kadish, Richard Wrigley, Janet and Peter Egelston, and Tod and Suzi Foster--these and others are the people who founded the movement and who have flourished with it. But there are others who have had an influence who are neither brewers nor owners. This chapter provides a cross section of the many people who have made a contribution to the good beer movement in New England.

Will Anderson invented the term "breweriana" to describe all types of beer advertising and packaging. Born in Yonkers, New York, Will is the consummate breweriana collector. It started his senior year at Cornell, way back in 1962. His roommate piled up 24 cans of Ballantine Beer he had just emptied. Will looked at the stack and asked himself, "I wonder how many different kinds of beer cans there are in the world?" The rest is history. His first book was *Anderson's Turn-of-the-Century Beer Directory* (1968) followed by *Beers, Breweries, and Breweriana; The Beer Book ; Breweries of Brooklyn; The Beer Poster Book; Beer USA; From Beer to Eternity;* and *Beer New England.* Will has written on many other subjects as well. His books include *New England Roadside Delights, Mid-Atlantic Roadside Delights, Was Baseball Really Invented in Maine?,* and *Good Old Maine.* Will lives in Portland, Maine, and is an ardent Red Sox fan.

Patrick Baker is the "Big Daddy" of homebrew supply shops. In 1968, while working for Olin Chemicals in Connecticut, he started a mail-order wine-making supply business. Over time, this developed into a partnership with Nancy Crosby. Crosby & Baker is now the largest U.S. homebrew supply wholesaler. In 1986,

Pat conceived of the Beer Judge Certification Program and engineered a joint venture between the American Homebrewers Association and the Home Wine and Beer Trade Association to bring it into reality. He continues as co-director of the program. In 1979 Pat wrote the *New Brewers Handbook*, which has sold over a half million copies. In 1988 he wrote *Pat Baker's Beer and Bar Atlas* (the second edition should be published in 1994). In addition, Pat has written columns for various beer magazines. Pat grew up in Connecticut and studied chemistry at Yale University. He is now retired and lives in Keene, New Hampshire.

Al Diamon is a big fan of craft brewed beer. From February 1992 until August 1993 he conducted a daily radio talk show on a Portland radio station. About twice a month, on Fridays, he would interview a New England beer personality. The beer programs, on which he interviewed everyone from David Geary to Jim Koch, developed a tremendous following. He has published articles concerning craft beer in *Down East* and *All About Beer*. Al is a political analyst and a writer whose columns are syndicated in several Maine newspapers. Al is a regular at Gritty's where, he says, you can find more interesting people per square foot than anywhere in the world.

Alan Eames has been an advocate of good beer for a long, long time. In 1974 he opened Gleason's Country Store in Templeton, Massachusetts, where he stocked hundreds of exotic bottled beers from around the world. Nine years later Alan opened Three Dollar Dewey's in Portland, Maine, which gained a national reputation for its outstanding selection of draft beers. In 1986 he opened his second Dewey's in Brattleboro, Vermont. Dewey's later became Brattleboro's first brewpub, McNeill's Brewing. Alan has led several seminars on beer at the Culinary Institute of America in Hyde Park, New York and is currently director of the American Museum of Brewing Arts and History at the Oldenberg Brewery in Ft. Mitchell, Kentucky. He has written one book on beer, *The Beer Drinker's Companion* and is working on two more: *The Oldenberg Beer Drinker's Bible* and *Blood Sweat and Beers*. He has made numerous appearances in the media including two appearances on the *Today Show*. He now resides in Brattleboro, Vermont, and spends about seven months out of every year traveling to breweries, taverns, restaurants, and beer festivals.

Terry Foster has written several books and articles about beer, breweries, and beer making. His first book, *Dr. Foster's Book of Beer* dealt with the English beer scene, both commercial and amateur. More recently, he has written two books in the *Classic Beer Style Series*: *Porter* and *Pale Ale*. Terry is originally from England, but has resided in Norwalk, Connecticut, for several years, where he is a chemist.

Donald Gosselin is the publisher of the *Yankee Brew News*, a bimonthly beer tabloid covering New England. He was inspired by the *Celebrator Beer News* out of California and some of the New England homebrew club newsletters. Since the *Yankee Brew News* first came out in May of 1989 it has brought news of the brews and breweries to New England beer aficionados. Donald has been interested in unusual beers since he was a teenager and became inspired by the new American beers, such as those of Anchor Brewing and the Boston Beer Co., which were fresher than the imports. Donald, a native of Boston, is a member of the Boston police force. He resides in Winthrop, Massachusetts.

Chris and Roger Levesque, both New England natives, have dedicated their lives to collecting anything and everything related to craft breweries. They began as just regular breweriana collectors in 1980 and were bitten by the micro bug in 1986 while attending the East Coast Breweriana Association (ECBA) annual convention, hosted by the William Newman Brewery in Albany, New York. Since then they have visited more than 70 craft breweries and brewpubs. In 1990 the couple chaired the convention committee for the 1992 ECBA convention in White River Junction, Vermont, hosted by the Catamount Brewing Co. Next, in 1992, they formed the ECBA Micro Chapter (or Microbes, as they like to call themselves). This organization counts a membership of more than 150 and publishes a quarterly newsletter called *The Micro Connection*. If you are interested in craft-brewpub breweriana, contact them at *The Micro Connection*, P.O. Box 826, So. Windsor, CT 06074-0826.

William Mares has been an active homebrewer for many years and helped found the Vermont Homebrewers Association. A freelance writer, in 1984 he authored the book, *Making Beer,* about homebrewing. Bill lives in Burlington, Vermont, where he continues his homebrewing hobby, and is a regular at the Vermont Pub and Brewery.

Stephen Morris, wife Laura, and dog Guinness, made a tour of American breweries about 1980. Their trip is chronicled in Stephen's hilarious *The Great Beer Trek: a Guide to the Highlights and Lowlites of American Beer Drinking*. Stephen and Laura now live in Randolph, Vermont.

Pierre Rajotte has helped three cottage breweries establish themselves in New England. More than being just an equipment salesman, Pierre delivers and installs the equipment, coaches the new brewers, and trains them at a brewpub in Montreal. Pierre was born in Montreal and received a degree in mechanical engineering from the Ecole Technique of Montreal. After working for the Ford Motor Co. in Dearborn, Mich., Pierre returned to Montreal where he helped a friend open the first brewpub in the city, the Cheval Blanc. He is actively researching the history and evolution of brewing and has written several articles for *Zymurgy*. Pierre recently published a book, *Belgian Ale*. When asked which Belgian ale he prefers, he answers, "I have never tasted a bad one."

Stephen Stroud is a homebrewer from Medford, Massachusetts. Although several homebrewers have won more competition medals than he has, Steve has worked tirelessly behind the scenes to promote homebrewing and good beer. He made his first batch of homebrew in March of 1983 and since then has made hundreds of batches of beer. Steve made beer from malt extract for about four years, then switched to malt extract combined with some grain, and has been making beer exclusively from grain for about four years now. He has taken many medals at local and regional homebrewing competitions. In 1989 Steve took the national gold medal for his pale ale and was flown to Boulder, Colorado, by the American Homebrewers Association to brew a batch at the Boulder Beer Co. He has been very active in his local homebrew club, the Boston Wort Processors, an outstanding homebrew club. Steve has edited or co-edited their wonderful club newsletter for six or seven years and has held the offices of treasurer, secretary, and vice-president. Steve has also been very active in the Beer Judge Certicatation Program, which trains and tests homebrewing judges in order to provide consistency in the judging process.

Jonathan Tremblay is manager of the Cambridge Brewing Co. and founder and director of the Boston Brewers Festival. After attending the Great American Beer Festival in Denver, Colorado, he felt that New England needed its own festival to showcase the many fine beers being produced here. With a background in restaurant management, an appreciation for good beer, and his many contacts in the new beer business in New England, he was able to put on a first-class festival in Boston in the spring of 1992. The second annual festival was held the following May and has become the premier beer festival in New England.

Richard Wrigley founded the first new brewery in New England in July of 1986. An English entrepreneur, Richard came to America with the idea of opening brewpubs. He did it in a big way, opening Manhattan Brewing in New York City in July of 1984. This was the first brewpub to open in the state of New York since Prohibition. In July 1986 he opened Commonwealth Brewing in Boston. Within a couple of years he sold his interest in the enterprises and moved to Seattle, Washington, where he opened Pacific Northwest Brewing.

What is Beer?

Beer is a fermented beverage made from cereal grains. In the modern world it has been traditionally made from malted barley. Other grains used in brewing include corn (from which the South and Central American chicha is made) wheat, oats, rye, and rice (from which saké is made). These grains are frequently used in addition to barley to change the character of the beer. In the United States beer is still made from malted barley, however, the use of unmalted corn and rice as adjuncts has become almost universal by the larger breweries. Corn and rice serve to lighten the body, diminish the malted barley flavor, and decrease the production costs because both are less expensive then malted barley.

Fermented beverages can be made from things other than cereal. Wine, for example, is made from fermented fruit. Although some beers have fruit in them, such as the Belgian fruit lambics, they are still brewed with malted grain. Hard cider, although popular in many pubs, falls in the wine category, because it is made from apples. Mead, made from fermented honey, is neither beer nor wine.

Two other necessary ingredients in beer are water, which constitutes up to 92% percent of the finished beer, and yeast, which creates alcohol. The alcoholic strength of beer can range anywhere from less than .5% (in the so-called "non-alcoholic" beers) to a high of almost 15%. Yeast can also give an estery character to the aroma.

Samichlaus Bier, brewed by Brauerei Hurlimann of Zurich, Switzerland, holds the world beer alcohol record at 14.93% by volume. In New England we have Olde Ale, brewed at Commonwealth Brewing to 9.3%. Other highly potent beers made in New England include Hercules Strong Ale, brewed at Boston Beer Works; Samuel Adams Double Bock; contracted for the Boston Beer Co.; Hampshire Special Ale, brewed at Geary Brewing; and Old 76'er Harvest Ale, brewed at Gritty McDuff's.

A fourth ingredient in almost all modern beer is hops. Hops give bitterness to beer (although over-roasted barley can make beer bitter also) and serve to counterbalance the natural sweetness of the malted barley. Hops can also contribute greatly to the beer aroma, giving it a floral character. Before pasteurization and industrial refrigeration were invented, hops served somewhat as a natural preservative for beer.

Craft brewers tend to be purists. They want their beer to be made with the the best ingredients, without adjuncts, additives, pasteurization, or microfiltration. For this reason many of them adhere to the *Reinheitsgebot*, or German purity law. In 1516 William VI, Elector of Bavaria, declared that only water, malted barley, and hops could be used to make beer. Yeast was not included in the ingredients, but taken for granted. The purity law was amended later to allow malted wheat. It was so important to the Bavarians that they made the continuance of the purity law a condition to their joining the German Republic in 1919. The purity law was struck down in 1987 by the European Court for being protectionist in nature (i.e., not allowing the importation of many foreign beers, which used all kinds of dreadful things in their beer). Despite the reversal in the European Court, German brewers have pledged to continue to adhere to the *Reinheitsgebot*.

How Is Beer Made?

There is a lot more to making beer than just throwing some barley and yeast into water and letting it ferment. If this laissez faire approach is taken, and one doesn't mind off-flavors and inconsistent beer, it can be made this way. But if you want to consistently brew a particular style of beer with an unadulterated flavor and aroma, which your customers will learn to like and return for again and again, you will have to be methodical and exact in the way you brew it.

The barley must first be malted, dried, and then roasted. This is always done at a malting house, never at the brewery. The way in which it is roasted affects its flavor. The hops have a very important effect on the beer's nose and palate, and, of course, they must be kept fresh if they are to be any good. The type of water can also influence the quality of the beer, although some marketing departments for the larger breweries have overemphasized its importance to the beer's quality. The type of yeast used (and there are dozens of varieties) can profoundly influence the flavor of the beer.

Finally, beer is very prone to spoilage, caused either by bacteria or wild yeast. All of these things and more, can affect the flavor and character of the finished beer. For this reason, brewing has become a very precise science, but still allows for the "artist" to express him or herself in the formulation of recipes.

Once the beer has been brewed, it must be stored and dispensed properly in order to guard against spoilage. Being a very perishable product, if you don't pasteurize it, cover it with a pressurized blanket of carbon dioxide, and microfilter it, like the big breweries do, you have a product which begins to decline in quality almost immediately. Like a freshly-baked loaf of bread, good beer is delicate and short-lived. The best beer is fresh, unfiltered, unpasteurized, and unpressurized. This is what makes brewpubs so attractive. A fresh, well-designed, well-brewed, and well-stored beer is a thing of indescribable, yet simple beauty.

The Ingredients

Beer is made from the following four primary ingredients:

    malted barley
    water
    hops
    yeast

MALTED BARLEY

Barley is a wheat-like cereal grain. It is important because it provides starch which is converted to maltose and other malt sugars during the malting and mashing processes. Later, the yeast converts the maltose to alcohol and carbon dioxide. The barley also provides flavor and color. Indirectly, it provides head, carbonation, and body to the beer. So, you can see barley is a key element in beer.

Two types of barley are used in making beer: six-row and two-row. Six-row gives a higher yield in the field and is therefore less expensive; however, it gives a lower extract yield in the mash.

Barley

The two-row is prized by craft brewers for its superior flavor and efficiency of extraction in the mash.

The way in which the barley is roasted is extremely important to the flavor and color of the beer. Ranging from lightest to darkest, they are:

> pale malt (including klages and
>   Harrington)
> caramel (or crystal)
> Munich
> chocolate
> black

Another type of malt which is frequently used is cara-pils (or dextrin). A largely unfermentable malt, cara-pils adds body and head retention to the beer.

WATER

Even though water is the main ingredient in beer, it is the least important in its effect on the finished product. You can't make a world class beer on the merits of the water--that's where the barley, hops and yeast come in (not to mention the brewer's art). However, to make good beer, the water must be pure. The hardness or softness of the water can be important in several styles. A European Pilsner, for example, should be brewed using relatively soft water. But you don't have to go to Bohemia to obtain soft water-- you can treat your local water.

HOPS

Hops are flower cones which grow on the hop vine (*humulus lupulus*, the Latin botanical name). Only flowers from the female vine are used in making beer. Hops were originally used to help preserve beer against spoilage and to provide bitterness as a counterbalance to the sweetness of the malt. Because hops must be boiled in order to bring out their bitter qualities, many feel that the introduction of hops to beer making contributed to the stability of beers. Hops can also provide a wonderful bouquet to the beer. There are dozens of hop varieties and most beer is made with a blend of hops. The variety of hop, the quantity and quality used, and time at which it is added to the wort or beer can make subtle differences in the flavor and aroma of the beer. The major American beer brands typically have very small amounts of hops in them.

On the next page is a chart showing the major hop varieties used by craft breweries and their characterisitcs.

Breweries may use hops in three forms: fresh, whole hops; pelletized hops; and liquid hop extract. The whole hops are most desirable for their freshness, but they are more bulky to store and are perishable.

Bittering hops are added at the beginning of the boil in the brew kettle because they need a full hour to bring out the bitterness. Flavoring hops are added during the boil. Aroma hops are added at the end of the boil or in the case of dry hopping, to the fermentation tank.

YEAST

Yeast is a type of microscopic fungus. During fermentation the yeast consumes the maltose and other sugars, converting it to alcohol and carbon dioxide. The many varieties of yeast used in brewing fall into two categories: *saccharomyces uvarum* (bottom fermenting) and *saccharomyces cerevisiae* (top fermenting). Each variety, or species, of yeast imparts its own distinct characteristic

Hops

to the beer's flavor. Two beers, brewed with precisely the same ingredients and in the same manner, but with different varieties of yeast, can taste very different. Because of this, and because there is wild yeast present in the air around us, brewers take great care to protect their beer against contaminating yeast.

At one time all, beers were brewed with top-fermenting yeast. Top-fermenting yeast float to the top of the beer and work best at warm temperatures, typically 59-77°F (15-25°C). Ales (see chapter on beer styles) are

Hop Varieties

Cascade	bittering and aroma hop, flowery, citrusy, spicy aroma
Chinook	very bitter; has a wild character
Cluster	bittering hop
Fuggle	mild, pleasant aroma; traditional hop for English bitter
Galena	very bitter
Goldings	traditional bittering and aroma hop for English bitter; those from England have an earthy character
Hallertau	very flavorful; flowery, spicy aroma
Hersbrucker	only grown in the Hersbruck region of Bavaria
Mittelfrüh	only grown in the Mittelfrüh region of Bavaria
Mount Hood	similar to Hallertau; nice, clean aroma
Northern Brewer	all purpose hop; for bittering, flavor, and aroma; has a wild character; used traditionally in lagers
Perle	all purpose hop, for bittering, flavor, and aroma
Saaz	very fine, spicy, flowery fragrance; associated with European-style Pilsner beer; grown in Czechoslovakia
Tettnang	very fine, flowery aroma
Willamette	mild, slightly spicy

almost always made with top-fermenting yeast.

Bottom-fermenting yeast sink to the bottom of the beer and work best at colder temperatures, typically 41-54°F (5-12°C). It was on the European continent, where beers were lagered (stored) at very cold temperatures for several months, where bottom-fermenting yeast was first recognized and cultured. All lagers are made with bottom-fermenting yeast.

OTHER INGREDIENTS

Other ingredients used in making beer include malted wheat, adjuncts, additives, herbs, spices, and fruit.

An adjunct is an unmalted grain, including barley, wheat, corn, rice, or oats, used in addition to the malted barley. In the United States adjuncts have been used by the large breweries to lighten the flavor and body of the beer.

Additives are chemicals, synthetic or natural, added to beer during brewing, packaging, or storing for a variety of reasons. Various sugars, such as lactose and sucrose, which are non-fermentable, are sometimes added to provide body and sweetness. Various types of clarifying aids are used, including Irish moss, isinglass, papain, and polyclar. Enzymes are sometimes added to give beer body and aid in head retention. Burton water salts are sometimes added in order to duplicate the hard water found in Burton-upon-Trent, England, a brewing town famous for its pale ales. Heading liquids are sometimes used to promote foaming action.

A variety of herbs, spices, and fruit have been used in making beer over the years. These include cinnamon, ginger, cherries, raspberries, coriander, peppers, licorice, and spruce. Brewpubs are likely to experiment with these different ingredients.

The Process

When you visit a craft brewery or brewpub you will see many tanks, hoses, and other unfamiliar contraptions in the brewing area. The following explanation is designed to provide you with the fundamentals of the brewing process so that you can make some sense of what you are looking at. Many brewpubs label the various tanks, which makes it easier to understand what's going on. But, to make things confusing, different brewpubs use different names for the same piece of equipment. The alternative names are provided in the text which follows. For a fairly complete description of the brewing process, see under Commonwealth Brewing later in this book.

If you are going to tour a brewery at a time other than when the regular tours are conducted, always call in advance. In fact, it's not a bad idea to let them know you are coming even for a regular tour. Brewing staff are usually happy to accommodate you if they can, but it may be difficult to fit a tour into the brewing schedule. Please realize that the brewing staff are doing you a favor in taking time out from their busy schedule to show you around.

One thing you won't see at a brewpub are fields of barley, like you would see a vineyard at a winery. This is because the orientation of wineries and breweries are toward the opposite ends of the process. Wineries are oriented toward the beginning of the process: the growing of the grapes; whereas, breweries are oriented toward the other end: the consumption of the beer. Logically, wineries exist where the grapes grow best. And also logically, breweries are situated near the consumer. For this reason, breweries will never grow their own raw ingredients nearby because you can't grow enough barley and hops in the cities and towns where the consumers are located.

Major Steps in the Brewing Process

-> malting

   -> roasting

      -> milling

         -> mashing

            -> boiling

               -> fermenting

                  -> maturing

                     -> kegging, bottling

Because of the space required, brewpubs don't malt their barley either. So, in understanding the making of beer, remember that the process within the brewery usually begins with the milling of the malted barley (see chart above).

MALTING

Malting is a process of steeping the barley in order that it sprout (germinate) and then drying the sprouted barley. This process converts proteins to starch, converts the starches already present into a more soluble form, and activitates the enzymes. The barley grains are sorted by size, soaked in water, removed and then spread out and allowed to sprout for about a week.

ROASTING

The malt is next dried and roasted in order to arrest the sprouting process. The longer they are roasted in the **kiln,** the darker and more caramelized the malt will become. This will affect the color and flavor of the beer. The malt is then sieved to remove the roots.

MILLING

Here is where the process typically begins at a craft brewery. Malt is taken from the **malt silo** or from paper bags and milled (or ground) in a **roller mill** to produce grist. Milling facilitates the extraction of sugars in the next stage. The silo is usually located outside and to the rear of the brewery. Many breweries purchase pre-milled malt, and so begin with the mashing stage.

MASHING

Next, the grist is transferred to the **mash tun** (or **mash-lauter tun**) where it is soaked and stirred in hot water of about 150°F (66°C) for one to two hours. The slurry of hot water and malt is called "mash." Mashing converts more of the starch to sugar and extracts the sugar and other solubles from the grist. At higher temperatures less starch is converted to simple sugars, which makes a sweeter, fuller-bodied beer. At lower temperatures more

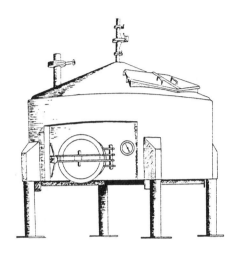

The Mash Tun

starch is converted to simple sugars, which produces a drier, light-bodied beer.

The mash tun is drained of solubles and the remaining sediment is sparged (sprayed) with hot water in order to extract as many solubles as possible. The sweet liquid which drains out through strainer plates in the bottom of the mash tun is called wort (rhymes with dirt).

The hot water for the mash is usually, but not always, stored in hot water tanks, called hot "**liquor tanks**" by brewers. Some brewpubs heat the water for the mash in the brew kettle and then transfer it to the mash tun.

Some brewpubs do not mill or mash their own grains. Instead, they use malt extract, a molasses-like substance, which they put directly into the brew kettle.

BOILING

The wort is transferred to the **brew kettle** (or **copper**) where it is boiled with the hops for about one-two hours. Bittering hops are added at the beginning of the boil. Flavoring

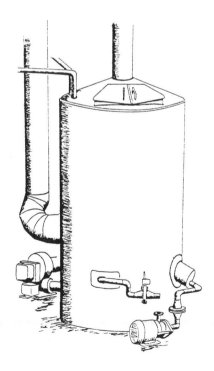

The Brew Kettle

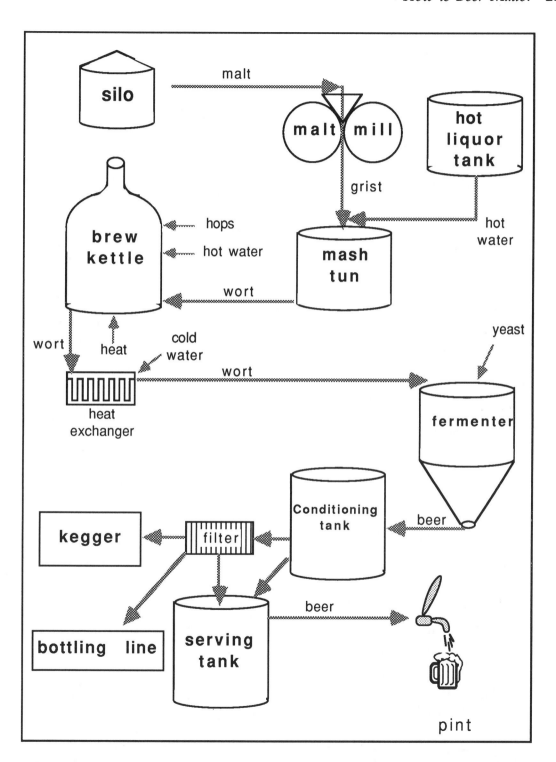

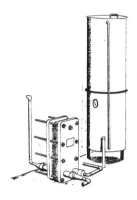

The Heat Exchanger & Hot Water Recovery Tank

hops may be added at any time, and aroma hops are added near the end of the boil. Some breweries dry hop their beer for extra aroma. In dry hopping, the hops are added after the boil is finished. The wort is transferred to the **whirlpool** where unwanted protein, hops, and other solids are separated through centrifugal force. Next the wort is forced to cool rapidly through a **heat exchanger** (or **cooler** or **wort chiller**).

FERMENTING

When the wort has cooled, it is transferred to a **fermentation tank** (also called **uni-tank**, **CIP tank** (CIP = clean in place), **fermenter**, or **primary**) and the yeast is pitched (added) to the brew. The wort is briefly stirred in order to provide oxygen to the yeast.

Most microbreweries use closed fermentation tanks; however, some use open fermentation vessels, where you can actually see the beer fermenting. At this stage you can see a great deal of foam at the top of the beer. What you can't see is the sediment (called "trub," rhymes with tube) forming at the bottom of the tank and the carbon dioxide being released into the air.

MATURING

When primary fermentation is complete, usually within 2-4 days, the green beer is transferred to a **conditioning tank** (also called **bright beer tank** (in a bright tank the beer is pressurized with CO_2), **serving tank**, **holding tank**, **finishing tank**, or **secondary**). Here the beer continues to ferment, but at a much reduced rate. The beer clarifies as small particles settle out and the flavors mature and blend. Conditioning tanks are closed; thus, as the beer ferments and the carbon dioxide can no longer escape, the beer becomes carbonated naturally. Conditioning may take anywhere from a few days to several months. The German lagering method, in which the beer is held for a longer cold conditioning period, results in a palate very low in yeast effects (i.e. esters), while the ale method, in which the beer is typically only matured at warmer temperatures, and only for a few days or a week or two, produces a more estery beer.

At this point the brewer has the option of filtering the beer before it is served or packaged. Filtration is usually done with diatomaceous earth. This is made up of microscopic skeletal remains of marine animals and does a very good job of filtering.

Brewpubs usually dispense their beer from serving tanks. Most pump the beer with CO_2 pressure (some with a mixture of CO_2 and nitrogen). If they opt to serve it unfiltered and unpressurized it is known as "real" beer and can be served with either gravity flow taps or with handpumps.

KEGGING, BOTTLING

An alternative way to package the beer is to put it into metal **kegs**. This way it can be tapped on premise or shipped to another bar or restaurant. Kegging is generally done by

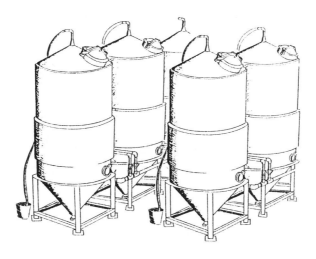

The Fermentation Tanks

adding carbon dioxide under pressure to the keg. Real beer does not use additional carbon dioxide and a wooden peg is placed in the bung, allowing the beer to continue to ferment and condition in the keg. This is sometimes called "cask conditioned" beer.

In addition, many microbreweries bottle their beers, a more expensive and time-consuming way to package the beer than kegging. Much of this bottled beer is pasteurized. However, some microbreweries do not pasteurize their bottled beer. This beer still has live yeast in it and is said to be "bottle conditioned." Cask beer and bottle-conditioned beer is much more delicate and perishable than pasteurized and kegged beer.

Most brewpubs offer their beers in bottles to customers to take home. Usually these bottles have been hand-filled and capped, a very labor-intensive process. As these beers have not been pasteurized, I recommend that they be consumed within a few days.

Some brewpubs will also fill buckets, jugs, or what have you, for take out. This beer should be consumed as soon as you get home (but not on the way).

What Beer Tastes Like

If you are confused about how beer should taste, you are not alone. Americans have forgotten what beer tastes like. Not only is the public confused, there are even a few brewers who haven't the foggiest idea what style they are trying to make. For this reason, it should be mandatory that every homebrewer who becomes a commercial brewer be given a six-week, working vacation to Europe to visit breweries, pubs, and beer halls to find out how the real thing is made and how it tastes. The itinerary should include England, Scotland, Ireland, Belgium, Northern France, Germany, and the Czech Republic. Undoubtedly, this suggestion will meet with favor among the new brewers.

It is important to remember that there are dozens of styles of beer, each one tasting different from the next (see the chapter which follows on styles). It takes time and dedication to become familiar with the style profiles and learn to recognize them. But, it certainly is enjoyable research.

Once you become knowledgeable, you will begin to realize there are three problems which make style identification difficult. First, it is not uncommon for a brewer to apply the wrong name to his or her beer. For this, I will forgive them. I remember, after trying a thick, malty, sweet ale, I told the brewer how much I liked his Scotch ale. He replied, "That wasn't a Scotch ale, that was a bitter." Could have fooled me!

Second, sometimes a brewer will experiment with recipes, with little thought to style, and then give it a name which gives no clue what style it is. These beers can be the source of interesting conversations (or arguments), which usually turn out to be inconclusive.

Third, there are many beers which are poorly made. When I began drinking imported and craft-made beers I was thrilled with the different flavors which assaulted my tongue. Later I learned that some of these beers were very poorly made and had flavors which should not have been there. These are known as off-flavors.

For the purpose of analyzing the taste of beer, we describe the taste in the order that we perceive it. Thus, we have the foretaste (or entry), which is the taste we perceive as the beer enters our mouth; followed by mid-taste, the taste we perceive as we swirl or hold the beer in our mouth; and the aftertaste (or finish), the taste left in our mouth after we swallow it.

Just to make things confusing, perception of flavor is different in everyone's palate. Sweet beer to one person may be dry to the second and sour to the third. So, don't be a beer snob and tell everyone who disagrees with you that they are wrong. Remember, you are drinking for yourself, not for everyone else.

To bring out the full aroma and flavor of beer, it must not be served too cold. Following are suggested serving temperatures for different styles of beers:

Serving Temperatures

category	temperature
ordinary beers	40°F - 45°F
quality lagers	45°F - 50°F
quality ales	50°F - 55°F
quality stouts/porters	55°F - 60°F

Major Flavor Components

malty - a disproportionately large amount of verbiage has been written about the minor flavors and off-flavors of beer. Little can be found about the major flavor, which is malt. Of course, to be part of the beer intelligentsia, you must never say something like, "Gee, that was a nice, malty beer." That would be like saying *A Portrait of the Artist as a Young Man* was a really good read. Still, identifying the malt is a good start.

Malt tastes like cereal, like cooked grain. It's that delicious aroma you smell at a brewery when the brewer is mashing. If you like that smell, you should love beer. To get a pure, malty flavor or aroma, you want to try a darker beer which is lightly hopped, such as an English brown ale or a Vienna-style lager; many porters, dark lagers, bocks, and Scotch ales can be good examples too, if not too heavily hopped.

bitter - bitterness in beer is usually derived from the hops. It can also come from highly roasted or burnt barley (either malted or unmalted). Bitterness is perceived toward the back of the tongue, so the bitterness comes on stronger near the finish.

hoppy - in addition to bitterness, hops also impart flavor and aroma to beer. It is possible for a beer to be bitter, but not very hoppy; hoppy, but not very bitter; and both hoppy and bitter.

Adding hops at the beginning of the boil adds bitterness, but very little flavor. Adding hops near the end of the brew (or boil) tends to develop hop flavor and some aroma. Adding hops during fermentation (after the boil) [called "dry hopping"] develops a hop aroma.

Hops impart varying degrees of floral, vegetal, bitter, tangy, spicy, citrusy, piny, and earthy flavors and aromas, and also counterbalance the sweetness of the malt.

sweet - dry - beers are either sweet, dry, or a combination of these factors. Beer is sweet because of the maltose from which it is made. The longer it ferments, the more maltose is consumed by the yeast, and the drier it becomes. Also, hops tend to counter-balance the sweetness of the malt. Most beers have both sweet and dry components. Sweetness tends to be perceived in the foretaste, as sweetness is perceived toward the front of the tongue. A normal profile is a sweet entry, followed by increasing dryness.

Other Flavor Components

alcoholic - creates a warming sensation in the mouth or throat. I can smell it too (beats me how to describe it).

caramel - comes from deeply roasted malt and/or boiling a small amount of the wort at a high temperature.

chalky - I sometimes pick this up when tasting an oatmeal stout.

chocolate - porters and stouts frequently have a chocolaty character to them. Even some lagers do too. This comes from the deeply roasted malt.

clovy - usually smelled or tasted in a weizen bier. This comes from the type of yeast used.

coffee - comes from deeply roasted, unmalted barley. Frequently apparent in stouts, sometimes in porters.

estery, fruity - comes from the yeast; frequently noted in fresh, unfiltered ales.

floral - comes from the hops; like fresh flowers.

nutty - deeply roasted malts sometimes have a nutty character.

roasted barley - similar to malted barley, but drier and harsher (sometimes a burnt flavor).

smoky - comes from smoked malts.

tart - slightly acid, lemony.

toffee - a sweet, caramely, nutty flavor.

woody - from beer conditioned in wood (in some cases, the brewer may add wood chips to the fermenter).

Off-Flavors and Aromas

Just like bread, beer is a delicate, perishable product and if not treated properly, off-flavors can develop very quickly. Beginning with fermentation, all equipment should be squeaky clean, or wild yeast and/or bacteria will develop. Exposure to oxygen promotes the growth of micro-organisms and spoilage. Lack of a vigorous fermentation is another cause for bacterial or yeast infection. Fermenting, conditioning, and storing beer at temperatures which are too high also tends to increase the rate of spoilage. Improper pH in the fermenter can promote the growth of bacteria. Light is an enemy of beer also (see below under skunky).

Beer will become stale in a matter of weeks or months; so, drink it fresh. Cask-conditioned ales, which are unfiltered and have no artificial CO_2 pressure to protect them, should be consumed within a few hours or days from the time they are tapped.

A well-run pub cleans its lines before serving to the first customer. If you ever want to experience the taste of rotten beer, try the first pour of the day from unpurged, unrefrigerated beer lines.

astringent - dry is okay, but astringent makes your mouth pucker.

buttery, butterscotchy - this is unacceptable in a lager, but a certain amount is okay in an ale. Technical term; diacetyl.

canned corn - technical term; dimethyl sulfide (DMS).

cardboardy, papery, musty - found in old, oxidized beer.

grassy - smells or tastes like grass or hay.

grainy/husky - harsh, dry, puckery.

medicinal - like cough syrup.

metalic - a bitter, metal taste.

phenolic - clovy, banana-like, or plastic tasting. Caused by bacteria or wild yeast.

skunky - cabbagy, a little like a skunk; caused by exposure to ultraviolet light.

sour, lactic, vinegary - comes from bacterial infection, considered a plus in a hefe weizen and many Belgian wheat ales.

sulfury - like sulfur or rotten eggs; if very strong, like a malfunctioning septic system. Caused by hydrogen sulfide. Beer served before its conditioning is complete may be sulfury.

Beer Styles

Variety has been a key element in the American beer renaissance. It was not too long ago that our choices among American-brewed beers were American Pilsner, American Pilsner, and American Pilsner. With these boring, watered-down choices it was only a matter of time before some Americans enthusiastically turned to the styles being revived by craft breweries and brewpubs.

As you visit brewpubs you will experience an amazing, even confusing, variety of beer styles. For one thing, the variety is so great. For another, brewers may call their beer just about anything they want to. And if marketing people are given a free hand in choosing a beer name, heaven help us. The names they apply may not reveal anything about their styles. One brewery may call its dark beer a porter; while another may call its dark beer, which is virtually identical to the other's, a stout. Or a brewery may identify its brand simply as a "lager" or an "ale." One major brewery's advertising department was calling its beer a "stout lager," which is a contradiction in terms.

There are two basic families of beers: ale and lager. The difference between ale and lager is one of the most asked questions. The answer is more important to the brewer than it is to the taster. Many authorities have tried to characterize the differences in terms of taste and aroma. I maintain that all such attempts are doomed to failure because the diversity in taste and aroma within each family is so great. There is simply no commonality in taste within either family. So, it is possible to describe the difference between a Pilsner and a bitter, but it is not possible to do the same for ale and lager.

Ales

Ales are made with a yeast which floats to the top of the beer and which works at warmer temperatures than lagers. The brewing process is shorter for an ale than it is for a lager. For this reason many brewpubs make ales. Ales are most prevalent in the British Isles, although in recent decades Germany has experienced a renaissance of its traditional top-fermented styles (weizen, alt, Kölsch).

Ales are frequently served at temperatures which are much too cold to allow one to appreciate the flavor. Americans tend to like their beers cold and it is not uncommon to see an ale served at 35° F in a frosted mug. This is a waste of good beer. If you really want to cool off, why not freeze the beer and serve it as a popsicle. If your beer is served too cold, try warming it up with the palms of your hands or placing it on a radiator. Even a microwave warm-up would be acceptable. Don't be embarrassed, the bartender might even get the message.

Lagers

Lagers are brewed with a yeast which sinks to the bottom of the beer and are fermented and served at cooler temperatures than ales. "Lager" is a German word meaning "to store." After the initial fermentation they are stored, or aged, for several weeks or months at very cold temperatures. The lagering or aging tends to give the lager a smoother, more refined taste. Lagers are more common on the European Continent.

Lagers made in brewpubs are often not aged as long as they should be because of the high demand for beer. The brewer is sometimes faced with the dilemma of serving lager before its time or serving no beer at all. Running out of beer would, of course, be a disaster from which the brewery might never recover.

OUTLINE OF BEER STYLES

ales

alt
barley wine
bitter
blonde ale
brown ale
Kölsch
light ale
mild
old ale
pale ale
porter
Scotch ale
stock ale
stout
Trappist ale
wheat beer

lagers

bock
Dortmunder
dunkel
helles
light beer
Münchner
Oktoberfest
Pilsner
Steinbier
Vienna

Hybrids, specialty beers, and misnomers

amber beer
Christmas ale
California common
cream ale
dry beer

fruit beer
herb beer
ice beer
lambic
red beer
smoked beer

abbey ale See under Trappist ale.

alt or altbier. This is a dark ale-style originating in Germany before the art of brewing lager developed. It is still popular in Dusseldorf and a few other locales. Altbier comes from the German, meaning "old beer," i.e., beer brewed before lager.

amber beer This is a term used frequently in brewpubs and craft breweries to describe beers which are tawny or copper in color. They may be ales or lagers. They tend to be fuller bodied and maltier than their golden colored counterparts.

barley wine A very potent ale, usually full-bodied, dark, and bitter-sweet. Its strength is typically between 6% and 11% alcohol by volume (the "wine" implies that it is as strong as wine).

bitter A well-hopped, relatively bitter-tasting ale common to England. The term originated to distinguish the "old" unhopped ales from hopped ales. Bitter is usually served on draft and is amber-to-copper in color. There are various subcategories of bitter depending on their strength. These include **ordinary**, **special**, and **Extra Special Bitter (ESB)**. Do not offend the English by calling it "bitters."

blonde ale A pale, light-bodied ale. Also called **golden ale**.

bock or bockbier. This style means different things to different people. In Germany it means a strong lager, at least 6.25% alcohol by volume. In America the name "bock" has been traditionally applied to dark lagers, at least until Sierra Nevada came out with its Pale Bock in 1990. There is an old wives' tale that bock beer is dark because it is made in the spring when the brewery cleans the dregs out of the brew kettles. There is

absolutely no truth in this and anyone understanding the importance of cleanliness in the brewing process will know that brew kettles are cleaned after every batch. There are two theories as to the origin of the name. One is that it is a corruption of "Einbeck," a German city which was once an important brewing center, and where the style may have originated. The other theory is that it is a corruption of the German term ziegenbock or "billy goat."

There are many kinds of bocks, including **pale bock**; **Doppelbock** [also called double bock or dopplebock], a strong, malty version; **Maibock**; **eisbock**, an extra strong bock finished by freezing the beer and removing some of the water; and **weizenbock**, a dark, strong wheat beer. Doppelbocks frequently end with the suffix "ator" and are easy to identify for this reason. The Paulaner Brewery in Munich started the trend of using the -ator suffix, with its Salvator.

brown ale A dark brown ale. There are three subgroups, based on geographic regions: those produced in southern England, which are relatively low in alcohol and hop bitterness, and sweet; those produced in northeast England, which are drier, but still weak and low in hop bitterness; and those produced in Belgium, which are stronger and more complex. English brown ales are equivalent to the bottled versions of mild ales.

California common A beer made with lager yeast, but brewed at ale temperatures. The style is typified by an amber hue, medium body, and hoppy character. For years it was known as steam beer, but since Anchor Brewing of San Francisco trademarked the name, the term California common was coined to identify the style in brewing competitions. This is the only beer style indigenous to the United States. California common beer originated in nineteenth century California, where brewers had access to lager yeasts but had no means to keep the beer at the proper temperature. At least two theories persist as to the origin of the name. One is that excessive amounts of pressure built up in the wooden casks and when they were tapped they made a loud hissing noise, like steam. The other is that steam power was used in the early California breweries, hence the name "steam beer."

Christmas beer A beer brewed for the yuletide (in Germany, fest bier). It is also called holiday beer. It is often dark and relatively high in alcohol, but styles vary widely. Many breweries put herbs and spices in their Christmas beer.

cream ale A pale, light bodied ale which is lagered at cold temperatures or mixed with lager. Sometimes called "lagale."

doppelbock See under bock.

Dortmunder A pale lager, with more body than a Pilsner, and less dry as well. Sometimes called "export."

dry beer A beer made by a special process, using enzymal additives in the mash, in which the yeast converts more of the malt sugars into alcohol than normal, making it drier tasting. In Japan, where the first modern dry beers became popular, they tend to be more potent than their counterpart lagers. In the U.S., dry beers tend to be of normal strength, but the breweries use lower hopping rates, rendering them almost tasteless. This is not the kind of beer you would expect to find in a brewpub.

dunkel (also, dunkle, dunkler, Munich [or

Münchner] dunkel, and dunkles) From the German for "dark." Any dark lager of average strength. Many bocks are dark, but are stronger than dunkels.

export See under Dortmunder.

framboise See under fruit beer.

fruit beer Beer with fruit in it, such as cherries, raspberries, or blueberries. Fruit beer has been brewed over the millenia, but the tradition was kept alive in Belgium. Its popularity has spread to the U.S. in recent years.

golden ale See under blonde ale.

helles Also called "Munich [or Münchner] helles." A pale lager. From the German for "pale." A helles tends to be maltier, less dry, and less hoppy than a Pilsner.

herb beer Any ale or lager with herbs or spices in it. Many Christmas ales have herbs in them. Common spices used are ginger, nutmeg, and cinnamon.

ice beer A beer which is frozen just enough to form a few ice crystals, which are then removed. This has little, if any, effect on the taste of the beer.

imperial stout See under stout.

Irish stout See under stout.

Kölsch A type of blonde ale brewed in and around Cologne, Germany. It tends to be delicate, dry, and fruity. The word "Kölsch" originated from "Cologne."

kriek See under fruit beer.

lager ale (or lagale) See under cream ale.

lambic A well-carbonated, spontaneously-fermented wheat ale, very popular in Belgium. There are several varieties, including fruit lambic (**kriek**-made with cherries, **framboise**-made with raspberries), **Faro** (a sweet version), and **Gueuze** (a blend of mature and young lambics).

light ale Meaning varies: 1. the bottled equivalent of a draft ordinary bitter; 2. a low-gravity ale, 3. a low-calorie ale.

light beer 1. A low-calorie, low-gravity beer. 2. A pale-colored lager, such as a helles or Dortmunder.

Maibock See under bock.

malt liquor An American tax term for a strong beer. In some states, law requires that beers above a certain alcoholic strength must be labeled as malt liquors. Malt liquors tend to lack malt and hop character.

Märzenbier See under Oktoberfest.

mild ale A lightly hopped ale. They are also frequently dark in color and low in alcohol.

milk stout See under stout.

non-alcoholic beer Also called alcohol-free beer and near beer. Any beer with less than .5% alcohol by weight. Reformed alcoholics should avoid such beers because they still have enough alcohol in them to put them back off the wagon.

Oktoberfest or Märzenbier. Originally, a beer brewed in Germany in March (hence, Märzenbier) and laid down for consumption during the summer and fall. Ceremoniously consumed in late September and early October. Oktoberfest is amber in color, medium-to-strong in potency, and malty. Similar to Vienna, but more robust.

old ale A medium-strong ale, usually dark in color, lightly to moderately hopped, and full bodied.

pale ale A copper-colored ale; a term frequently used to describe a brewer's premium bitter, usually in the bottled form. In recent years the term pale ale has frequently been used to describe draft bitter. The name is seemingly a misnomer, since there is nothing "pale" about pale ale. It was originally used to distinguish it from porter, a very dark ale. It is sometimes referred to as **Burton ale**, because it originated in the town of Burton-upon-Trent, England. A slightly stronger and hoppier version is known as **India Pale Ale** or **IPA**. It acquired this name because it was originally brewed for export to India.

pale bock See under bock.

Pils See under Pilsner.

Pilsner (also spelled Pilsener and frequently referred to as *Pils*) A dry, golden lager, originating in Pilsen, Czechoslovakia. European-style Pilsners tend to be dry and crisp, highly hopped, and have a flowery aroma. Most American premium beers (i.e., from the big brewers) are technically in the Pilsner style, but, in character, are mere shadows of their European counterparts. They are paler in color, less hoppy and malty, and have less body. The major American breweries usually substitute corn or rice for a significant portion of the malt, which weakens the malt character.

porter A very dark-to-black ale. Porter originated in eighteenth century London and was first popular among porters (hence, its name). It is traditionally malty and bitter. Many have a dry coffee taste as well. The stronger and more bitter varieties later became known as stouts, because (it is said) they were appreciated by the "stoutest" of the London porters.

premium and **super premium** 1. These are price categories used by large

American breweries. Premium is usually in the middle price range and super premium is higher priced. These names imply quality, but have been so misused, microbrewers avoid using them. 2. Beer of high quality.

rauch (smoked) or rauchbier. Beer made with smoked malts. The classic examples come from Franconia, near Bamberg, Germany.

Red ale A reddish colored ale, sometimes called Irish red.

Scotch ale A strong, amber-to-dark, malty, full-bodied ale, originally from Scotland. Also known as "wee heavy." It has also been brewed in Belgium for many years.

spiced ale See under herb beer.

steam beer See under California common.

stock ale (or stock beer) A strong ale originally brewed to be stored for a long period of time.

stout A very dark-to-black, full-bodied ale; a stronger variety of porter. Two main subcategories exist: **dry stout** (also known as **Irish stout**) and **sweet stout** (sometimes called **milk stout**, because it has lactose [milk sugar] added to it), more common to England. In addition there is **imperial stout** (also known as Russian imperial stout), **oatmeal stout**, and **cream stout**. Imperial stout was originally brewed in England and exported to Catherine the Great's court in St. Petersburg. Cream stout is not really considered a style; this term is used in referring to its creamy mouthfeel or to its sweetness.

strong ale See under old ale.

Trappist ale An ale style originally brewed by Belgian and Dutch Trappist monks. A true Trappist ale should be relatively strong, use candy sugar in the brewing process, and be bottle conditioned. They tend to be assertive and complex. Some are full bodied, with a rich and rounded palate; others are tart and fruity. Stronger versions of the same brand are frequently referred to as "double" or "triple." Also known as abbey ale.

Vienna A reddish-amber lager; usually malty and moderately hopped. The style originated in Vienna in the 19th Century.

wee heavy See under Scotch ale.

wheat beer Any beer using malted wheat. There are many styles. **Berliner Weisse** is an unfiltered, tart, low-alcohol, light-bodied, well-carbonated beer, originally from Berlin. It is frequently served with fruit syrup. Other varieties originating from southern Germany are variously called **weizenbier**, **weisse**, or **weissbier**. These beers are of a more conventional alcohol strength and body, but are also tart and fruity. They are frequently served with a twist of lemon. Wheat malt content varies from 50%-80%. Bottle-conditioned wheat beers are usually called **hefeweizen**. Other styles include **dunkelweizen** (dark wheat) and **weizenbock**, or wheat bock. Weis means "white" in German, and refers to the very pale color of the beer. Weizen means "wheat" in German. Wheat beers are generally brewed with ale yeasts.

Witbier is a Belgian version of wheat beer with an orangey character and a honeyish aroma.

white beer See under wheat beer.

witbier See under wheat beer.

winter warmer A beer brewed for consumption in winter, frequently dark, malty, and fairly high in alcohol, but there are some that are light colored and emphasize hops instead.

Beer Vocabulary

additive - chemicals such as enzymes, preservatives, and antioxidants which are added to simplify the brewing process or prolong shelf life.

adjunct - fermentable, unmalted grain, including wheat, corn, rice, or oats, used in addition to the malted barley. In the United States the larger breweries have used adjuncts extensively to lighten the flavor and body of the beer.

alcohol - an intoxicant created through the fermentation process. Alcohol content is expressed as a percentage of the volume or weight of the beer.

all-grain - an adjective describing the brewing process in which the brewer begins with grist, as opposed to using malt extract.

all-malt - an adjective describing beer made with malted barley and without adjuncts.

attenuation - the degree to which the beer has fermented, also stated as the reduction in the wort's specific gravity. Other things being equal, the higher the level of attenuation, the drier, more alcoholic, and lighter bodied the beer becomes.

Balling - a measure of beer's density, devised by Carl Joseph Napoleon Balling in 1843. To convert Balling to specific gravity, take the Balling measure, multiply it by .004, and then add 1.

barley - a cereal grain used in making beer.

barrel - 31 gallons. In Great Britain it is 36 Imperial gallons (43.2 U.S. gallons).

beer - a fermented beverage made from malted cereal grain.

body - the thickness of beer as perceived by its mouthfeel. The density and level of carbonation can affect this mouthfeel.

bottle conditioned - unpasteurized beer, naturally carbonated in the bottle.

breweriana - beer-related memorabilia.

brewhouse - the equipment used to make beer.

brew kettle - the vessel in which wort from the mash is boiled with hops. Also called a copper.

brewpub - an establishment which brews beers and sells it for consumption on the premises.

bright beer tank - see under conditioning tank.

bung - the stopper in the hole in a keg or cask of beer through which the keg or cask is filled and emptied. The hole is <u>also</u> referred to as a bung or bunghole. Cask-conditioned beer must use a wooden bung, also called a spile.

cara-pils - complex, unfermentable carbohydrate in the malt. Dextrin contributes to the finishing gravity, body, and sweetness of the beer.

carbon dioxide - a gas created from the the fermentation process. Carbon dioxide gives beer its effervescence.

carboy - a glass bottle, usually five gallons in size.

cask - a closed, barrel-shaped container for beer. They come in various sizes and are now usually made of metal. The bung in a cask must be made of wood, which allows the beer pressure to be released from the fermenting beer and to naturally carbonate itself.

cask conditioned - unfiltered, unpasteurized beer, and not served under CO_2 pressure.

conditioning tank - a vessel in which beer is placed after primary fermentation where the beer matures, clarifies, and is naturally carbonated through secondary fermentation. Also called bright beer tank, and secondary.

contract beer - beer made by one brewery and then marketed by a company calling itself a brewery. The latter uses the brewing facilities of the former.

copper - see under brew kettle.

Cornelius keg - a five-gallon keg used primarily in the industry to dispense soda syrup. Used to serve beer in some of the smaller brewpubs.

dextrin - see under cara-pils.

diatomaceous earth - skeletal remains of ancient microscopic marine animals. Used in breweries to filter beer.

finishing gravity - see under specific gravity.

gravity - see under specific gravity.

grist - malt which has been ground.

Grundy - a seven-barrel tank manufactured in England and used for fermentation, conditioning, or serving.

guest beer - a beer offered by a pub which is not brewed at the pub or at the parent brewery.

hand pump - a device for dispensing draft beer using a pump operated by hand. The use of a hand pump allows cask-conditioned beer to be served without the use of pressurized carbon dioxide to force it up.

hard cider - a fermented beverage made from apples.

hops - seed cones which grow on the hop vine (*humulus lupulus*, the Latin botanical name). Only cones from the female vine are used in making beer.

house beer - a beer brewed in the pub or at the parent brewery.

keg - a closed, metal, barrel-shaped container for beer. It is usually pressurized and has a capacity of 15.5 gallons (1/2 barrel). A half keg (7.75 gallons) is referred to as a "pony keg."

krausen - the foam which appears on top of fermenting beer.

krausening - the process of conditioning beer by adding unfermented wort to fully fermented beer before kegging or bottling.

lauter tun - a tank used to sparge the mashed grain. If mashing and sparging takes place in the same tank, it is frequently referred to as the mash-lauter tun.

liquor tank - a tank used to store water (sometimes referred to by brewers as "liquor") for the brewing process. They may store either hot or cold water .

malt - barley which has been soaked in water, allowed to sprout, and then dried.

maltose - a water-soluble, fermentable sugar contained in malt.

mash tun - a tank where grist is soaked in water and heated in order to convert the starch to sugar and extract the sugar and other solubles from the grist. The process is called "mashing." "Mashing in" is the expression used to describe the process in which the grain and grist enter the mash tun in a slurry.

mead - a fermented beverage made from honey.

microbrewery - a brewery producing small amounts of beer. The upper limit of annual production has been variously set at 10,000, 15,000, and 20,000 barrels.

original gravity - see under specific gravity.

pasteurize - the application of heat to bottled, canned, or kegged beer in order to arrest the activity of micro-organisms, including yeast and bacteria. Pasteurization was first developed by the French scientist Louis Pasteur, who conducted several studies on the pasteurization of beer. Pasteurization may be either flash pasteurization (usually for kegs) where the beer is held at a high temperature for less than a minute and then rapidly cooled, or tunnel pasteurization (usually for bottles) where the bottles go through a tunnel of hot water for up to an hour.

pitch - to add yeast to wort.

Plato - a measure of beer's density, first devised by Carl Joseph Napoleon Balling and later corrected by Dr. Plato. One degree Plato is equal to 0.97 degrees Balling. The Plato measure is prevalent in Germany.

pony keg - see under keg.

pub - an establishment serving beer and sometimes other alcoholic beverages for consumption on the premises. A pub usually serves food as well. The term originated in England and is the shortened form for "public house."

publican - The owner or manager of a pub (not to be confused with a RE-publican).

rack - to transfer beer from one container to another, a process which generally leaves sediment in the first container.

Reinheitsgebot - German purity law. In 1516 William VI, Elector of Bavaria, declared that only water, malted barley, and hops could be used to make beer. Yeast was not included in the ingredients, but taken for granted. The purity law was amended later to allow malted wheat. It was so important to the Bavarians that they made the continuance of the purity law a condition to their joining the German Republic in 1919. The purity law was struck down in 1987 by the European Court for being protectionist in nature.

room temperature - the temperature of the surrounding air where the beer is stored, typically around 55°F (13°C). "Room temperature" is actually a misnomer; people are referring to "cellar" temperature. Beer served at actual pub room temperature would be unappetizing.

seasonal beer - a beer brewed at a particular time of the year, such as bock or winter warmer.

serving tank - a tank from which beer is dispensed.

session beer - Any beer of moderate to low alcoholic strength, that can be consumed during a long "session" in a bar.

sparge - to spray grist with hot water in order to remove soluble sugars (maltose). This takes place at the end of the mash.

specific gravity (s.g.) - a measure of beer's density in relation to the density of water, which is given a value of 1 at 39.2°F (4°C).

When fermentation begins, the wort's density is measured--this is called original gravity (o.g.) The o.g. is always higher than 1 because of the solubles, such as maltose, which are suspended in it. As the yeast converts the maltose into alcohol the gravity drops, alcohol being lighter than water. When brewers are ready to serve, bottle, or keg their beer, they take a final gravity reading, known as the finishing gravity (f.g.).

wort - the sweet liquid which is created from the mashing and boiling process. When the wort is cooled and fermented, it is called beer.

wort chiller - see under heat exchanger.

yeast - a micro-organism of the fungus family. During the fermentation of beer, the yeast consume maltose and in the process create alcohol and carbon dioxide.

zymurgy - the science or study of fermentation.

The Boston Brewers Festival

Of the many beer festivals held throughout the region, there is one which stands out above the rest. This is the Boston Brewers Festival, held every spring at the World Trade Center. It is here that you will get the chance to try almost every beer brewed in New England. Just as important, you will be able to meet the people who make the beer, as well as others, like yourself, who enjoy good beer.

The first festival was held on May 15 and 16, 1992, at the Boston Park Plaza Hotel. The objective of the festival was to give New England breweries a chance to showcase their beers and take a public bow. To the welcome surprise of the festival organizers, the event attracted about 5,000 beer lovers. One hundred beers from 34 breweries from the Northeast were represented.

The second annual festival was held at the World Trade Center on May 1, 1993. This time 54 breweries came from as far away as Montreal, Canada; Seattle, Washington; and Abita Springs, Louisiana. They brought almost 200 brands of beer to a crowd numbering more than 7,000.

The third festival is being held May 14, 1994, again at the World Trade Center, and should attract more beer lovers and breweries than ever.

Good Beer Bars (BB) and Package Stores (PS)

The beer is always best at the brewery. However, many breweries are not allowed by law to sell packaged beer to go. I have provided below a list of recommended good beer bars and package stores. I learned about most of them through second-hand sources, and cannot recommend them from personal experience.

Connecticut

New Haven
    Richter's (BB)
    900 Chapel Street

Norwalk
    Yankee Spirits (PS)
    on Old Route 7

West Hartford
    The Spigot (BB)
    468 Prospect Street

Maine

Portland
    The Great Lost Bear (BB)
    540 Forest Avenue
    (virtually all of the New England micros
    on tap, not to be missed)

    Three Dollar Dewey's (BB)
    446 Fore Street

South Portland
    Hops & Barley Import Tavern (BB)

Massachusetts

Amherst
    The Spirit Haus (PS)
    338 College Street

Boston
    Blanchard's (PS)
    741 Centre Street (Jamaica Plain)

Blanchard's (PS)
418 LaGrange (W. Roxbury)

Blanchard's (PS)
103 Harvard Avenue, Allston

Boodle's (BB)
The Back Bay Hilton
40 Dalton Street
(best hotel beer bar in the U.S.)

Cornwall's (BB)
510 Commonwealth Avenue (Kenmore Square)

Doyle's Braddock Cafe (BB)
3484 Washington Street (Jamaica Plain)
(great beer bar and atmosphere)

Jacob Wirth's (BB)
31-37 Stuart Street
(one of Boston's oldest, German atmosphere)

Kappy's Liquors (PS)
126 Liverpool (East Boston)

Marty's Liquors (PS)
675 Washington Street

Sunset Grill & Tap (BB)
130 Brighton Avenue (Allston)
(not to be missed)

Cambridge
    Christopher's (BB)
    1920 Mass. Ave.

The Wursthaus (BB)
4 JFK Street (Harvard Square)

Brookline Liquor Mart (PS)
1354 Commonwealth Ave. (Allston)

The Plough and Stars (BB)
912 Mass. Ave.
(this tiny Irish pub serves a good pint of
Guinness)

Medford
Kappy's Liquors (PS)
10 Revere Beach Parkway

Revere
Blanchard's (PS)
286 American Legion Highway

Somerville
Downtown Wine & Spirits (PS)
225 Elm Street (Davis Square)
South Amherst
Amherst Alehouse (BB)

Sturbridge
Yankee Spirits (PS)
on Route 20

Homebrewing

Before American craft brewing, what was there? As far as most people can remember, there was a beer wasteland. If you wanted good beer, you had to drink imports or make it yourself. Unfortunately, until 1979 the latter option was illegal. Undaunted, many rugged individualists were doing it in their basements.

After legalization the homebrewing movement began to flourish. Equipment and supply shops began to pop up, clubs were organized, newsletters were published, how-to guidebooks were written, competitions were held, and the quality of homemade beer improved considerably. Gone are the days of exploding bottles, corn sugar, and Fleischmann's bread yeast. Homebrewing has become sophisticated. The current generation of homebrewers are using liquid yeast cultures, heat exchangers, making their beer from malt instead of malt extract, and fermenting in glass or stainless steel containers.

New England homebrewers contributed on a national scale. In homebrewing competitions they took medals far in excess of their numbers.

One of the clubs, the Boston Wort Processors, has consistently placed second in national club competitions. Their club newsletter, to which I have subscribed for many years, is perhaps the best in the country.

The flourishing of the homebrewing movement led directly to the birth of craft brewing. It increased beer appreciation and also contributed the skilled craftspeople who could create the beer at the new breweries.

Homebrewing is more active in New England than it has ever been. If you are not already part of this scene, you might consider doing so. The best way to start is to stop by your local homebrew supply shop where you can talk with the owner, meet homebrewers from your area, and find out about the local homebrew club. At the shop you can find out about ingredients, methods, costs, and virtually everything you will need to get started.

On the following pages is provided a list of homebrew supply shops around New England.

Homebrew Retail Supply Shops

Connecticut

Brothers Logan Homebrewing Supplies
60 Jerry Daniels Road
Marlborough, CT 06447

The Mad Capper
P.O. Box 310126
Newington, CT 06131-0126
(203) 667-7662

Maltose Express
391 Main Street
Monroe, CT 06468
(203) 452-7332; (800) MALTOSE

S.E.C.T. Brewing Supplies
C/O SIMTAC
20 Attawan Road
Niantic, CT 06357
(203) 739-3609

Wine & Beer Art of Smith Tompkins
1501 E. Main Street, Route 202
Torrington, CT 06790
(203) 489-4560

Maine

Cookin' With Spirits
Squire Hill Plaza
Upper Main Street
Winthrop, ME 04364
(207) 377-3237

Homebrew Emporium
RR. #1, Box 1815
Upper Main Street
Winthrop, ME 04364
(207) 377-3128; (800) 400-MALT (in state)

The Purple Foot Downeast
116 Main Street
Waldoboro, ME 04572
(207) 832-6286

The Whip & Spoon
161 Commercial Street
P.O. Box 567
Portland, ME 04108
(800) 937-9447

Winter People
P.O. Box 45 A
Cumberland, ME 04021
(207) 829-3745

Massachusetts

Aubut's Liquor & Party Center
1768 Main Street, Rt. 38
Tewksbury, MA
(508) 851-2031

Barleymalt & Vine
4 Corey Street
Boston, MA 02132
(800) 666-7026

Barleymalt & Vine
280 Worcester Street
Framingham, MA 01701
(800) 666-7026

Barleymalt & Vine
26 Elliot Street
Newton, MA 02161
(617) 630-1015

Barnstable Brewers Supply
P.O. Box 1555
Windmill Square, Rt. 28
Marstons Mills, MA 02648
(508) 428-5267

Beer & Wine Hobby
180 New Boston Street
Woburn, MA 01801
(617) 933-8818; (800) 523-5423

Beer & Wine Supplies, Inc.
154 King Street
Northampton, MA 0106
(413) 586-0150

Biermeister
P.O. Box 9334
Lowell, MA 01853
(508) 458-5899

Boston Brewers Supply
48 South Street
Jamaica Plain, MA 02130
(617) 983-1710

The Brew Shack
50 High Street
Amesbury, MA 01913
(508) 388-FOAM

Brewers Choice
120 W. Center St., Rt. 106
Howard Farms Marketplace
W. Bridgewater, MA 02379
(508) 580-6850

The Brewers Kettle
331 Boston Post Road, #12
Marlborough, MA 01752
(508) 485-2001

The Frozen Wort
Box 988
Greenfield, MA 01302
(413) 733-5920

The Hoppy Brewers Supply Co.
555 Central Avenue
Seekonk, MA 02703
(508) 761-6615

Julio's Liquors
33 Lyman Street
Westborough, MA 01581
(508) 366-1942

The Keg & Vine
697 Main Street
Holden, MA 01520
(508) 829-6717

The Malt Shop
P.O. Box 81005, Box 139
Springfield, MA 01108
(413) 783-0242

The Modern Brewer Co., Inc.
2304 Massachusetts Avenue
Cambridge, MA 02140
(617) 868-5580; (800) SEND ALE

Nashoba Brewing Supply
12 Hemlock Road
Groton, MA
(508) 448-3301

Partners Village Store
999 Main Road
Westport, MA 02790
(508) 636-2572

Stella Brew
P.O. Box 23
207 Center Depot Road
Charlton Depot, MA 01509
(508) 248-6823

The Vineyard
123 Glen Avenue
Upton, MA 01450
(508) 529-6014; (800) 626-2371

Walpole Wine & Spirits
660 Main Street
Walpole, MA 02081
(508) 668-3338

The Witches' Brew
25 Baker Street
Foxboro, MA 02035
(508) 543-2950

New Hampshire

Beer Essentials
92 Renshaw Road
Weare, NH 03281
(800) 608-BEER; (603) 529-4664

Brewer & Associates
112 State Street
Portsmouth, NH 03801
(603) 436-5918

Brewers Market
10 N. Main Street
Ashland, NH 03217
(603) 968-7016

Granite State Natural Food, Inc.
164 N. State Street
Concord, NH 03301
(603) 224-9341

Jasper's Home Brew Supply
11D Tracy Lane
Hudson, NH 03051
(800) FOR BREW

Orford Home Brew Supplies
RR 1, Box 106 A
Orford, NH 03777
(603) 353-4564

Stout Billy's
61 Market Street
Portsmouth, NH 03801
(603) 436-1792; (800) 392-4792

The Stout House
Eastern Slope Plaza
North Conway, NH 03860
(603) 356-5290; (800) 842-BREW

Rhode Island

Brew Horizons
884 Tiogue Avenue
Coventry, RI 02816
(800) 589-BREW

Northeast Brewers Supply
Mariner Square
140 Point Judith Road, #C-45
Narragansett, RI 02882
(401) 789-9963; (800) 352-9001

Vermont

Something's Brewing
196 Battery Street
Burlington, VT 05401
(802) 660-9007

Something's Brewing
65 Elm Street
Montpelier, VT 05602
(802) 223-1185

Vermont Homebrewers Supply
K & K Beverage
1341 Shelburne Road
South Burlington, VT 05403
(802) 658-9595 and 985-9734

Connecticut

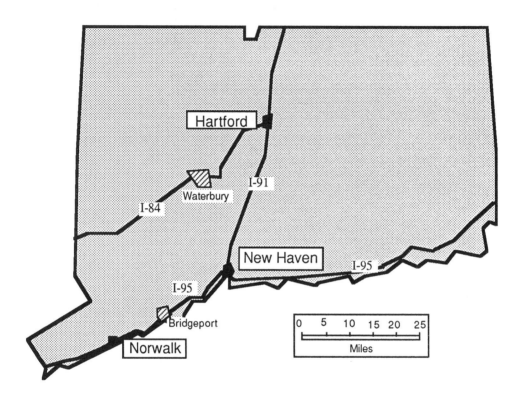

Connecticut can take credit for the second brewery in New England, with the opening of Sargeant Baulston's Brewery in New Haven in 1638. Only a handfull of breweries operated in the state until the mid-nineteenth century. By 1890, Connecticut had reached its golden age of brewing with 30 breweries across the state.

From that point consolidation took place in the industry and by the time Prohibition went into effect in 1920 the number of breweries had declined to 18. In the two years after Repeal, 21 breweries opened, but few were able to withstand the hardships of the Depression and by 1940 only eight remained. Hull Brewing of New Haven, the last remaining brewery finally closed its doors in 1977.

The first new brewery in Connecticut opened in September 1989. This was New Haven Brewing, a craft brewery. In February of the following year New England Brewing opened in Norwalk. In August of the same year Charter Oak Brewing opened in Bristol. Unfortunately, Charter Oak closed two years later. The state's newest brewery, and its first modern brewpub, opened in August of 1991, the Hartford Brewery.

Hartford Brewery
Of all the Beer Joints in all the Towns of the World

Well, why not Hartford? While most of us may only know Hartford as "insurance city" because so many insurance companies call it home, employing one-fourth of the local work force, there is much more to Hartford than that mass of high rise office buildings off to our left as we make the trip northward on I-91 from the Big Apple to northern New England. Many call this city their state capital, their place of work, and even their home. And they can claim Mark Twain and Noah Webster as their famous sons.

The opening of the Hartford Brewery, Ltd. in August 1991 gave a new aspect to downtown Hartford and gave a lot of folks who work in the downtown something to be happy about. Hartford Brewery, Ltd. is housed in a former Friendly's Restaurant in the Gold Center, a complex of glass office towers, just two blocks from the Old Statehouse historical area. The exterior is a contemporary black, bronze, and tinted glass storefront with the brewery name stenciled in goldenrod yellow letters above the double-door entry and windows. From the outside, it looks pretty upscale.

Once inside, the urban chic is replaced by the distinct atmosphere of a neighborhood tavern, one which has a barroom as well as a dining area. The floor is red tile, the walls are white and the ceiling is nondescript acoustical tile, painted black in the dining area. The furnishings are simple slat back chairs and square tables, although the tables are set with white cloths and starched napkins in the dining area. Breweriana including antique beer trays and framed collections of beer mats are hung about, and one wall in the dining area is a showplace for hunting trophies.

The pub section has a bar with a brass foot rail and a wooden-clad brewhouse on display directly behind it. For entertainment there are dart boards and a pool table. There is a large selection of board games for those who like a friendly game of chess, backgammon, or the like with their fellow drinkers. The owners, Phil Hopkins and Les Sinnock have created a place for people to congregate at the end of the workday for some fun and relaxation. A wide screen television set is tuned in for all of the Whalers ice hockey games. The midday crowd - the insurance and banker types - tends to be a little more staid, coming in for their noontime meal and something to lift their spirits.

Phil and Les go back a long way, even though they were only 29 and 30 years of age when they opened their doors. They had been brewing beer together for years, with the special blessing of Phil's parents who gave him a homebrew kit for his eighteenth birthday. They enjoyed what they were doing and decided to open a brewpub. Their preparation included visiting about 50 brewpubs across the country and a stint at Geary's in Portland in order to prepare themselves for the rigors of commercial brewing.

Both owners grew up around Hartford and have chosen to recognize people and places from Hartford by naming two of their brews after them. The Arch Amber Ale is named for the Soldiers and Sailors Memorial Arch built in the 1880s to commemorate those who fought in the Civil War, and the Bushnell Burton Ale celebrates the contributions of one of Hartford's oldest and most accomplished families. The menu is sprinkled with captioned photos of Hartford in bygone days.

The Menu

The Hartford Brewery Ltd. serves pub grub, reasonably priced. There is a special emphasis on the freshness of the food served and for two reasons. First, they believe freshly brewed ales deserve to be served with only the freshest of foods. Secondly, as the inside cover of the menu explains, "Because the brewery uses 80% of available refrigeration on the premises, our chef orders small amounts of fresh produce, meats and seafoods daily...this practice ensures a high degree of freshness."

Appetizers include a full range of nacho, chip, salsa, chili and quesadilla finger foods as well as a hot and gooey baked brie served with apple slices and French bread. The sandwiches are ample and there are many to choose from, many served with a house dressing or special sauce. The brats are steamed in Hartford brews for the open-face Archwurst sandwich. The seven varieties of sirloin burgers are half-pounders and like the sandwiches, are served with an interesting choice of German potato salad, cole slaw, rotini salad, a Red Bliss Pesto Salad, hot parsleyed potatoes, or the special side dish of the day. If beer and pizza are your thing, you can order several combinations of classic and nouveau toppings on freshly baked focaccia. Soups and salads round out the menu and some serious desserts (translate - mostly chocolate) complete the offerings here.

The Brew

Phil and Les are using a seven-barrel, Peter Austin brewing system with an open fermenter (it used to be used at the Frog & Frigate brewpub in England). The yeast is the same as Geary's in Portland, Maine. It takes only two days in the primary fermenter, and must be aerated and cooled because it ferments so fast it heats up and robs the wort of oxygen.

Phil and Les is using primarily two-row, English malts, plus some Munich malt from Germany. They use all American leaf hops.

Most of the beers are served from serving tanks under CO_2-nitrogen pressure. They usually have six on at a time, but you may only purchase one sampler at a time, because Connecticut law does not allow a customer to be served more than three beers at a time. The beers are available in ten-oz. mugs ($2.25), pints ($3.00), and pitchers ($9.50). A set of three samplers costs $4.25.

Phil and Les like to provide their customers with a broad range of beers and normally have six beers on at all times. In addition to the beers listed below, they have brewed another two dozen recipes.

Kolsch - bright, dark gold; fresh, estery-sulfury aroma; off-sweet entry; malty in the middle with a dry, hoppy finish

IPA - bright copper; dry, hoppy-malty finish

Porter - dark, reddish brown; on the sweet side, malty with some caramelized maltiness

Bachus - deep reddish brown; lots of sweet, caramelized malt with a nice malty-hoppy finish; chewy; a rich and delicious brew; an old ale

Arch Amber - not sampled

Pitbull Golden - not sampled

Imperial Russian Stout - brewed once a year, not sampled

Barrel of Miscellany

Address:	35 Pearl Street Hartford, CT 06103
Telephone:	(203) 772-2739
Hours:	Monday - Thursday: 11:30 a.m. - 1:00 a.m.; Friday: 11:30 a.m. - 2:00 a.m.; Saturday: noon - 2:00 a.m.; occasionally open on Sunday
Credit cards:	American Express, Discover, Mastercard, Visa

non-smoking area -- handicapped access - pub games: pool, pinball, backgammon, darts (Wednesday night is league night), multitude of board games

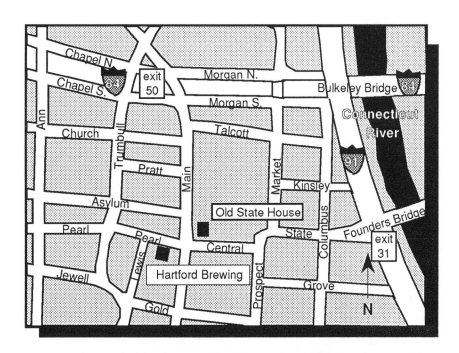

New Haven Brewing

Ale University

Ever since the early 1700s, Yalies have taken their Latin and Greek along with liberal doses of ale, brewed, of course, at local Connecticut breweries. Over the years, things have gone downhill. Latin and Greek; who studies that anymore? And ale, brewed in Connecticut? That gradually disappeared and finally went out altogether when the state's last brewery, Hull Brewing of New Haven, closed its doors in 1977. (Hull, by the way, was well known for its "Export Beer." After some investigation, author Will Anderson discovered that the only "countries" to which it was exported were New York and Massachusetts.) In the twentieth century, most "Yale gentlemen" stooped to drinking lager and some even put their creative talents to inventing moronic, fraternity, beer-drinking games. Tang, the most infamous, ensured that the greatest number of people would be totally wasted in the shortest amount of time.

New Haven, in general, has fallen on hard times. The city's famous elm trees have all but disappeared. The mid-twentieth century saw the growth of urban blight, followed by a bout of urban renewal, and then followed by more urban blight. The city was so uncompromising in its zeal to knock down old buildings, several of which were old breweries, it even tried to destroy Louis' Lunch, the place where the American hamburger was invented back in the nineteenth century. When I worked in New Haven in the seventies the "in" bumper sticker to have on your car said "Save Louis' Lunch." And they did, and you can still have a hamburger at Louis', made just the way it was over 100 years ago.

Another ray of light in New Haven has been the revival of brewing, just a short distance from the university. And, hallelujah, ale is what is being made. You will find New Haven Brewing in the waterfront, urban village of Fair Haven (wasn't Popeye from Fair Haven?), where Grand Avenue crosses the Mill River. The brewery is in a handsome old brick building with huge arched windows, which originally housed the generating station for the New Haven trolley line. It later became a trolley barn and has served as a transfer point for steamships and railway lines.

Being a revivalist industry, it is appropriate that New Haven Brewing is located on the banks of the Mill River. For it was just a mile or two north of here, on the banks of the same river, that Eli Whitney, a graduate of Yale, built his arms factory in 1798. The birth of the industrial revolution traces its roots to this location, where interchangeable parts were mass produced for the first time. I think Whitney also had something to do with gin. Ah, but our subject today is beer.

It is also most appropriate that New Haven's brewer, Blair Potts, is a Yale graduate. Blair first developed a fondness for real ale in 1984 while representing Yale at the Henley Regatta in England. Blair graduated with a degree in history the same year.

What can you do with a B.A. in history? Tend Bar. Upon graduation, Blair landed a bartending job at Richter's in New Haven and quickly moved up to beverage manager and then manager of the whole restaurant. Richter Elser, the owner, became fascinated with good beer and began stocking what he could in the bar. He inundated Blair with books about beer and brewing. The craft brewing movement was gathering strength by now and a little light bulb clicked on in Blair's brain. An accomplished chef, he began brewing at home and soon attracted the attention of two Connecticut natives with whom he had business dealings as beverage manager: Jim Gordon, who had been importing and selling wines, and Mike Gettings, who was a Coca Cola salesmen. In 1987 the three incorporated the New Haven Brewing Co. and began raising capital.

The first beer rolled out the door on October 1, 1989. They started with Elm City Connecticut Ale, a low-hopped ale modeled after an English mild. The partners felt that locals were fairly averse to highly hopped ales and they wanted to go after the mainstream beer market. Interestingly, Blair is allergic to hops (he can taste the beer, but can't swallow it). This would be about as ironic as W. C. Fields being allergic to alcohol, which, in fact, he was.

Other brands have been added gradually. Production has increased steadily, with output reaching 4,500 barrels during 1993.

The Brew

Blair is making fifteen-barrel batches with the brewhouse, which are then put into 60-barrel fermenters or sometimes split into two 30-barrel fermenters. All the handsome equipment was manufactured by JV Northwest. They have doubled their capacity since they opened and would like to double it again. The ales are filtered and packaged under CO_2 pressure. All domestic pre-ground, two-row malt is used, along with pelletized, domestic hops. Sixty percent of their sales are draft.

Mr. Mike's Light Ale - brilliant, pale gold; fresh straw aroma; light malt and hop flavor; made with two-row pale and 35% wheat malt; hopped with Hallertau

Elm City Golden Ale - bright gold; fruity-malty-grass aroma; sweet and malty; made with two-row pale and cara-pils; hopped with Galena

Elm City Connecticut Ale - bright amber; off-sweet and malty; clean tasting; very drinkable; made with two-row pale and caramel malts; hopped with Northern Brewer and Willamette

Blackwell Stout - clear with a dark brown color; rich, dry malt aroma; rich and malty; lightly bitter; on the sweet side; a delicious and very drinkable stout; made with caramel, roasted barley, black barley, chocolate, Munich, and cara-pils; hopped with Northern Brewer, Willamette, and Cascades; named after Blair's Labrador retriever

Belle Dock New Haven - a beautiful, brilliant beer with a reddish copper color; fruity, perfumed, alcoholic aroma; rich, nutty, alcoholic, and caramelly; full bodied; sherry-like; a barleywine to be sought after; released once a year before Christmas

Imperial Stout - not sampled, but it has an enthusiastic following

Barrel of Miscellany

Address: 458 Grand Avenue
                    New Haven, CT 06513

Telephone: (203) 772-2739

Tours: 10:00 a.m. Saturday; for other times, please make advance
                    reservations

Availability: throughout New England

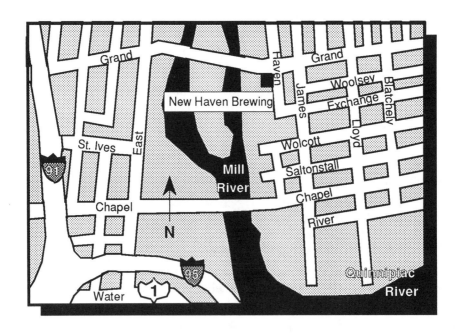

New England Brewing

Barreling Along in an Aling Economy

Connecticut's economy has suffered a big down turn in recent years. But you wouldn't know it if you visited the New England Brewing Co. in Norwalk. Ever since it opened in February of 1990 it has done nothing but move onward and upward.

Why all the success? Answer: their ales are fantastic. And, of course, behind every good beer, there is a good brewer. However, in this case, there are two very good brewers: head brewer Phil Markowski and assistant Ron Page. Both began as homebrewers and both have won their share of competition medals. Ron, in particular, has won more national awards than any other homebrewer in New England.

Phil, age 32 and an electrical engineer by training, first became interested in imported beers in the early eighties, and then discovered some domestic beers he liked, such as products from Anchor Brewing of San Francisco, California, and Yuengling Brewing of Pottsville, Pennsylvania. Then in 1984 he began homebrewing. He later took two courses at the Siebel Institute in Chicago and one at UC-Davis. However, Phil says he has learned most through independent reading and practice.

Company owners Richard and Marcia King, originally from Meriden, Connecticut, first became inspired after trying Catamount ales while traveling through Vermont. They decided that Connecticut needed its own brewery and that they were the ones who were going to open that brewery.

New England Brewing Co. was incorporated in February of 1989 and their first brew, Atlantic Amber, hit the shelves in February of the following year. Their seven-barrel brewing system was manufactured locally. However, they quickly had to upgrade to a nineteen-barrel system. The beers were all kegged at the beginning. Later they began bottling in 12-oz. bottles, using a third-hand bottling line.

By 1994 their distribution had spread out of Connecticut to Rhode Island, Massachusetts, Vermont, New York, and New Jersey. They are making plans to move to a larger facility.

The Brew

Phil Markowski and Ron Page are making nineteen-barrel batches and are using a variety of sizes of closed fermenters, including 30-, 65-, and 70-barrel tanks. They use English, two-row pale malt and domestic, six- and two-row specialty malts, which they mill in house. They use a combination of domestic and imported hops in pellet form. All the beers are filtered.

Atlantic Amber - pale copper; light hop aroma; complex, spicy, hop flavor; malt in the background; a little buttery; nice finish; took the gold medal in the alt class at the 1993 Great American Beer Festival; made with English two-row pale and English crystal malt, Cascade, imported Saaz, and Northern Brewer hops; California common style (1.048)

Gold Stock Ale - nice, hoppy-spicy aroma and flavor; made with American two-row pale malt, imported Saaz, Perle, Northern Brewer, and Hallertau Hersbrucker hops, dry hopped with a blend of hop pellets (the pellets are placed in a slurry of hot water and then dumped into the fermenter); aged with beechwood planks (1.058)

-- seasonal --

Light Lager - fresh hop aroma and flavor; made with American two-row pale malt, Hallertau Hersbrucker, Saaz, and Perle hops; available in the summer (1.033)

Holiday Ale - bright, deep copper; fresh ginger aroma; fresh, tart, spicy, and malty; medium to full body; loaded with cinnamon and nutmeg; warming mouthfeel; made with English two-row pale, crystal, roasted malts, Perle and Northern Brewer for bittering; blend of spices (1.054)

Oatmeal Stout - made with English pale and roasted malts (eight different malts used) flaked oats, roasted, umalted barley, and Northern Brewer hops for bittering; a touch of Tettnang flavoring (1.053), not sampled

---

Barrel of Miscellany

Address:	25 Commerce Street
	Norwalk, CT 06850
Telephone:	(203) 866-1339
Tours:	call for information

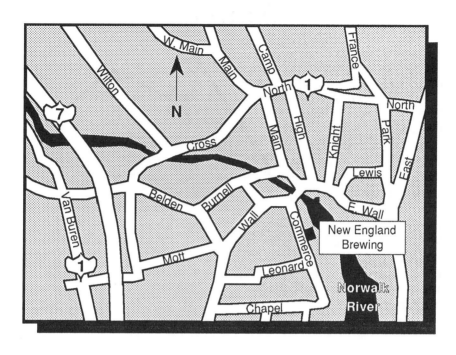

Maine

Quiz time: when was the heyday of Maine brewing? 1890 would have been a good guess, but, of course, it would have been WRONG. The correct answer is 1994, because before the current trend in brewing, only five breweries had ever operated in the state, and none of them managed to survive for more than two years.

The first new brewery in the state was the Geary Brewing Co., which opened in Portland in 1986. Ten other brewery openings have followed since then. That has more than tripled the total number of breweries to have ever operated in Maine. Brewing in Maine is here and now.

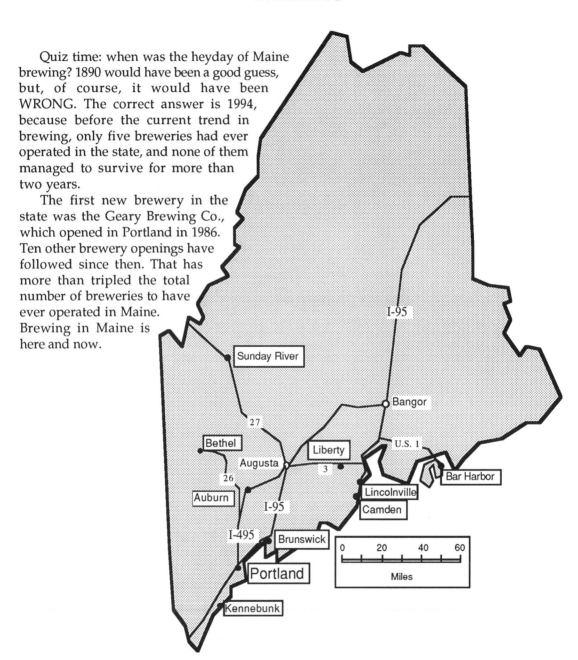

No Tomatoes Restaurant
Great Falls Brewing

Yes, we have no tomatoes

No Tomatoes was another one of the late-breaking brewpub openings about the time *On Tap New England* went to press. I found out about No Tomatoes when I overheard someone at the Lompoc Café say a restaurant in Auburn was buying their old equipment. As I was going to be traveling through Auburn the next day, on my way to the Sunday River Brewing Co. in Bethel, I stopped by, unannounced, to have dinner.

No Tomatoes is located at one of Auburn's busiest intersections, the corner of Main and Court streets, where U.S. Route 202 crosses the Androscoggin River from Auburn's sister city, Lewiston. The restaurant is in the old section of town, with brick sidewalks and antique gas street lamps. The place had a turn-of-the-century charm to it, with high, stamped tin ceilings, ceiling fans, old-fashioned wallpaper, carpeting, antique light fixtures, hanging ferns and potted plants, oak tables, and bentwood chairs. The dining area was lit with candles. Large windows looked out onto the historic street. Kind of a Gay Nineties feel. The large bar had a bare brick wall behind it.

My first question to the waitress was, "Do you serve tomatoes." "Mister," she said, "do you wanna know how many times I get asked that question every day?"

Legend has it, the original owner hated tomatoes as a boy. When his mother would ask him what he wanted on his dinner plate, his answer was always, "You can put anything on it, but NO TOMATOES!" There is a vicious rumor going around that it got its name because when the restaurant first opened the staff was all male. But, that is about as accurate as the old wives' tale that bock beer is made when the brewers clean out the brewing vats in the spring.

Yes, they do offer tomatoes--in the house salad. In addition, they had an ample list of appetizers, soups, sandwiches, burgers, chicken, veal, beef, and seafood dishes. The specialties included Shrimp Wellington, Tournedoes Oscar, Baby-back Ribs, and Steak Au Poivre Madeira. I tried the Baked Stuffed Haddock accompanied by a bottle of Shipyard Export Ale (from Kennebunkport Brewing). They were both very tasty.

At press time, brewer Cass Bartlett was planning on making a pale ale, an amber ale, and a porter to start. He will add seasonal ales later. Cass has been homebrewing for twelve years, however, this is his first experience on a commercial scale. He will be making four-barrel batches with a gas-fired kettle and fermenting in closed fermenters. The pale and the amber were to be filtered, but not the porter. The ales were to be served from kegs under CO_2 pressure. He hopes to make some cask-conditioned ales in the future. Cass is using English two-row malts. The pale malt is pre-ground, but he grinds his own chocolate and Munich malts. He plans to use East Kent Golding and Fuggle hops from England and Saaz from Czechoslovakia. He planned to have his ales on line by late spring 1994.

Barrel of Miscellany

Address: 36 Court Street
                      Auburn, ME 04210

Telephone: (207) 784-3919

Hours: 11:00 a.m. - midnight daily

Credit cards: American Express, Mastercard, Visa

non-smoking area

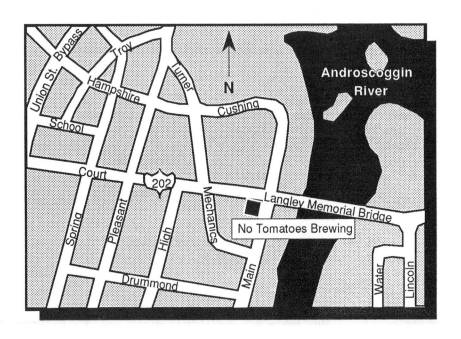

Bar Harbor Brewing

Brew Pilgrims' Way Station

Tod and Suzi Foster's life is devoted to making beer--Tod brews it, Suzi manages it, and they both receive brew pilgrims with open arms. You see, the brewery, located in the basement of their home, is surrounded by Acadia National Park. With four million tourists driving by their house every year, they get lots of visitors. In fact, a major part of their summer is taken up with welcoming brew pilgrims.

Typically, they see the station wagon filled with mom, pop, the kids, and the dog go whizzing by their sign; the brake lights come on; the back-up lights come on; they pull onto the front lawn and the whole family comes piling out of the car (pop, with a twinkle in his eye). The Fosters are well prepared for these daily occurrences. Out back they have a hospitality log cabin, where they can sell beer and other merchandise to go, with a porch where visitors can rock in the chairs, sample the brews, and talk about beer and brewing. In front of the porch is Alewife Pond, where the kids can play among the cattails and hunt for frogs. While not occupied with brewing, Tod, 41, spends much of his time explaining to curious visitors how beer is made and answering multitudinous questions (What is racking? How long does it have to cook? How do you make different styles of beer? How much alcohol is in beer? etc., etc.). Suzi, 39, has an amazing memory for faces and names and has more stories to tell about the visitors than Chaucer did in his *Canterbury Tales.* For those who really want to spend a lot of time at the brewery or in the park, the Fosters have an efficiency apartment to rent by the week, right upstairs from the brewery. What a splendid place to use as your vacation headquarters!

Although Tod's brewery is tiny--he makes only two barrels at a time--it is a national trend setter. Since it opened in July of 1990 it has been the first cottage brewery to succeed. Few people have taken note of this, with the exception of a small band of do-it-yourselfers who wanted to do the same thing, but were reluctant to go against the advice of virtually everyone in the brewing business. In fact, the only person who had faith in Tod was Suzi. Taking heart from Tod and Suzi's success, there has been a rash of cottage brewery openings across the country (Colorado, Montana, North Carolina, Idaho, California, Washington) but most notably in New England, which now counts five such breweries.

Brewing comes naturally to Tod. He can remember helping his dad make some homebrew when he was only seven. Years later, two very good things happened to Tod. First, he took up homebrewing while attending the University of California at Santa Barbara, and second, he met Suzi Murphy, a native of Bar Harbor. After college he set homebrewing aside and worked on his career as a fisheries biologist, working in a federally funded project to protect dolphins in Southern California. When funding for the project dwindled, Tod and Suzi moved to Bar Harbor where she waitressed and he tried his hand as a scallop fisherman. After spending a winter diving in 32° water in a leaky wet suit he decided to try his hand at house painting.

In the mid-eighties Tod renewed his interest in homebrewing. Soon, he heard about the craft brewing movement and visited Geary's and Gritty's in Portland. The idea of opening his own brewery began to creep into Tod's mind. So, the couple traveled back to California where they conducted an extensive tour of the brewpubs and craft breweries. The advice they received was to forget about the whole thing if they couldn't come up with $350,000, minimum.

Tod and Suzi returned to Maine very discouraged and disheartened. But, a few years later Tod saw an ad in the homebrewing magazine he subscribed to, for a two-barrel commercial brewing system. He called the number advertised. Pierre Rajotte, of Montreal, answered. Sure, he could get them started with their own malt-extract brewery for under $20,000. They thought, "Farewell house painting and waitressing; brewing, here we come!"

The couple decided to first test their market on an even smaller scale. Tod bought a fifteen-gallon brewpot, and constructed a 160 square-foot brewery in their cellar. Tod had been fermenting in five-gallon plastic buckets, so, he reasoned, he could just buy 25 more buckets and ferment upstairs, in the couple's bedroom. Suzi still remembers the mornings she would wake up to the the pleasant gurgling and bubbling of the fermenting beer.

Tod and Suzi decided to name their brewery after the town, because using the name Foster was out of the question, with Foster's Ale from Australia being distributed in this country. Their first beer, Thunder Hole Ale, was named after an Acadia National Park landmark. Later they suffered what they call "the Bass Ale fiasco." In 1991 they were going to name their newest ale Bass Harbor Light, named after another local landmark. While the first batch was still fermenting, they received a phone call from a New York law firm so fast it made their heads spin. The gist of the call was, if they used the word Bass, they would find themselves in court. By the time the beer was released the name had been shortened to Harbor Light.

Brewed and bottled by the
Bar Harbor Brewing Company
BAR HARBOR, MAINE

Tod and Suzi kegged the Thunder Hole Ale in five-gallon Cornelius kegs and on July 20, 1990, began selling it to their first account, in downtown Bar Harbor. The ale was a tremendous hit, and within a few days it was completely gone. For the rest of the summer it was all Tod could do to keep his one account supplied.

In February 1991, they purchased a two-barrel brew kettle and six, two-barrel fermenters from Pierre Rajotte, and expanded the brewery in their cellar. The next two summers distribution spread to other restaurants in Bar Harbor and onto the mainland. By now they were able to quit their other jobs. In the winter of 1992 they moved out of Bar Harbor proper to their current location near the village of Otter Creek, surrounded by the Acadia National Park. In April of 1993 they did a 180° turn and switched from a completely kegging operation to a bottling operation only. The move and the packaging change slowed things down somewhat, but they have now recovered and are actually selling 30% of their ales directly from the brewery to the customer.

What are Tod's and Suzi's plans for the future? They certainly are not going to be the next Anheuser-Busch of Maine. They want to keep theirs a small and simple operation. They like the hands-on approach to running a business, working out of their home, and being able to relate directly with their customers, or brew pilgrims, as they call them.

The Brew

Tod is making two-barrel batches of ale using malt extract and specialty grains, which he grinds himself (Tod has ordered a four barrel kettle and plans to convert to all-grain brewing in April of 1994.) He then ferments in stainless steel, closed tanks. Pelletized hops are used exclusively. The ales are unfiltered and bottle conditioned in 22-oz. bottles. The bottles are primed with a small amount of corn sugar. During the colder months, when he has more time to brew, Tod makes two batches every week, compared with two batches every other week in the summer. Production during 1994 should be around 200 barrels.

Harbor Light Pale Ale - hazy amber; malty; long, dry, hoppy finish; made with malt extract and crystal; hopped with Cascades (1.043)

Thunder Hole Ale - deep brown with a pronounced reddish tint; very active carbonation; estery; nice and malty; slightly woody; nice hoppy finish; made with malt extract and crystal and chocolate malts; hopped with Willamettes for bittering, Cascades and Willamettes for aroma; an American brown ale (1.048)

Cadillac Mtn. Stout - opaque brown; pleasant malty-roasted barley aroma; sweet malt up front with a deliciously rich, drier bitter finish with oodles of roasted barley; full body; a great cold-weather beer made with chocolate and black malts and roasted barley; an imperial stout (1.070)

Barrel of Miscellany

Address: Route 3, Otter Creek Road, Bar Harbor, ME 04609

Telephone: (207) 288-4592

Tours & tastings: July & August: Monday - Friday 3:30 - 5:30 p.m. June, Sept. & Oct: Tues., Thurs., & Friday; on weekends and during the off-season by appointment or just stop by; if they're not busy, they'll be happy to show you the brewery.

Distribution: Cadillac Mtn. & Thunder Hole Ale -- 22-oz. bottles in central-Maine; Harbor Light -- only at the brewery

Apartment: They offer an efficiency apartment for rent; call for reservations

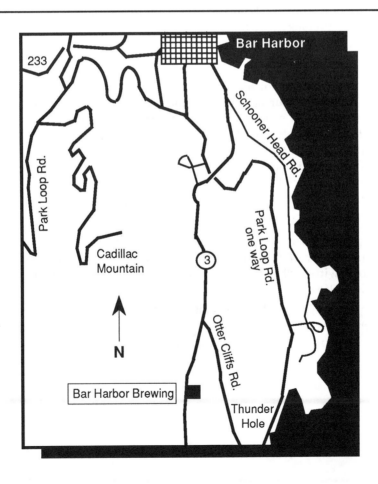

Down East Brewing

The New Kid on the Block

As *On Tap New England* was going to press, Tom St. Germain was opening Bar Harbor's third brewery. Tom has been brewing at home for some time and, inspired by the rash of brewery opening in Maine, has decided to go public with his beer.

He had applied for a license and was in the process of installing his equipment. Once open he plans to hold tours. The brewery is located at 154 Main Street in the basement of the Butterfield Delicatessen. You may reach Down East Brewing by phone at (207) 288-0355.

Lompoc Café
Atlantic Brewing

Save the Ales: *Support Your Local Brewpub and Microbrewery*

While the skippers down at the Bar Harbor docks are taking the tourists out to sea to view the humpbacks spouting, and then selling them souvenir bumper stickers with the rallying cry, "save the whales," the owners of the Lompoc Café and Brewpub, just a couple of blocks inland, are doing what they can to "save the ales." With much good humor Barbara Patteu and chef Doug Maffucci teamed up to create a cozy cafe with a slightly zany, off-beat ambience. Naming the restaurant after the Old Lompoc Cafe featured in one of W.C. Field's classics, *The Bank Dick,* was a great way to start in 1990 and the place has been attracting colorful characters, both customers and employees, ever since.

Bar Harbor is, of course, the quintessential Down East summer resort, located at the entrance to Acadia National Park where ancient mountains meet the sea. Once the summer playground of the really, really rich folks, it now caters to just plain old rich folks, the ones with really, really nice boats. The rest of us are welcome to watch them.

The Lompoc Café is located on a side street, across from the municipal parking lot and one block from the touristy shops. It is housed in a typical, two-story New England salt box, nothing fancy on the outside except their gilt edged sign which hangs above the doorway. Inside is perhaps the world's smallest brewpub, with only fourteen tables and a small bar. The atmosphere is bright and cheery with medium green walls, bright white woodwork, and polished wood floors. The windows are over-sized and make the small space seem larger than it is. Purple table cloths and multicolored cafe curtains on the windows add pizzazz and a funky Bohemian quality to the space. Artsy photographs taken by the head brewer and other local photographers complete the decor.

The mahogany-topped bar seats twelve friendly people or eight just getting to know each other. Above it hang the mugs of Lompoc's Mug Club members, handsome pottery mugs with the name of the cafe lettered on a band around the rim. Head brewer Roger Normand owns numero uno.

Thirteen of the fourteen dining tables have numbers, but one, just one, has a name. She is Cindy, short for Cinderella, and every night at nine Cindy has to be whisked away

The Menu

The menu at the Lompoc Café reflects the ethnicity of its creator, Doug Maffucci, of Milanese origin. The Persian Plate appetizer is a sampler of marinated feta cheese, hummus, tabouli, and stuffed grape leaves topped with lemon yogurt sauce. Sandwiches include a shawarma, a Middle Eastern pita sandwich filled with curried lamb, tomatoes, onions and lemon yogurt sauce and a sauteed chicken breast sandwich topped with a Berber marinade described as a "unique blend of North African spices." Pizzas are made with thin crusts and range from the more or less conventional Italian versions to the imaginative goat cheese and Greek pizzas with marinated feta. Dinner entrees include several vegetarian dishes, such as the Curried Vegetables: tofu and vegies sauteed in a spicy green curry coconut sauce. Tamr Hindi combines vegetables, figs, cashews and a sweet tamarind sauce with your choice of tofu or chicken. Doug prepares fresh seafood specials daily as well as three very different sea scallop dishes, including Julie's Stuffed Sweet Red Peppers filled with rice pilaf, scallops and shrimp topped with a jalapeño cream cheese sauce. Save room for dessert--Doug creates his own apricot-almond baklava, chocolate mousse, a triple chocolate truffle and some truly serious cheesecakes.

to make room for the band. That's right, they get a six-piece jazz band in Lompoc's.

When the band isn't playing, you may still find yourself royally entertained by the characters who are famous for frequenting the place. Take for example the mad poet, a regular who once had his poetry published in the New Yorker. He's got a story to tell, and he's been telling that one story to anyone who will listen at the Lompoc for many an evening. If you want to buy him a beer, he likes the pale ale. Or you might run into "Codfish Jerry." It seems that Jerry ran out of cash one evening before he ran out of desire for more house brew. The bartender would not run a tab for him so they moved on to bartering--a fish for another beer. The story told is that Jerry rowed out to a fishing boat in the middle of that bitterly cold January night and liberated a 30-pound codfish

which he then presented in payment for his honest debt. Guess what the chef's special was the following day?

The Lompoc Café attracts tourists, locals, those who enjoy jazz, and after ten o'clock during the summer, the place is a haven for the waiters, waitresses, and bartenders of other Bar Harbor restaurants. On a regular basis residents of lompoc, California, show up. Word of mouth has reached the West Coast and the poeple in the western version have just got to see this joint. Many postcards, photographs, and letters on the walls attest to the relationship which has grown up between the two Lompocs. There is also a photograph of a very stern-looking General Eisenhower, with a bogus, handwritten message on it saying, "Great food, great beer-- Dwight D. Eisenhower.

The Brew

The good food, good music, and good times were here from the start. The beer was fine too for that matter, "imported" from other states and from Geary's in Portland. In 1990 they began serving locally made ale. But it wasn't long before Doug decided to brew his own stuff. He purchased a small brewing system from Pierre Rajotte in Montreal and sent Roger Normand to the Cheval Blanc in Montreal to learn how to brew. When Roger got back to Bar Harbor, he began with "a sink, a kettle, two fermenters, sixteen Hoff-Stevens kegs, and himself." With his antics to keep up with the never ending demand for beer, Shawn, the assistant brewer was soon known as the "brewmonkey."

Roger began making ale with malt extract and brewing in a one-barrel kettle. He was running out of beer constantly. The next year he added a four-barrel mash tun, replaced the kettle with a larger, four-barrel one, and began making the ales with a full mash. Beer was still running out on a regular basis, so in 1993 they replaced the whole system with a seven-barrel mash tun and kettle and fourteen-barrel fermenters. Roger is still kegging into Hoff-Stevens kegs and says he still can't keep up with demand, even though he is brewing five-to-six days each week. He does bottle a small amount of the ale and it can be purchased for take out at the brewery.

Roger is making his ales from two-row, English malts and American pellet hops. The ales are clarified with a combination of Irish moss and whirlpooling. The Lompoc Pale Ale and the Bar Harbor Real Ale are filtered as well. They are all served under CO_2 pressure.

They always have three house ales on tap, and sometime have a fourth. Ales are available in 12-oz. servings ($2.50), pint servings ($3.00), 20-oz. servings ($3.50), and 4-oz. sampling sets of four for ($3.00).

Roger says a lot of customers make a black and tan with the pale and the stout, and a few wierdos try the blueberry with the stout. They also offer on tap Sam Adam Boston Lager, Guinness, Pete's' Wicked Ale, Woodchuck Cider, and Newcastle Brown Ale. Beer to go can be purchased in 12-oz. bottles at the brewery, next door.

Lompoc Pale Ale - made with pale and Munich malts, and a little malted wheat; not sampled (1.050)

Bar Harbor Real Ale - clear, deep reddish amber; faint nutty-malty aroma; good hop-malt balance; nutty; on the dry side; made with pale, crystal, and black malt (1.048)

Blueberry - cloudy; orange-red; fruity-blueberry aroma; a little hop bitterness and some malt; light and fruity with lots of blueberry; made with 259 pounds of real, crushed blueberries (1.060)

Coal Porter - opaque; deep brown-black; nice roasted barley hoppy taste; delicious roasted barley bitterness in the finish; starts rich and sweet and finishes dry; made with pale, crystal, chocolate, black, and Munich malts (1.050)

Roger's Three Frog Stout - served in the fall; made with pale and crystal malts and roasted barley; pumped with a CO_2-nitrogen mix, named after Roger and the two assistants, who are French Canadians; not sampled (1.052)

Spiced Ale - Roger adds nutmeg, cinnamon, and a little allspice; not sampled (1.050)

Barrel of Miscellany

Address:	34-36 Rodick Street Bar Harbor, ME 04609
Telephone:	(207) 288-9392 (restaurant); 288-9513 (brewery)
Hours:	May - October: 11 a.m. - 1:00 a.m. daily; closed the rest of the year
Tours:	May - October: every afternoon at 4:00
Gift shop:	at the brewery they sell bottled ale to go, homebrewing supplies, T- shirts, bumpers stickers, etc.
Music:	live music nightly at 9:00
Credit cards:	MasterCard, Visa

free off-street parking -- non-smoking area

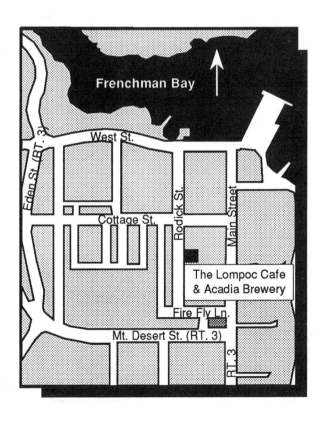

Sunday River Brewing
The Moose's Tale

The Floor Plan from Hell

It was Al Diamon, New England beer gadfly, who felt compelled to dub Sunday River as the brewpub with a "floor plan from hell" after surviving one of Sunday River's weekend nights. If form is supposed to follow function, then somebody forgot to convey to the architect that on weekend nights during the ski season, very large numbers of happy revelers would want to get to and from the bar, the fount of some pretty amazing brews. The problem in a nutshell is too few entrance and exit points from the raised bar platform which is surrounded by booths and sturdy safety rails. The solution is to visit some other time if you like your bar stool with breathing room, or why not have a seat at a table and let the waitstaff deal with the hellish crunch.

Let us go back to the parking lot to start our tour. Sunday River Brewing Company is a large, contemporary red-roofed structure set out in the Maine countryside, a few miles from the little town of Bethel. Like the hero from "Field of Dreams," Grant Wilson erected his dream of a brewpub in the middle of a corn field, believing that if he built it THEY would come. In Grant's case "they" would be the ski crowd from nearby Sunday River and Mt. Abram ski resorts. And come they have. A deck handles overflow crowds for the 200+ seat restaurant and brewpub.

Enter the front doors and you are greeted with a second set of doors and transom windows created by glass etcher, Clint Magoon. Clint was given several illustrated books on brewing and was commissioned to decorate Sunday River. There are panels decorated with barley and hops, a scene of maidens gathering hops, an illustration of an old English gravity-fed brewing system, and a huge, fanciful work on one wall of a group of comical looking Elizabethan revelers making merry with pints of ale around a tavern table. Once through Magoon's doors, you enter The Moose's Tale (Grant's girlfriend came up with the name of the restaurant in the brewery). It is an open and airy space with the definite feel of a ski resort with its exposed rafters and the wood-paneled ceiling high above, the rock faced fireplace, and wood floors. The walls are white and provide the backdrop for an eclectic mix of art, mostly old photos and tin beer advertisements, along with some snow skis.

Another local artist, Ken Irons, has his own gallery of Sunday River art hanging

The Menu

The menu caters to those who have put in a hard day on the slopes and who want to swap tall tales over drinks and a meal. There are several appetizers to choose from, including chicken wings served with a choice of dipping sauces, nachos, chips and salsa, beer battered onion rings, and a seven layer dip which includes various cheeses and veggies. Or try the house specialty, "Head Poppers," jalapeño peppers, stuffed with cheese, coated in beer batter and fried. Salad plates include a traditional cobb salad as well as grilled salads of marinated chicken or beef, charbroiled and served atop mixed greens. For those who look forward to a bowl of steaming soup when they come in out of the cold, Sunday River offers clam chowder, chili (vegetarian or beef) as well as a daily special.

The sandwich section of the menu features something for everyone including a choice of sirloin burgers, including the Yukon burger--rolled in cracked black pepper, charbroiled, and then covered with melted Monterey Jack. Vegetarians will find not one, but two "veggie burgers" to choose from.

Dinner entrees tend toward steaks, seafood, grilled chicken, and BBQ items, "smothered in Grant's Black Bear Porter Sauce." And for those who like pasta, the menu offers spaghetti, chicken parmesan, and a vegetarian lasagna. Don't hesitate to bring along the kids; Sunday River has four items for the "Mogul Monsters."

above the bar. Ken draws on the back sides of cardboard beer mats when the muse tells him to pick up his pen between sips of his favorite ales. His drawings are typically spoofs on the seasonal brews, such as the Black Bear Porter, which Ken illustrated with a kilt attired Scotsman toting around a barrel of the brew with pipes sticking out of it as if it were a bagpipe. Ken's collection has inspired other patrons to draw on beer mats, but not everyone's renderings pass inspection for either artistic merit or appropriateness and make it to the overhead gallery.

The wood of the floor, furnishings, trim and paneling around the beautiful square bar are all in mellow tones, a nice contrast to the white walls and dark green booths. The bar and glass-enclosed, stainless steel brewery are dead-ahead as you enter the front door of the Moose's Tale, booths and tables are to your right, a pool room is to your left.

The winter clientele is predominantly skiers and ski bunnies, but Sunday River has a loyal following of locals and those who work the slopes. The rest of the year you will find yourself amongst those who come to Western Maine for its beautiful and cool mountains. Mountain bikers who frequent a nearby mountain bike park have found the brewpub, as well as a group of Canadians who know a good time when they see one.

The management is young and they love their music. In fact, the owners along with the bartender, the head brewer, the cook and the restaurant manager are organizing their own band, the Shway Daddy's, which promises to be heavy on the percussion with three out of the six being drummers. In the meantime, The Moose's Tale rocks to the sounds of established bands three to five nights a week, depending on the season. Other times the air waves are a movin' to sounds supplied by a mega-sized CD collection.

The Brew

I took one look at Sunday River Brewing and figured this was going to be yuppie beer par excelance. Boy, was I wrong. The brews are exceptionally good and authentic here. So, follow Al Diamon's advice and wade through all those yuppies to the bar where you will be rewarded with some very satisfying brew.

When it comes to making good beer, leave it to head brewer Peter Leavitt. Peter's inspiration was at Triple Rock, where he used to hang out when he lived in the San Francisco Bay area, doing carpentry, construction, and restaurant cooking. The story goes, he talked the people at Triple Rock into running a tab, which they didn't usually do. When they insisted he pay up and he found himself short on cash, he volunteered to help brew (anything to avoid washing dishes, right?). He was hired on as assistant brewer at the brewpub and then moved on to 20 Tank Brewing across the Bay in San Francisco. Later Peter attended brewing classes at the Siebel Institute in Chicago and also helped the San Juan Brewing Co. get started in Telluride, Colorado.

Peter is working with a new JV Northwest, seven-barrel mash-brew system, with three seven-barrel and four fourteen-barrel fermenters and twelve conditioning/serving Grundies. The fermenters are closed. He is using two-row pale and six-row specialty malts, which he grinds at the brewery. The hops are all American in pellet form. The water comes from an artesian well. All of the beers are filtered (although the porter receives only a very minimal filtration) and are pushed using CO_2, although Peter was going to try one cask conditioned ale last winter, as well as experiment with a CO_2-nitrogen mixture.

Four to seven ales are on tap, depending on the demand. During his first full year brewing at Sunday River, Peter produced about 1,200 barrels. About 10% of the output is distributed in kegs to the Portland area. Beer prices are seasonal in the Moose's Tale; eight-ounce glasses cost $1.50 in the winter and $1.25 in the summer; pints go for $2.75 in the winter and $2.25 in the summer, while a 60-oz. pitcher costs $9.00 in the winter and $8.00 in the summer. They offer a six-set sampler on a wooden paddle for $5.00 in the winter and $3.50 in the summer. Cask-conditioned ales are served on Thursday. Since my visit they have added two new ales: **Reindeer Rye** and **Stone Ridge Oatmeal Stout** (served under a nitrogen-CO_2 mix.

Pyrite Gold Ale - light and refreshing; made with Cascade hops; for the beginner

Mollyocket IPA -bright; deep gold - amber; nice fresh hops at the end; clean with a nice dry finish; made with Galena hops; Mollyocket was a local Indian princess who stayed after the Europeans arrived and was known for her powers of healing

Redstone - amber; medium bodied; nutty and fruity with caramelized malt; fresh and hoppy too; made with Chinook, Cascade, and Mt. Hood hops

Sunday River Alt - bright; nice, copper color; a cold conditioned ale (fermented warm, conditioned cold) fruity and malty; sweet entry, dry finish; medium body, made with Cascade, Mt. Hood, and Cluster hops; very enjoyable

Harvest Fest - similar to an Octoberfest, but not a lager; seasonal; not sampled

Black Bear Porter - opaque; dark brown with a reddish tint; sweet and chock full of coffee and chocolate

Mai Bock - not sampled
Brass Balls Barleywine - not sampled

Barrel of Miscellany

Address:	1 Sunday River Road (P.O. Box 847), Bethel, ME 04217
Telephone:	(207) 824-4ALE
Hours:	11:30 a.m. - 1:00 a.m. daily
Tours:	by appointment
Music:	live music three nights a week
Credit cards:	MasterCard, Visa

two televisions for sporting events -- fireplace -- handicapped access -- free off-street parking -- non-smoking area -- darts and pool inside, horseshoes outside -- beer garden

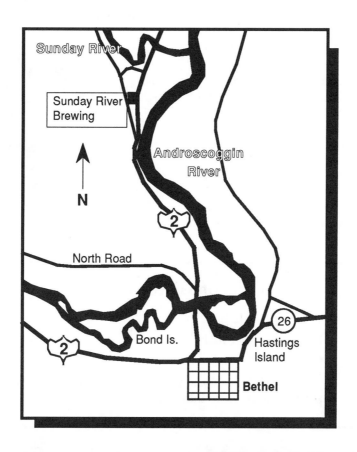

Casco Bay Brewing

Great Mountain, Great Beer

Question: what do you do when you have achieved your goal in life? Answer: set a new goal. That's what award-winning, home-brewer Michael Lacharite did after winning numerous regional homebrewing competitions and achieving national status in the beer judge certification program.

The new goal of Mike and partner Bob Wade is to open their own craft brewery. To this end Mike has graduated from the Siebel Institute in Chicago. It looks as if their goal will be achieved by the time *On Tap New England* sees the light of day. When I last talked to Mike, the building was selected, the equipment was ordered, and licensing was well under way.

Mike is a fourth-generation homebrewer, born and raised in Brunswick, and founder and former president of the 150-strong homebrew club known as M.A.L.T (Maine Ale and Lager Tasters). His ales are to be named after Maine's highest mountain, Mount Katahdin. The lofty appeal to the public will be "Great Mountain, Great Beer." His first beer to go into production will be Katahdin Golden, followed shortly thereafter by Katahdin Red. Mike says the Golden will be a cream ale in style (brewed with ale yeast and then cold lagered). He will finish the brew with imported Saaz hops and says the beer will have a delicate hoppy finish. The Red will have a full, malty body, balanced by a hoppy finish. Both will be distributed in kegs and 12- and 22-oz. bottles. Mike has on order a 20-barrel brewing system from DME in Canada. The closed, conical fermenters will be 40-barrels in size, meaning Mike will have to do double brews to fill one up.

I hope Mike and Bob reach the pinnacle of success with their new brewing adventure.

Barrel of Miscellany

Address:	14 Industrial Parkway Brunswick, ME 04011
Telephone:	(207) 729-5522
Tours:	Mike and Bob were planning on conducting regular weekly tours; please call for more information.

Sea Dog Brewing

Schooners of Good Beer

Close your eyes and imagine, if you will, the sight of a sleek sailing vessel slipping across the waves, sails full of wind, blue sky reflecting on the green sea waters. Imagine where she's been or where she is going--what ports of call. Remember her proud heritage and the time in our history when these fast running schooners, built in New England's pre-eminent shipbuilding centers, revolutionized sea travel, made a class of sea merchants wealthy, and gave birth to an era of romance with the sea and its trade winds. Got it?

Great, because you are set for your visit to the Sea Dog tavern-restaurant and brewery, located in one of those venerable shipbuilding ports, Camden, Maine. Pete Camplin, owner and long-time sailor, and his family have created a dream of a place in a four story water-powered woolen mill built in the 1790s. The mill stands just two blocks from the home of the largest fleet of living schooners in the world--these are the beauties that still go out to sea.

Pete's love for the sea and her schooners is reflected in the nautical theme which dominates the Sea Dog, named for Pete's faithful sailing partner, Barney, the family's pet Great Pyrenees. Scale models of two windjammers are proudly displayed behind the bar, a ship's boom hangs from the exposed rafters of the ceiling, and nautical charts, maritime memorabilia, and pictures of sailing vessels adorn the walls. Seating is at both tables and booths, and the Camplins have chosen to commemorate each of the 26 living schooners with a brass plaque on each of its booths. Light oak is used throughout in the furnishings which provides

a nice contrast to the old and darkened woods of the mill structure.

Other elements of the woolen mill which have been left intact are the original stone walls and wood plank floors, as well as the overhead drive belts, wheels and pulleys which once transferred the power of the water outside to the machinery inside. Now, from anywhere in the restaurant you can sit sipping a cask-conditioned ale in a comfortable Windsor-backed captain's chair and watch through picture windows the waterfall that once turned a giant wheel. In the summer months you can sit on the deck with your brew and hear the rush of the water as well as see it tumbling down into the sluice which runs along the building.

Sea Dog is a family operation and it is the eldest son, Pete, Jr., who manages the bar area. The bar itself is paneled in vertical hardwood boards, topped with planks that remind you of ship's decking. Behind the bar,

The Menu

Younger son, Brett, a graduate of the New England Culinary Institute, is the head chef. The menu is eclectic, a mix of international favorites and a large selection of faithfully rendered Down East dishes such as lobster roll and crab roll sandwiches, smoked shellfish, haddock chowder, and lobster stew. There are plenty of char-broiled items, many of which are marinated in house ales such as the brochettes of chicken, shrimp, and French garlic sausage. A beef and ale soup is made with Old Gollywobbler. Brett creates daily specials, usually beef, seafood, and pasta offerings.

mounted on twin cabinets, are antique models of the "Ruth Mary," which was a coaster or cargo schooner, and the "Helen Vida," a Grand Banks fishing schooner and racer. At the end of the bar are the Sea Dog's pride and joy, four, white oak casks set in the wall from which Old Baggywrinkle ESB is dispensed through gravity taps. Above the casks and elsewhere hang an impressive collection of antique beer trays. Above the bar, suspended from hooks attached to ship's hauser line, hang ceramic tankards ready for filling.

The Sea Dog has been a howling success since the day it opened, May 17, 1993 when the local fire marshall had to ask people to leave. The crowd that managed to stay drained the beer tanks dry in very short order, and have been keeping the head brewer busy ever since. The Sea Dog attracts folks who appreciate good beer, good food, attractive and interesting surroundings, and hospitable service by a family that genuinely enjoys what it is doing.

The Brew

Pete is assisted in the brewery by head brewer Dennis Hansen. Neither had commercial brewing experience, but Pete had done some homebrewing many years ago while in college and Dennis has been brewing at home for many years. In addition, Pete took a brewing course at the Siebel Institute in Chicago and plans to send Dennis for a course there, just as soon as there is a let up in brewing at Sea Dog.

They are brewing with a Peter Austin system, complete with seven-barrel open fermenters and the hop percolator. They use English and Belgian, two-row malt and mill the malt in house. They use a combination of foreign and domestic hops--pellets for bittering and whole leaf for finishing.

Most beers are filtered and pushed from serving tanks with a mixture of nitrogen and CO_2 pressure, while the Old Baggywrinkle and the Old East India IPA are cask-conditioned and fined rather than filtered, in the English tradition. The Old Baggwrinkle is dispensed by gravity from American white oak casks behind the bar. The IPA is drawn by a beer engine and has a blanket of nitrogen on it, but is not pressurized in any way.

Owl's Head Light - bright gold; fresh malty, hoppy aroma; nice, fresh hops; thin body; refreshing; finished with Tettnang and Hallertau, a touch of Cascade too; named after a local lighthouse

Windjammer Blonde Ale - dark gold to light amber; nice maltiness with a little caramel; off-dry, Cascades all the way through; trying to make true-to-style California blonde ale

Celtic Red Ale - fiery red hue; distinctive nutty, malty flavor balanced by the citrussy tang of fresh Oregon hops; brewed in the American ale style

Penobscott Pilsner - bright; dark gold; nice Saaz aroma; some hoppy bitterness, caramelized malt flavor; a little tangy; dry and crisp; a very friendly lager; cold conditioned for 25 days; made with pale malt, imported Saaz hops, and lager yeast

Old Gollywobbler Brown Ale (Midlands style) - bright, deep, reddish brown; fairly malty; nice hop-malt balance; smooth and appetizing; made with six different hops--Willamette, East Kent, Cascades, Tettnang, Hallertau, and Saaz

Old East India IPA - deep reddish brown; quite strong with a very assertive hop finish and a curious fruitiness

Black Irish Winter Stout - deep black; substantial, yet soft and supple from nitrogen carbonation; dry, malty, smooth, and warm

Oktoberfest - bright copper; sweet and malty; medium to full body; nice caramelized malt; hops and malt come together to make a great finish; reminded me more of a Vienna style; made with Saaz and a little Hallertau

Old Baggywrinkle (ESB) - tawny, reddish copper; very malty; very dry and woody, almost astringent; , subtle, yet complex; a little bit of a dry, red winey character at the very end; conditioned in white oak for five weeks; now sold off-premises to other restaurants and bars

Jubilator Doppelbock - dark garnet brown; overwhelming maltiness with a hint of hops

Barrel of Miscellany

Address: Sea Dog Brewing
                  43 Mechanic Street
                  P.O. Box 1055
                  Camden, ME 04843

Telephone: (207) 236-6863

Hours: 11:30 a.m. - 1:00 a.m. daily

Tours: June-Oct.: 11:00 a.m. daily; Nov.-May: Saturday at 3:00 p.m.

Beer to go: 64-oz. polystyrene bottles to go

Music: live music weekends and frequently during the week; including Irish,
                  Scottish, and maritime; also folk and blues

Credit cards: American Express, Discover, MasterCard, Visa

two wide-screen televisions -- handicapped access -- free off-street parking -- non-smoking area -- many board games -- beer garden overlooking the river

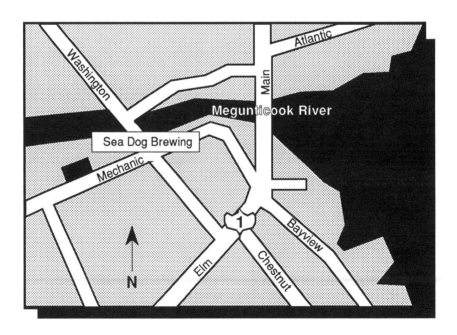

Kennebunkport Brewing
Federal Jack's Brew Pub

Beer with a View

Federal Jack's Brew Pub offers one of the loviest views of any brewpub in North America. Belmont Brewing in Long Beach, California, has a very nice view of the Pacific Ocean; the White Cap Brew Pub in Hood River, Oregon, has a lovely view of the Columbia River Gorge; and Spinnakers of Victoria, British Columbia, offers a beautiful view of Victoria Harbor, but nothing can beat the panorama from the deck of Federal Jack's on a clear autumn afternoon. Directly below is the marina with sail boats, fishing boats, and pleasure craft of every size bobbing in the waters of the tree-rimmed Kennebunk River. Across the river is the picturesque town center of Kennebunkport (founded about 1650) with the steeple of the South Church towering above the many colonial buildings and homes, which now house gift shops, artists' studios, and antique stores.

Casting your eyes back to your immediate environs, inside Federal Jack's you will see a room simply decorated with light wood furnishings, deep blue carpeting and white walls. A skylight bathes the room in natural light during the daytime. Paintings of fish and green glass fishing floats complete the decorating scheme. Federal Jack's bar is a simple wood counter, lined with Windsor backed bar stools. Overhead hangs a collection of mugs owned by the various members of Federal Jack's Brew Crew. Behind the bar is a game room with pool tables, foosball, two dart boards, a second bar and four--count 'em, four--wide-screen televisions. Acoustic and folk music groups

appear on Wednesday evenings during the warmer months.

Federal Jack's Brew Pub is frequented primarily by tourists during the summer, but a diverse and loyal crowd hangs out all year round. George and Barbara Bush have not sampled the cuisine yet, nor played a round of pool in the game room, but maybe one of these days. As a matter of fact, co-owner Don Benoit says the presidential couple once toured the the brewery and later ordered a keg of T'aint Town Pale Ale for a lawn party. The president later sent an autographed photograph, which now hangs on one of the brewpub walls.

If necessity is the mother of invention, then Federal Jack's is one of her finest prodigies. The story is that Fred Forsley, a real estate developer, decided in 1992 to buy The

The Menu

As good as the brews might be, the balance sheets revealed that the brewpub needed to expand its menu and become a full service restaurant. Mother of Invention was put back to work, a chef was secured and a delightful menu was born which included lots of fresh local seafood and herbs. House brews have been put to culinary use in the shrimp steamed in spices and T'aint Town Pale Ale and in the mussels steamed in Goat Island Light Ale. There's lobster in puff pastry, swordfish with a lobster and tarragon cream sauce, and scallops sauteed with artichoke hearts, cherry tomatoes and fresh garlic served over lemon fettucine. Those who prefer their vittles come from dry land will also find an interesting selection of items to choose from and the pizza is made with house-made whole wheat herb dough and special sauces. The soup offerings which include both clam and fish chowder, as well as a rich cheddar and asparagus soup, change daily and are very popular.

Shipyard, a contemporary two-story structure of retail and office spaces which look out on the Kennebunk River and picturesque Kennebunkport. In spite of its great location, a string of management failures had resulted in repossession by the mortgage lender. Fred believed a brewpub, such as those operating successfully in other parts of Maine, would be just perfect for putting new breath back into the ailing complex and he sought out a brewpub owner whom he hoped would be willing to open a second location. A Portland brewer wasn't interested, but he convinced Fred that he could do it himself, so the real estate developer became a brewery and brewpub owner.

Fred's forte for putting together an attractive commercial space is evident in Federal Jack's, a wonderful amalgam of historic and nautical themes which have been personified by a most fictitious namesake, Federal Jack. Just as beer is brewed in the basement level of the brewpub, Federal Jack was similarly "cooked up" in an adjacent basement painter's studio. Artist Ken Hendrickson is a civil war buff who created the persona of Federal Jack after the real life hero, Joshua Lawrence Chamberlain who distinguished himself as the Colonel of the 20th Maine Infantry, especially at Gettysburg, and who accepted Lee's sword in the surrender at Appomatox. Chamberlain went on to become governor of Maine and later served as president of Bowdoin College. Federal Jack was actually the name of a ship built in the last century on the banks of the Kennebunk River which sailed only briefly before sinking in an untimely demise.

But what a dashing Captain, Hendrickson has created out of canvas, paint and imagination. Chamberlain's portrait which hangs as a prominent piece of art in the brewpub restaurant is that of a handsome and thoughtful gentleman viewed in profile, wearing his officer's uniform, sword at his hip. He stands with his arms crossed, looking out at who knows what--his men? the future? Or perhaps, just daydreaming about his beloved Maine. Or, maybe, how good a freshly brewed beer would taste?

The Brewer

Meet the brewpub guru of all times, and "Johnny Appleseed of Maine microbrewing," Alan Pugsley. A native of England, Alan graduated from the University of Manchester with a degree in bio-chemistry. In 1981 he landed an apprenticeship at The Ringwood Brewery, founded by one of the fathers of the modern craft brewing movement in England, Peter Austin. Alan began setting up breweries around the United Kingdom for Peter Austin and later the two formed a partnership to continue their venture on a more ambitious level. To date, Alan has assisted in the opening of almost 50 breweries scattered across the globe. He can lay claim to breweries in such far away places as China, Siberia, and Nigeria; and as close as Montreal, Canada; Cambridge, Maryland; Chambersburg, Pennsylvania; and Hartford, Connecticut; not to mention five in Maine.

Alan's entree into the North American craft-brewing movement came in 1984 when he met David Geary at the Ringwood Brewery. David was studying British craft breweries in preparation for opening his own brewery in Portland. The two men hit it off well and the result was an agreement that Alan would help David start his brewery and stay on for two years. From there he branched out, helping to start four other breweries in Maine: Gritty McDuff's, Kennebunkport, Sea Dog, and most recently the Shipyard Brewery in Portland.

Alan Pugsley

In 1993 Alan turned the Kennebunkport Brewing into a training ground for budding brewers, offering a hands-on course which lasts anywhere from one day to two weeks. It has been immensely popular and covers everything from sanitation to handling yeast cultures. The day I visited the brewery a young couple was taking the course while on their honeymoon. Now that's true devotion!

The Brew

Alan and assistant brewer Paul Hendry are very busy fellows; they are making seven-barrel batches twice a day, five days a week. The infusion method is used in the mash. After the one-hour boil, the wort cools for an hour and is then forced through the hop percolator, an Alan Pugsley-Peter Austin invention. The hop percolator is a metal cylinder about three feet tall and a foot and a half across. It is filled with fresh, leaf hops, sealed, and the hot wort is forced through it. This is not exactly the same as dry hopping, in which the hops are added to the fermenter, but the next best thing. After this, the beer is fermented in open fermenters and then transferred to closed conditioning tanks. With the exception of two fermenters, all of the equipment was manufactured in

England. The beer is filtered and dispensed from serving tanks under CO2 pressure. I found them to be served at the right temperature.

Two-row, English malts are used, which are milled at the brewery. Flaked maize is used in the Goat Island, in addition to the malted barley. Domestic Northern Brewer, Cascade, and Willamette hops are used in pellet form, with the exception of the stout, which is finished with East Kent Goldings. Whole-leaf Tettnangs are the finishing hop in most of the beers (they are put into the hop percolator). The ales are fermented with Ringwood yeast, an old strain which goes back about 120 years. It attentuates very quickly--fermentation takes less than two days, and the ale is ready in eight days from start to finish. In 1993, 2,600 barrels were produced, of which 1,900 was sold to off-premise accounts. There is no beer to go at the brewery, but you can go down the street to the Maine Traders Market, where Shipyard Export is available in 12- and 22-oz. bottles and five-liter cans.

Beers are available in 10-oz. servings ($2.00), pint servings ($2.50), a half yard ($4.00), 22-oz. bottles ($3.75), and a 5-oz. sampling set of six ($4.00).

Goat Island Light Ale - bright gold; sweet malt entry; off-dry, malty finish; flowery; slightly grainy

Brown Moose Ale - dark amber; sweet, caramelized malt; slight graininess; off-dry finish; more malty than hoppy, my favorite

Shipyard Export Ale - bright, gold-amber; fresh, hoppy-fruity aroma; very fresh, hoppy-tangy palate; fresh hop finish with a little metalic bitterness; very drinkable; best seller by far--60% on the premises and 95% off the premises

T'aint Town Pale Ale - so named because vicinity where the pub is located has been known to locals as T'aint Town ("T'aint Kennebunk an' t'aint Kennebunkport" (not sampled)

Winter Ale - deep brown with reddish tint; nice, sweet, caramelized malt

Captain Eli's Kennebunkport Porter - not sampled

Blue Fin Stout - opaque; dark brown with light brown, creamy head; fairly light bodied; nice, roasted-coffee taste; medium to short finish; roasted barley character; a sweet stout; my favorite

Barrel of Miscellany

Address: 8 Western Avenue #6
     Kennebunk, ME 04043

Telephone: (207) 967-4322 (restaurant); 967-4311 or (800) BREWALE (brewery)

Hours: noon - 1:00 a.m. daily

Tours: during the summer, every half hour from 5:00 p.m. - 9:00 p.m.

Availability: throughout New England

Beer to go: at the Maine Traders Market, where Shipyard Export is available in 12- and 22-oz. bottles and five-liter cans

Music: frequently live music on weekends, including blues, blues, and rock 'n roll

Credit cards: Mastercard, Visa

four wide-screen televisions -- handicapped access -- free off-street parking -- non-smoking area -- pub games, including darts, pool, foosball, and backgammon -- beer garden overlooking the river

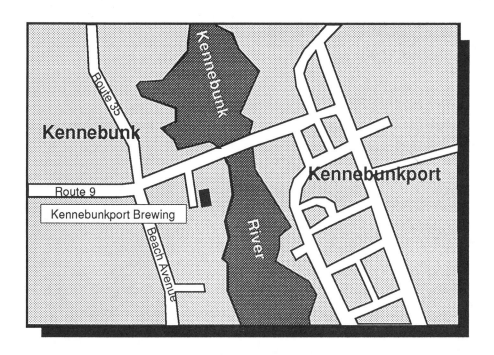

Lake St. George Brewing

Brewing on the Back Porch

June 30, 1993 saw the opening of New England's newest cottage brewery. The brewery is located in an unlikely, but lovely setting: the home of Dan McGovern, in the countryside near Lake St. George. The house is surrounded by stacks of firewood, fields of wild blueberries, and pine woods.

Partners Dan McGovern, a 41-year-old meat cutter, and Kellon Thames, 38, sales manager for Liberty Graphics, teamed up after Kellon read a newspaper article about the nation's first successful cottage brewery, Bar Harbor Brewing. When Kellon read the article, he said, "Hey, we can do this," and rushed over to Dan's house to show it to him.

Dan had done some homebrewing back in the seventies, stopped, and then restarted the hobby in the mid-eighties. Kellon was introduced to homebrewing on a trip to Great Britain in 1984 and started brewing on his own when he returned. The duo first began playing volleyball together, then started brewing together, and finally decided to start their own commercial brewery.

In order to economize, they installed the brewhouse in Dan's enclosed back porch and put three, used Grundy tanks in the basement for fermenting and conditioning. They converted a used, stainless steel dairy tank into a mash tun and got a local sheet metal person to make the the brew kettle for them.

Since they are located in the township of Liberty, they considered calling their brewery Liberty Brewing, but decided against that because of Liberty Ale, made by Anchor Brewing in San Francisco, California. The pair decided to make a brown ale because the New England market for pale ales seemed saturated. They are currently selling ale as fast as they can make it and distributing it throughout central Maine in kegs. Dan and Kellon have taken advantage of Maine's enlightened distribution laws, which allow small breweries to distribute their own products. The duo has decided to forego bottling for now, because of the expense of purchasing a bottling line.

Lake St. George Brewing is a good example of the revolution that is taking place in the brewing industry. Brewing in America started out as a cottage industry by the pilgrims, flourished, and then consolidated into a few brewing super powers making a product designed with shelf life in mind, rather than flavor. Now it is coming full circle, with small breweries leading the charge, making fresh, all-natural beer. The cottage breweries are the latest phase, bringing us back to our roots. It is no wonder that the public is beating a path to their doors. But enough of philosophy. Let's have another beer!

The Brew

Dan and Kellon are making six-barrel batches of Dirigo Ale and Lake St. George Amber using a single-step infusion mash and closed fermenters. They use pre-ground, English, two-row pale malt, domestic six-row specialty malts, malted wheat, and domestic hops. They use their local well water. The ales are unfiltered, but clarified with isinglass finings and a kettle coagulant. They were planning to introduce Lake St. George Pale Ale in the summer of 1994.

Dirigo Ale - clear, dark mahogany color with a stiff, frothy, light brown head; rich, yeasty, malty aroma; sweet, malty flavor with an interesting, tangy nutty character and soft and smooth texture; very drinkable; made with English, two-row pale and American six-row crystal, chocolate, and cara-pils barley malts and malted wheat (less than 5% wheat malt); hopped with Willamette pellets (bittering) and Goldings (flavoring); a brown ale, true to style; "dirigo" is the state motto, meaning "I lead," or "I direct" (1.048)

Lake St. George Amber - made primarily with English, two-row pale malt, with minor additions of crystal and wheat and just a touch of chocolate malt; hopped with American Hallertau and Willamette; not sampled (1.040)

Barrel of Miscellany

Address:	RR. 1, Box 2505 Liberty, ME 04949-9738
Telephone:	(207) 589-4180 or 589-4690
Tours:	Because the brewery is in Dan McGovern's home, unannounced visitors are not welcome. Please call at least one week in advance.
Availability:	on tap at restaurants and taverns in central Maine

Andrew's Brewing
Brewing in the North Woods

Andy Hazen is fascinated with brewing. When you hear him talk about it--and he does love to talk about it--you will note a sense of intellectual curiosity mixed with an affectionate familiarity with the equipment and the ingredients. If you want to learn more about the process, Andy is the perfect tutor, being both knowledgable and patient. However, your lesson on brewing could be suddenly interrupted by a signal from the local Lincolnville fire department, in which case Andy will go dashing out the door to douse the flames at some neighbor's home. Andy cocks his head to one side and listens attentively to the rings on his telephone--the right pattern notifies him that the fire department needs him. Boomer, the golden retriever, or Boomie, as Andy affectionately calls him, sprawled near the mash tun, takes note of none of this, preferring to "keep watch" over the brewery.

Andrew's Brewing is located in rural Lincolnville, a few miles west of the wooded Camden Hills area. Andy built the brewery in the old carriage house which is attached to his home. He had been making ales for himself for more than twelve years. What better thing to do during those cold Maine winters? His ales were getting better and better while at the same time he began to take interest in the many craft breweries which were popping up in the region. He did a lot of reading and experimenting and found Dave Miller's book, *The Complete Handbook of Home Brewing* particularly helpful. He worked on perfecting his Old English Ale recipe for more than five years. Andy never entered any homebrew competitions. As he says, "I'd rather have a buck than a blue ribbon."

When Andy decided to take the plunge into small-scale commercial brewing, he found that his regular occupation as a cabinet maker came in very handy. He knocked out the back wall of his wood-working shop, which had previously been the old carriage house, expanding into the apple orchard in order to make room for the new equipment. He did all the renovations himself, including the electrical and plumbing work. However, there were two tasks he hadn't counted on doing, and he couldn't do himself. These were drilling a well and installing a new septic system. The two of them together cost almost $7,000, a very large expense for such a small operation.

Andy purchased a one-barrel brewhouse from a West Coast firm and a slew of five-gallon glass carboys to ferment in. His first ale went out the door two days before Christmas, 1992. But he soon learned that an awful lot of work went into making a very small amount of beer. The next step was to purchase a four-barrel wine fermenter and convert it into a mash-lauter tun himself, making the false bottom out of stainless steel perforated screen. A sheet metal company in nearby Rockland made a five-barrel, stainless steel brew kettle and three 52-gallon fermenters for him. He has since added two, 66-gallon and three, 105-gallon fermenters, and three four-barrel fermenters.

From the fermenters he racks it into five-gallon 15.5-gallon kegs with ten pounds of

CO_2 pressure. He is brewing two, four-barrel batches each week and distributes the ales in his pickup to bars and restaurants in the Rockland-Camden area. Andy has produced more than 100 barrels during his first year.

The Brew

Andy makes his ales exclusively with imported English malts. He uses pre-ground pale malt and grinds his own specialty malts. He uses only domestic, whole leaf hops, including American Hallertaus, and Willamettes in the boil and Cascades to finish. The ales are unfiltered and clarified with finings, right in the five-gallon kegs from which they are served.

Andrew's Old English Ale - clear, deep gold to amber; fruity, flowery aroma with malt evident also; more malty than hoppy flavor; slight metalic hop bitterness in the finish; made with pale and crystal malts; his flagship beer; an American pale ale

Andrew's Brown Ale - cloudy brown; fresh hop-malt aroma; sweet and malty entry; drier, tangy-hoppy finish; very fruity; made with pale, crystal, chocolate, and cara-pils malts and roasted barley; a little brown sugar is added after the mash and before the brew; a very tasty brown ale

Andrew's Porter - dark brown with tan head; estery nose; fresh hop palate; fruity and malty; very nice; long, bitter finish; made primarily with chocolate malt and brown sugar, also uses pale, crystal, and cara-pils malts and roasted barley; an older bottle I tried had a nice, alcoholic-licorice finish

---

Barrel of Miscellany

Address:	RFD #1, Box 4975, Lincolnville, ME 04849
Telephone:	(207) 763-3305
Tours:	Call for an appointment. As this is located in the brewer's home, unannounced visits are not welcome.
Distribution:	restaurants and bars in central Maine

D. L. Geary Brewing
Beer Pioneer

In 1986 David and Karen Geary opened the first craft brewery in New England since Prohibition. It has served as a source of inspiration and a fount of information for the dozens of New England breweries that have opened since then.

It took a lot of daring to be the first. David is a romantic at heart. He quips, "you get one chance in your life, if you're lucky, to do something really, really stupid, and I did it." To avoid becoming just another failure in the dust bin of brewing history, David knew he had to add a healthy dose of realism to his dream. So, he used a conservative, back-to-the-basics approach in designing and operating the brewery. This is reflected in things like sticking to making only one brand for the first two years, spending countless hours keeping the equipment sanitized; choosing a simple brewing system and an efficient yeast, and making an ale instead of a lager (ale is cheaper to produce).

The founding of the brewery is due in large measure to the influence of three men on David--Alan Eames, Peter Maxwell Stuart, and Alan Pugsley. Back in the late 1970s David was a medical equipment salesman who loved good beer. He got to know Alan Eames while hanging out at the popular beer bar in Portland, Three Dollar Dewey's. Alan was the owner back then and was a beer visionary. He encouraged David to open his own craft brewery. At first, David thought it was a crackpot scheme. But Alan kept telling him it was the wave of the future. Finally, in the early eighties, David visited a few American craft breweries and became convinced that it was not such a wild idea after all.

Then Alan introduced David to Peter Maxwell Stuart, a Scottish nobleman, the twentieth Laird of Traquair. Stuart was on a trip to the U.S. to promote his renowned Traquair House Ale, brewed in the basement of the oldest inhabited house in Scotland. David expressed an interest in learning how to brew and in opening his own brewery. The Laird responded with an invitation to visit his small brewery in Scotland. David had now taken the brewery idea, hook, line and sinker.

In October of 1983 he incorporated the D.L. Geary Brewing Co. At the time, there were only thirteen operational craft breweries in the United States. Early the next year he flew to Scotland where Stuart showed him the basics of making beer in the tiny brewery beneath the chapel of the Traquair Castle, on the banks of the Tweed River. The brewery's 300 years showed--it still had earthen floors, open, wooden fermenters, and centuries-old brewing equipment. After that, David spent more than a month on a trip, arranged by the Laird, visiting small breweries throughout England, including two of the David Bruce Ferkin brewpubs.

But the most beneficial visit was to the Ringwood Brewery in Hampshire. There he met Peter Austin, the well-known designer of breweries, often viewed as the father of the small brewery movement in the British Isles, and the youthful Alan Pugsley, who had spent six years setting up the Peter Austin brewing systems around England. David and Alan hit it off marvelously from the outset and David quickly realized that Alan was a brewing wizard. Alan expressed interest in setting up David's brewery back in Portland, and was soon hired not only to do that, but to be head brewer as well.

While David was in the British Isles, his wife, Karen, was creating a business plan. Once back in the States, David learned that it would take longer to raise the capital than to build the brewery. They eventually put out a private stock option and between their own resources and nineteen investors from around Maine, raised $500,000. They broke ground for the brewery in 1985 in a small industrial park on the western edge of Portland. Initially there were only three employees: David, Karen, and Alan.

The brewhouse was custom manufactured in England and included a hot liquor tank, mash tun, brew kettle, hop percolator and five open fermenting vessels. The conditioning tanks came from JV Northwest in Oregon. The hop percolator was one of Peter Austin's inventions. It is a cylinder which sits in the brew line between the brew kettle and the heat exchanger. Whole leaf hops are placed in it and the hot wort is passed through it on the way to the heat exchanger. This is similar to, but not the same as dry hopping, in which the hops are placed in the fermenter after the wort has cooled. The brewhouse size was 24 barrels.

The yeast strain was obtained from Ringwood. Actually, it is a combination of two strains; one which is particularly vigorous and ferments the beer in just a few days, and the other is an excellent flocculating yeast, promoting rapid clarification of the beer. The fermentation is so vigorous that the open fermenters have cooling coils which serve to keep the heat down.

They initially did not have a bottling line, so, all of their production was in kegs. The first keg went out the door in December of 1986 and was tapped, appropriately enough, at Three Dollar Dewey's, where David heard someone say for the first time, "Gimme a Geary's."

In early 1987 the "bottling line from hell" arrived. And what a bottling line it was, a 1929 crown cork and seal soda filler. Calling it old and decrepit was putting it mildly. It was so old the valves had leather gaskets. And it became shaky enough that they had to put up six-by-six wooden posts to keep it from vibrating itself to death. The old bottler did 32 bottles per minute with about a 15% loss. About two years ago the old boy reached retirement age at 63, and was replaced by a new filler. The new one fills and seals 100 bottles per minute, with negligible loss. (A note to brewery historians: you can still see the remains of the old monster, resting at the edge of the parking lot behind the building.)

Then there was the time the frangible rupture disk on top of a conditioning tank failed. The crew was working on the bottling line from hell one day when they heard a boom--a two inch column of beer shot straight up, hit the ceiling about twenty feet above the conditioning tank, and in an instant beer was flowing everywhere. So, while the bottling line guys ran to get their mugs, David ran to get his lawyer. Looking back, David says he wonders how they ever got by, compared to the way they do things now.

From the outset the Maine beer distributors needed little convincing to carry Geary's product. The consumers and restaurant owners were another story. This new stuff from Geary's tasted "kinda funny" and it didn't have the panache of a wine. Over the years craft-brewed beer has gone from being weird to being mainstream, and now every good restaurant in the state has to have at least one micro on its beer list. It is so mainstream that Portland's new minor league baseball team, the Sea Dogs, will have three beers sold in the stadium: Bud, Bud Light, and, you guessed it, Geary's.

The Brew

Geary's makes its ales exclusively from two-row, English malts and domestic hops. Pellet hops are used in the boil and whole leaf hops in the hop percolator. Most of the year they are making two, 24-barrel batches, five days a week. Each day's double batches are fermented in open, 60-barrel tanks. The ales are whirlpooled and filtered for clarity, and packaged under CO_2 pressure, but are not pasteurized. About 20% of their output is sold in kegs; 80% in bottles. They are currently developing a second, full-time product. The 1993 output was over 8,000 barrels. They are planning an expansion which will boost annual capacity to 25,000 barrels.

Geary's Pale Ale -light copper; fresh, hoppy, flowery, fruity nose; beautiful, long, dry, bitter, malty finish; a very drinkable pale ale; made with pale, crystal, and chocolate malts; hopped with Cascades and Hallertaus in the boil and whole-leaf Tettnangs, and Fuggles in the hop percolator (1.047)

Hampshire Special Ale - very malty; long, bitter-sweet, alcoholic; earthy aroma and palate; made with pale, crystal, and chocolate malts; hopped with Cascade and Mt. Hood for bittering and finished with imported East Kent Goldings -- "Available only when the weather sucks"-- as Al Diamon says, it "warms the body, soothes the soul, and makes even the silliest of saloon soliloquies seem profound." A strong ale, to be sipped (1.070)

Barrel of Miscellany

Address:	38 Evergreen Drive (in the Evergreen Industrial Park) Portland, ME 04103
Telephone:	(207) 878-2337
Tours:	call for appointments
Beer to go:	six packs and cases
Distribution:	throughout New England

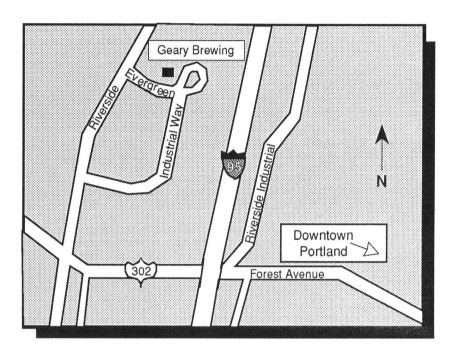

Gritty McDuff's

True Grit

To quote Al Diamon, beer guru, Gritty regular, and former Portland radio show host to craft brewers and other brewing celebs, "There is no way to describe Gritty's, it's a state of mind." That may be so, but the attempt will be made here to convey the essence of Gritty's and the physical environment in which Gritty's particular magic takes place.

Portland was a city of Revolutionary patriots who would not surrender their arms to the British and paid the price of having their homes and businesses destroyed. In the eighteenth century it became one of the principal ports of New England. It is now Maine's largest city (pop. 64,000), a major manufacturing and wholesale distribution center; and a center for the visual, musical and performing arts. It is also the birthplace of Henry Wadsworth-Longfellow who waxed poetic about Portland as "The beautiful town that is seated by the sea." Sounds ideal, doesn't it?

Gritty McDuff's is a clear reflection of its city and the diverse patronage Portland can supply. Gritty's didn't come into existence like most other brewpubs, establishments thoroughly planned for an identified target market, the ambience set by an interior design scheme, a memorable theme, or a novel menu. Gritty's owners Rich Pfeffer (age 29) and Ed Stebbins (age 31) were more interested in producing fine brews than fiddling around with interior designers. They put in just the basics in an old fishing supplies warehouse and let the rest sort of evolve. Heck, even the name was a spur of the moment, inspiration that came to owner Rich only when asked by a friend what his pub would be named.

The fishing supplies warehouse once sat on Portland's waterfront, but after a catastrophic fire in 1866 which leveled most of Portland, the waterfront was extended. The Fore Street warehouse is now more aft, two blocks from the docks. Like other old New England waterfront districts, Gritty's neighborhood is now full of shops, boutiques, galleries and restaurants catering to the tourists and locals who have money to burn. Above the shops live the city's artists and students who gravitate to low rent digs. The exterior is unpretentious, the window and door frame painted red, Gritty McDuff's lettered on the window with the subtext, "Portland's Original Brew Pub."

Inside, Gritty's is two rectangular rooms of exposed brick walls, a white acoustical tile ceiling and unfinished wood floors original to the building. The opening between the two rooms features a mammoth sliding door which rests up against one wall, takes us back to that fire of 1866. The metal clad door, with metal straps and large studs looks like the entry way of some medieval castle, but is, in fact, just a nineteenth century fire door. Long, heavy, trestle tables and benches are lined up along the walls where patrons can huddle, elbows on the tabletops. If you want a chair you'll have to hope for one of the eight Windsor backed stools that sit along the bar. The bar itself is paneled in dark oak, topped with copper sheeting and sports a traditional brass foot rail. Pretty basic stuff here.

On to the "decorating." A collection of antique beer trays graces one wall. An obligatory stuffed buck head hangs elsewhere for the manly-men types. Co-owner Rich is a member of the Portland Rugby Club so he hung up some photos of his Rugby buddies in all their gritty glory (pun intended!) and the neighborhood sports bar touch was added. On the wall behind the bar hang the mugs of the members of Gritty's mug club, which in true Gritty fashion, is imaginatively named the Mugs Behind the Bar Club. Certainly few have been put off by the name. Mugs Behind the Bar currently has 320 members and a waiting list of 400 eager souls. Al Diamon owns mug #107, David Geary was an early believer and drinks from #6. The mug number of movie star Judd Nelson is not public information, but it has its own special identity as # 007.

Are you getting a sense of this joint? Well, lots of others have and have gone on to make themselves part of that ambience. We use the term eclectic elsewhere to describe the clientele of other brewpubs, but that doesn't fully convey the mix at Gritty's--tourists, professionals, blue collar workers, students, fishermen, artists and musicians, and a liberal sprinkling of local and visiting "characters."

The place, no, uh, "the state of mind" attracts colorful personalities, as well as those who enjoy the atmosphere created by these larger-than-life types.

One colorful character who has literally left his mark at Gritty's is Claude Schmutz, a local artist, who hangs out at Gritty McDuff's when he isn't painting or tending bar at a nearby tavern. Claude decided Gritty's needed some murals, and after some talking, persuaded Rich and Ed to approve the project. Claude, referred to affectionately as a crazy Alsatian, set to work on some very striking visuals. The first is that of the brewing process with four brewing steps--mashing, brewing, fermenting, and conditioning, illustrated with the appropriate tun, kettle and tanks wreathed in hop vines. Seated, perched, reclined and even flying about are five naked brewing angels to which Claude has painted the faces of Gritty's owner, head brewer, assistant brewer, a waitress, and a female bartender. These folks obviously have a well developed sense of humor! The second mural guards the entry to the rest rooms. There a

The Menu

In contrast to the, "gee, that might look good" system of pub decorating at Gritty's, the management did set a clear course for the ales they would brew and the food they would serve: English pub grub. The menu cover is a silhouette of Parliament and Big Ben in London. Inside, the "Publican's Fare" is a faithful recreation of what you would find in a British pub from the curried Mulligatawny soup, to the house-made potato chips, to the entrees which include steak and kidney pie, shepherd's pie, a ploughman's lunch, and beer battered fish and chips. House ales are also used for steaming clams and stout is added for character to both of the pie dishes. There are non-English items to choose from especially in the appetizers and sandwiches columns where you will find Buffalo wings and nachos, a cajun burger, or a Maine crab roll. There are a few vegetarian items to select from and Gritty's chef always has a few daily chalk board specials.

large barebreasted woman nurses a baby under a banner which reads, "Blessed be the mother who gives birth to a brewer," a Czech proverb which hangs in almost every bar in the republic.

The Brew

Ed Stebbins is making his ales using a seven-barrel, Peter Austin brewing system, featuring open fermenters. He uses two-row, English malts, which he mills in house. To his base of pale malt, he adds chocolate and black malts, and unmalted roasted barley, the proportions depending on the style of beer. Each beer is made with about 10% torrified wheat with the exception of the Summer and Winter Wheat, which are made with a 60% mixture of malted wheat.

Both whole leaf and pelletized hops are used; the whole-leaf hops are put into the hop percolator, through which the hot wort is pumped on the way to the heat exchanger. Most of the hops are domestic. Galena and Cluster are used for bittering. Ed uses whole-leaf East Kent Goldings in several of the ales for aroma, and whole-leaf Cascade and Willamette in others. The IPA and the Christmas Ale are dry hopped. The Halloween Ale doesn't need any dry hopping because Ed uses about seven pounds of East Kent Goldings in the hop percolator.

None of the beers are filtered and all are dispensed from serving tanks. CO_2-nitrogenpressure is used to push many of the ales. However, there are usually two which are cask conditioned. These include McDuff's Best Bitter, IPA, Halloween Ale, Christmas Ale, Old Porter, and Nuptial Ale. On my visit to the pub I found the ales to be well-attenuated, clean tasting, and brewed according to style.

Ed is brewing six days a week and normally has five regulars and two seasonal ales on tap. In 1993 he made 1,500 barrels. The Portland Headlight Pale Ale is their best seller. The ales are sold in pints for $2.50 with the exception of the Halloween Ale, which goes for $3.25. Five, four-oz. samplers are available for $3.00.

Sebago Light Ale - served much colder than the others, bright gold; light, hoppy, and refreshing (1.035)

Portland Head Light Pale Ale - light copper; nice head; faint hop aroma; nice, dry hop finish (1.040)

McDuff's Best Bitter - slightly hazy copper; fairly flat; nice hop aroma; nice mouthfeel; good balance; on the malty side, but good hop bitterness (1.048)

Lion's Pride Brown Ale - nice bright brownish red color; mainly malty, but with a good amount of fresh hops; hoppy rather than bitter (1.043)

Black Fly Stout - black with a creamy, brown head; roasted barley and chocolate flavor; dry; very smooth with a great mouthfeel; a superbly made stout (1.045)

-- seasonal - rotating --

Halloween Ale - cloudy, dark amber with nice reddish tint; fresh hoppy-malty aroma; tangy-malty-hoppy; very fresh; cask conditioned; one of my favorites; they put a limit on the amount served because it is so strong; an ESB (1.076)

None of the following ales were sampled: **Christmas Ale** (1.064), **Nuptial Ale** (1.042), **IPA** (1.050), **Summer Wheat** (1.042), **Winter Wheat** (1.045), **Old Porter** (1.050), **Mild** (1.038), **Abbey Style Tripple**.

Barrel of Miscellany

Address:	396 Fore Street Portland, ME 04101
Telephone:	(207) 772-BREW
Hours:	Monday - Saturday: 11:00 a.m. - 1:00 a.m.; Sunday: noon- 1:00 a.m.
Tours:	Saturday at 1:00 p.m.
Gift shop:	five-gallon kegs of ale to go, T-shirts, bumpers stickers, etc.
Music:	live music on Tuesday evening and Sunday afternoon; blues, folk, Irish
Credit cards:	American Express, Discover, Visa

darts -- handicapped access -- TV -- free off-street parking in the evening

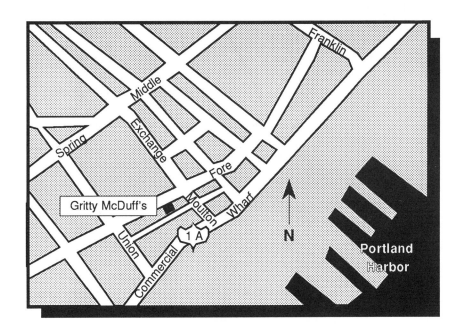

The Shipyard Brewery

By the shores of Casco Bay
By the shining big-sea-water
Stood the brewery of Alan Pugsley,
Maker of good ale, Pugsley.

There has been such an incredible demand for the ales from Kennebunkport Brewing that the owners have constructed a second brewery in Portland, named after their most successful ale, Shipyard Export. Appropriately enough, the brewery is located in an old foundry building which commands a view of a shipyard and Casco Bay.

Of interest is the fact that the location for the new brewery is the very site of the birthplace of Henry Wadsworth Longfellow, famed author of "Hiawatha," "The Village Blacksmith," and "Tales from a Country Inn."

At press time, the equipment was en route from England, and the owners hoped to have their first batch off the line by late spring 1994. Alan and his assistant brewers will be making 50-barrel batches in open fermenters. Actually, the same brewing methods were to be employed as now in practice at the Kennebunkport Brewing Co. The ales will be available in both kegs and bottles. They planned to begin with the Shipyard Export and then have three to four year round and a rotating seasonal. The ales were to be Goat Island Light Ale, Brown Moose Ale, Shipyard Export Ale, T'aint Town Pale Ale, Winter Ale, Captain Eli's Kennebunkport Porter, and Blue Fin Stout.

Barrel of Miscellany

Address:	75 Newbury
	Portland, ME 04101
Telephone:	(207) 761-0807
Tours:	call for information

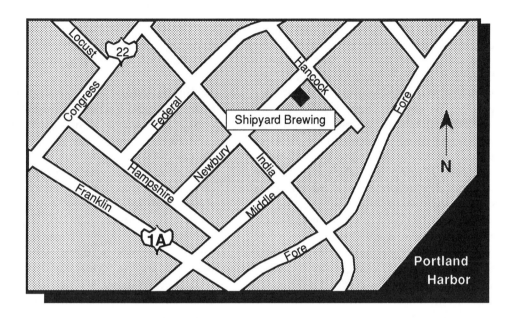

Sugarloaf Brewing -- Theo's Pub

Ice Beer

Quiz time. The first question is easy. What do snow, ice, and beer have in common? Give up? They are all cold and wet. The similarity ends there. But partners Dick Leeman and Jim McManus figured they could make a winning combination by putting these three elements together. But, unlike some of the major breweries, they are keeping the ice out of the beer (thank God). At press time they were about to test their theory by opening their brewpub at the Sugarloaf Ski Resort, one of the snowiest places in Maine. And with their plans for Theo's Pub, the largest brewpub in the state, they will make it the beeriest too.

Next question (the level of difficulty increases significantly here): Theo who? Answer: they named the pub after Theo A. Johnson, ski enthusiast and author of the book, *The Art of Skeeing,* published way back in 1905. The book propounded the health benefits of skiing and exercising in the out-of-doors.

Last question (this one is really easy): do Dick and Jim like to ski? Answer: you've gotta be kidding--why else would they build a brewpub within a mile of the ski slopes?

When Sugarloaf Brewing opens it should be the largest brewpub in the state of Maine, with seating for 250. It is housed in an attractive, two-story, rough-sawn, naturally-weathered, pine building. Located only 100 feet from the south branch of the Carrabassett River, and on the access road to Sugarloaf, you can't miss it.

The interior has a beautiful construction of post and beam white pine. The main floor is a family-oriented, non-smoking dining and lounge area with thirty-foot high ceilings and windows looking into the brewery. On the lower level you will find Theo's Pub, with a dark oak, copper-topped bar.

The dining room will have a full menu focusing on chicken, fresh pasta, and seafood. The pub will feature appetizers, finger food, and lighter fare.

Jim McManus has homebrewed for a few years and also took Alan Pugsley's pupilage course last year at Kennebunkport Brewing. He will be using a Peter Austin system, with fourteen-barrel mash tun, brew kettle and open fermenter. There will be a combination of fourteen- and 28-barrel conditioning tanks. After filtration, the ales will be dispensed from serving tanks using CO_2 pressure. Jim will be using English, two-row malt, milled on site. He will be using a combination of domestic and imported hops. His flagship ale will be Carrabassett Pale Ale. He plans to come out with a porter and a stout after that, followed by a light ale. There will be one guest tap.

Barrel of Miscellany

Address:	RR #1, Box 2268 (Access Road, Sugarloaf) Carrabassett Valley, ME 04947
Telephone:	(207) 237-2211
Hours:	11 a.m. - 1 a.m. daily
Credit cards:	American Express, MasterCard, Visa

non-smoking area -- darts
off-street parking

Massachusetts

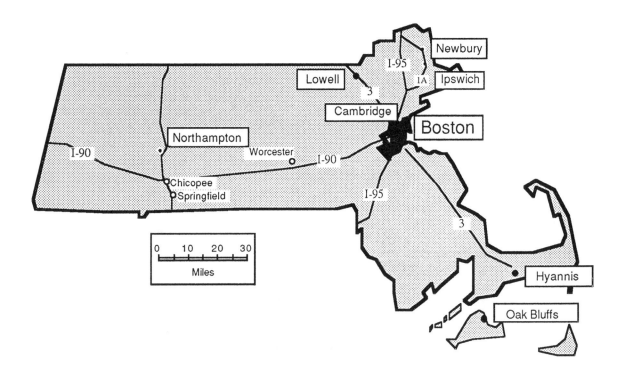

The Commonwealth of Massachusetts has a long history of brewing. The Pilgrims first set foot on Plymouth Rock because they had run out of beer, among other provisions. It also claims the establishment of the first commercial brewery in New England, Captain Sedgwick's Brewing in Boston (1637). By the Gay Nineties the state had 41 breweries. When Massachusetts instituted its own prohibition in 1918, two years prior to national Prohibition, only 23 breweries remained. Nineteen reopened during 1933-34, immediately after Repeal. But they began closing one after the other, until the last brewery closed in Lawrence in 1970, the Diamond Spring Brewery. A New York brewer, Jacob Ruppert, operated a brewery in New Bedford from 1967-1977.

Recent years have witnessed a resurgence of brewing activity, with thirteen breweries opening across the state. The first was Commonwealth Brewing in Boston in the summer of 1986, followed by Mass. Bay Brewing and Northampton Brewing the next summer. As breweries continue to open (the count is now up to 14), it will be interesting to see if the number of new breweries surpasses the all-time high of 41 way back in 1890.

Atlantic Coast Brewing

Boston

New Kid on the Block

As *On Tap New England* went to press, yet another brewery was set to open in the Boston area. That will make eight breweries in the area. The new brewery is Atlantic Coast Brewing Ltd., and is located in an old shipping warehouse on the docks of the Mystic River, in the Charlestown area, just across the Charles River from Boston. The brick building dates to the late nineteenth century and is located at the foot of Bunker Hill.

Owner Alex Reveliotty pointed out to me that this will be at least the third brewery to operate in Charlestown, the first being Van Nostrand Breweries (closed by Prohibition) and the Commercial Brewing Co., which managed to stay open until 1940.

Alex and co-brewer Chris Lohring will be making a line of ales named Tremont. The peninsula Boston sits on was first named Tremountaine by John Winthrop, because of the three steep hills he could see from his home in Charlestown. Upon settlement, the name was changed to Boston. But, the shortened version of Tremountaine, Tremont, is still used in several Boston street and landmark names.

The 20-barrel brewing equipment arrived from the U.K. in December 1993. Alan Pugsley of the Peter Austin Co. assisted with designing and setting up the brewery. It was ready to go into production at press time. Their flagship ale was to be Tremont Ale (o.g. 1.049), an English pale ale. It will be made with English, two-row malt and East Kent Goldings and Fuggles hops. It will initially be kegged and distributed to bars and restaurants in the Boston area. Tremont Best Bitter (1.049) was to follow off the production line shortly after the Ale. They plan to distribute the best bitter cask conditioned (i.g. unfiltered and unpressurized). Alex and Chris have plans for four seasonal ales: ESB, IPA, Strong Ale, and Stout.

Barrel of Miscellany

Address:	50 Terminal Street
	Boston, MA 02129
Telephone:	(617) 242-6464
Tours:	by reservation, please call

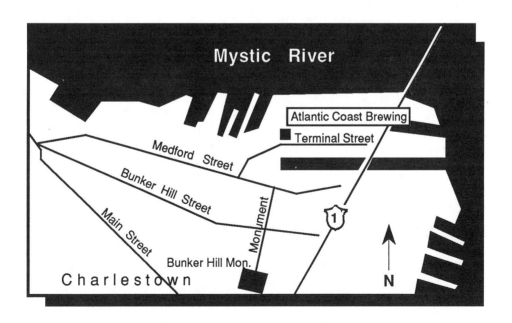

Boston Beer Co.
Boston
Born to Brew

The Boston Beer Company's brewery in the Jamaica Plain area of south Boston is four things wrapped up in one: (1) the brewery for Boston Lager and Boston Stock Ale for the Boston market, (2) a distribution center for all of the Boston Beer products for metropolitan Boston, (3) a pilot brewery where skilled brewers develop new products, and (4) a showcase visitors center dedicated to the art of brewing, the history of breweries in Massachusetts, and the Koch family brewing heritage.

The Brewery Tour

Over 20,000 visitors come to the old Haffenreffer Brewery each year. On your 90-minute tour you will get to see the brewing-fermenting operation; visit the museum featuring an exhibit of the history of brewing in Massachusetts and history of the Boston Brewing Co., including brewing artifacts, photographs of the six generations of the Koch brewers; and finally, get to try many of the Boston Beer Co. products in the hospitality room. Note the front of the bar--it was made from an old church pew. On your way out be sure to check your blood alcohol level with the breathalizer.

The Koch Brewing Heritage

Jim Koch has beer in his blood. You see, Koch (pronounced "cook"), age 44, founder, head brewer, and president of the Boston Beer Co., is no less than a sixth-generation brewmaster. Jim's father, soured by the many failures of American breweries in the mid-twentieth century, unsuccessfully tried to steer his son away from the brewing business. He

managed to put Jim through college, after which Jim launched a very successful career with the Boston Consulting Group. You can imagine his father's dismay when in 1985 he received a phone call from his son announcing that he was going to start a brewery.

The family's brewing heritage goes as far back as early nineteenth century Germany, where Jim's great-great-great grandfather made beer. He taught the art of brewing to his son, Louis Koch, who later emigrated to the United States in the 1840s. Louis found his way to St. Louis, Missouri, where, in 1860, he founded the Louis Koch Brewing Co. Louis brewed the beer and his wife Elisabeth managed the company. When Louis died, Elisabeth continued the business. The Louis Koch Brewing Co. finally closed in 1895, after having attained an annual output of 25,000 barrels.

Louis' son, Charles Jerome Koch, carried on what was now a family tradition, working at Otto Stibel's Union Brewery and later at the Empire Brewery, both in St. Louis. Louis' grandson, Charles Joseph Koch, graduated from the Siebel Institute, America's premier brewing school. Charles Joseph was working at Anheuser-Busch when Prohibition shut it down. In the years which followed, he made supplies required by homebrewers and even patented a process for making powdered malt.

Charles Joseph's son, Charles Joseph, Jr., became an apprentice brewer in 1942 and received a degree from the Siebel Institute in 1948. He worked in numerous small breweries in Ohio, including Burger Brewing, Hudepohl Brewing, Wiedeman's Brewing and the

Wooden Shoe. At the Wooden Shoe, he brewed a small batch of his great grandfather's recipe (now Boston Lager). As the story goes, the manager sampled it and turned it down. What he wanted, he said, was a beer that looked like water, tasted like water, had some alcohol, and kept a good head. Charles took the keg home and he and a friend finished it off that weekend.

At this time, American breweries were shutting down by the droves. Seeing the handwriting on the wall, Charles left the brewing business and started a wholesale chemicals firm in Ohio. He discouraged his son Jim from getting into the beer business.

Genesis of the Brewery

After receiving his B.A. at Harvard College, Jim became a mountaineering instructor for Outward Bound. After a few years of this, he returned to Harvard where he simultaneously received an M.B.A. and a law degree. Everything seemed to be in place for a very successful career with the Boston Consulting Group, when, in 1984 on a visit to the family home in Ohio, Jim discovered an article in *Inc. Magazine* about Fritz Maytag and Anchor Brewing. He immediately became excited about the beer renaissance and even entertained thoughts of one day opening his own brewery. Needless to say, his father would hear of no such nonsense.

Jim began researching the new trends in brewing and decided he wanted to create the first craft-brewed beer in New England. After a weekend of frantic phone calls, Jim raised $240,000 to get started. What he needed next was a recipe for making a world-class beer, and he felt surely his father had it in the attic of his home. After reassuring his father that he would be competing with the imports rather than with Anheuser-Busch, to whom Charles still maintained a great deal of loyalty, his father provided him with the dusty, old

recipe for the original Louis Koch Lager. This eventually became Samuel Adams Boston Lager.

With recipe in hand, Jim decided to brew the beer first and build the brewery later, the first of several controversial decisions he was to make. He hired world-renowned brewmaster Joseph Owades as his consultant. Jim reached an agreement with Pittsburgh Brewing Co. to brew his beer. Jim chose to identify his product with Samuel Adams, native Bostonian, American patriot, leading instigator of the Boston Tea Party, signer of the Declaration of Independence, and owner of a brewery on State Street. The symbolism was perfect, as Jim planned to tackle the imported beers head on.

Samuel Adams Boston Lager was first brewed on December 12, 1984. It was released at dozens of bars and restaurants around Boston on April 19, Patriot's Day 1985, a holiday commemorating the Battle of Lexington and also the same day as the running of the Boston Marathon. This was more than a year before the first brewery was to open in New England.

SAMUEL ADAMS

The unveiling was followed by a series of publicity coups, including several articles and TV appearances in key media spots. In June of the same year Boston Lager won the popular voting at the Great American Beer Festival, held in Denver. This was followed by many more years of ribbon gathering at the annual festival. Then, in November, Boston Lager became the first American beer to pass the German Reinheitsgebot purity law and be exported to Germany (it is now brewed at the Gambrinus Brewery in Germany). In 1986 Boston Lager was introduced to Washington, DC, at which time the President Reagan's White House staff asked to have Samuel Adams delivered to the White House Mess, Air Force One, and Camp David.

Jim kept his promise with his father--he tackled the imported beers head on, using the advertising slogan, "When America asked for Europe's tired and poor, we didn't mean their beer," referring to the fact that imported beers were old and stale. The campaign maintained that Heineken, Beck's and St. Pauli Girl, and many other European imports, would not pass the German Reinheitsgebot purity law. When it was rumored that the importers were going to sue, Jim responded that he was not worried in the slightest--he had done his homework and lab analysis showed that many of the imports contained adjuncts. He never was sued.

After creating his beer, Jim moved quickly to build his brewery. He located the old Haffenreffer Brewery in Jamaica Plain, closed in 1965. He thought it was just what he wanted, even though the brewing equipment had long been removed-- the building was a National Historic Landmark and it seemed to be a sound structure. He worked with the City of Boston, the Bank of Boston, and the Neighborhood Development Corporation to restore the old building. Due to structural problems, they eventually had to raise $8 million to restore the building and install the equipment.

Ground breaking took place in April of 1986, one year after the release of Boston Lager. The brewhouse from the old William Newman Brewing Co. in Albany, New York, was purchased and annual capacity was estimated at 25,000 barrels. Due to delays in construction, they were not ready to make their first test batch until two and a half years later, in November of 1988. In the meantime, Mass. Bay Brewing had opened down on the waterfront in 1987. By January 1989 the first Boston Ale rolled out the door of the entirely renovated brewery. In June of the same year the visitors center and tasting room were opened to the public.

In creating his brewery, Jim Koch had to overcome many obstacles. For example, when the first batch was made at the Pittsburgh Brewing plant, it had to be thrown out. Completely baffled at first, they later discovered that Bavarian hop varieties had changed over the years, so the quantity of hops added to the beer had to be adjusted. Then, when Jim was ready to have the beer distributed, he could not find a single Boston distributor to carry his product. He had to form his own distributorship and personally went door to door selling Boston Lager, frequently putting in sixteen-hour days. When he arrived at his first Great American Beer Festival in 1985, he discovered the beer hadn't arrived yet. Upon phoning the brewery in Pittsburgh, Jim discovered someone had forgotten to ship it. Within hours a Flying Tiger full of beer was winging its way towards Denver.

Being at the forefront of the American beer revival, Jim Koch has had his detractors. For one thing, he doesn't fit the stereotype--a conservative business suit and a briefcase don't endear him to the rubber booted, bearded, pony-tailed set. For another, almost all of his beer is brewed at plants in Pittsburgh, Pennsylvania, and Portland, Oregon. Some beer festivals have gone so far as to ban any beers brewed under contract. Importers are angry because he has cut into their profits and showed some of them up for being stale, spoiled, and impure. Others point out that he is primarily a marketer of beer, and they feel his publicity is inaccurate, at best. And finally, success does tend to create envy in the hearts of others.

In its defense, the Boston Beer Co. has produced a consistently fresh, pure, flavorful, and I might add, superior, product, reviving our German-American brewing heritage. In addition, all craft breweries have benefited from the visibility of Boston Beer products. Many aficionados of craft brewed beer were first introduced to it through Samuel Adams Boston Lager. Finally, the Boston Beer Co. has been on the forefront of consumer education, in particular promoting freshness. In July of 1988 the Boston Beer Co. introduced freshness dating on the bottle label, and was the first modern American brewery to do so in an unencoded format.

The Brew

The brewery in Boston is producing two products for the Boston metropolitan market: Samuel Adams Boston Lager and Samuel Adams Boston Stock Ale. Both of these were developed from family recipes; the Lager from Jim Koch's great-great-great grandfather and the Stock Ale from his grandfather. The only modification made to the Boston Lager recipe was the additional step of dry hopping.

In addition, Jim Koch and his staff develop new recipes at this brewery. They have recently been working on a nut brown ale. The four, full-time professional brewmasters include David Grinnell, 36, from the Siebel Institute and New Amsterdam Brewing in New York; José Ayala, 37, previously brewmaster at the Dominican Republic Presidente Brewery; Richard Dubé, previously brewmaster at Labatt's brewery in Halifax, Nova Scotia; and Jim Pericles from the Samuel Adams Brewhouse in Philadelplhia.

The newly installed brewhouse has a capacity of twelve barrels, in which they are brewing two to three days a week. The annual output is less than 10,000 barrels. They have eight, 70-barrel, closed fermenters and conditioning tanks with conical bottoms. The mash is the double decoction, method, something which is very unusual outside of the traditional Germany breweries. In the double decoction mash, a portion of the mash is brought to a boil and then added back into the main mash. This, more complex method, provides higher consistency to the mashing process. All of the beers are filtered. They use pre-ground, two-row malt. Pelletized, imported hops are used exclusively.

Boston Beer Co. beers tend to be assertive and complex, yet well balanced, clean, and very drinkable.

Brewed in Boston

Sam Adams Boston Lager - bright amber; delightful fresh; floral Hallertau aroma; good hop-malt combination to give it a soft, yet complex character; lovely, long, dry hoppy finish; made with two-row Klages, Harrington, and caramel 60; hopped with Hallertau Mittelfrueh and Tettnang Tettnager; has won numerous awards at the Great American Beer Festival, including best beer in the popular voting 1985-1986, and 1989, and best Pilsener 1987 and 1990 (1.052)

Samuel Adams Boston Stock Ale - a beautiful beer with bright amber color and a tight, creamy head; complex, earthy-fruity-floral aroma; fruity, caramelized malt; hoppy and complex; a little butterscotch; delightful, long, off-dry finish; made with two-row Klages, Harrington, and caramel 60; hopped with Fuggles, some Saaz, and dry hopped with East Kent Goldings; the flip side of California common - brewed and fermented as an ale and then stored like a lager; won the gold medal in the ale category at the 1987 Great American Beer Festival; another gold in 1992 and a silver in 1993 (1.056)

Samuel Adams Cream Stout - ruby tinted, dark brown/black; tall, tan, compact head; burnt, roasted grain, coffee aroma; sweet, roasted grain-malt-coffee up front; long, dry, rich, and bitter finish; made with two-row Klages, malted wheat, roasted, unmalted barley, caramel 60, chocolate malt, and black malt; hopped with Saaz, Fuggles, and Goldings; introduced as a seasonal in 1992, made a regular in 1993 (1.056) (sometimes brewed at other locations)

Brewed elsewhere
Boston Lightship - very fresh, hoppy aroma; crisp, hoppy flavor; light body; made with two-row Klages, Harrington, and Caramel 60; hopped with Hallertau Mittelfrueh, Saaz, and Tettnang Tettnager; won popular voting at the 1987 Great American Beer Festival (named Festival Lager) and took a gold medal in the light category in 1988 (1.032)

-- Seasonal --
Samuel Adams Octoberfest - beautiful copper color; nice toasty barley aroma; caramelized malt and tangy-zesty hops palate; made with two-row Klages, Harrington, caramel 60, chocolate, black, and Munich malt; hopped with Hallertau Mittelfrueh, Saaz, and Tettnang Tettnager (1.056)

Samuel Adams Double Bock - full body; very rich and malty; slightly alcoholic; made with two-row Klages, Harrington, and caramel 60; hopped with Hallertau Mittelfrueh, Saaz, and Tettnang Tettnager; available in the early spring; introduced in June of 1987 at the Great American Beer Festival where it won a gold medal (1.081)

Samuel Adams Winter Lager - bright amber; rich and malty, complex, well balanced, long, and very drinkable; made with two-row Klages, Harrington, caramel 60, and malted wheat; hopped with Hallertau Mittelfrueh, Saaz, and Tettnang Tettnager; available in the winter

Samuel Adams Cranberry Lambic - bright, deep gold-amber; lightly malty and fruity aroma; light and dry and with a tart fruitiness; somewhat gassy; made with two-row klages, caramel 60, and malted wheat; hopped with Saaz and Tettnang Tettnager; in addition, pure maple syrup is added; made with a wheat beer yeast; available in the late autumn and winter; not a true lambic, as it is not spontaneously fermented, nor bottle conditioned (1.052)

Samuel Adams Wheat - light clove taste; fruity and refreshing; made with malted wheat, two-row Klages, Harrington, and caramel 60; hopped with Hallertau Mittelfrueh, Saaz, and Tettnang Tettnager; available in the summer; first released in 1991 (1.042)

Samuel Adams Dunkelweizen - not sampled; hopped with Hallertau Mittelfrueh, Saaz, and Tettnang Tettnager; won a silver medal at the 1992 Great American Beer Festival; available in late spring and early summer

Barrel of Miscellany

Address: 30 Germania Street
Boston, MA 02130

Telephone: (617) 522-9080

Tours: Thursday & Friday at 2:00 p.m. and Saturday every half hour between noon and 2:00 p.m. No reservation needed. A one dollar donation to a local youth services groups is requested. Call the brewery anytime for a recording giving complete times and directions.

Distribution: Boston brewed products - in the Boston metropolitan area only

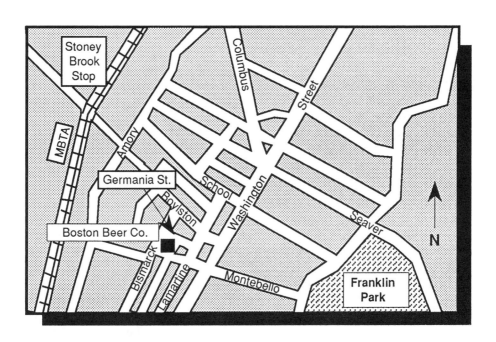

Boston Beer Works (Slesar Brothers Brewing Co.)
Boston

The Nuts and Bolts of Beer

Grab your blue denim work shirt and your Boston Red Sox ball cap on your way out the door, and you will find yourself most appropriately attired for your drinking and dining experience at the Boston Beer Works. Partners Joe and Steve Slesar and Marc Kadish found themselves an old Goodyear tire warehouse on Brookline Avenue across from Fenway Park and fully capitalized on the building's strengths. Industrial strengths, that is.

What greets you at street level is your basic yellow-brick, granite and glass facade and entryway, circa 1960, an obvious add-on to an otherwise nondescript red brick factory building. The aluminum and black sign, which runs the length of the building above the windows and entry, hints at the interior motif, but the real show is on the inside. There, galvanized pipes, sheet metal and a palette of grays and black have been artfully combined with no-nonsense blonde oak seating for a heavy duty industrial look. Gaze up and you'll see exposed ductwork, industrial style drop lights and large metal fans hanging from the 16-foot ceilings. Look down and you are walking on either black slate flooring or metal ramps and stairs. Massive concrete columns with oak wainscotted bases punctuate the room which seats 225.

Boston Beer Works has two bars, one which greets you as you open the front door, the traditional English "public bar," and a second, longer bar located in the main dining room. The second bar features front row seats onto the glass-enclosed brewery. Both bars are faced with vertical oak board paneling handsomely trimmed out with bands of gray steel. The bar tops are just the reverse,

The Menu

The menu is eclectic American and features favorites from cuisines around the world such as Thai curried chicken with peanut and red chili sauces, the house-made Italian pasta dishes, or the Mid-East hummus and tahini appetizer served with pita chips, black olives, artichoke hearts and grilled eggplant. Or you can choose something from a cuisine developed here like the Tex-Mex nachos and quesadillas or the Ragin' Cajun Jambalaya. For the more traditionally minded, there are plenty of barbecue and grilled items, including a classic half pound burger which they baste with their own beer sauce. Other items which include house brews in the ingredients are their Onion Ale Soup and their most popular dish, the grilled mako shark kabobs which are marinated in a blend of fresh herbs and raspberry ale, charbroiled and served with rice pilaf. They have an extensive selection of California wines.

polished steel banded in oak trim, as are the table tops throughout the bar and restaurant.

Along the opposite outer wall sunlight pours in through ten-foot tall windows, filtered at the bottom by panels of woven wire mesh and at the top by four continuous rows of beer bottles--over 1,000 columns of shimmering amber, green and clear glass. Adjacent to the window wall is a huge mural of an old-fashioned delivery truck parked in front of Boston Beer Works. The side of the bright red truck is emblazoned with the logo for Boston Red. Elsewhere, art imitates life in a colorful mural of food pantry shelves.

Boston Beer Works advertises that it features the nation's first "naked brewery'" Sure enough, kettles, fermenters, conditioning and serving tanks are all on full display behind the main bar, allowing patrons to watch the manufacturing of the house ales and lagers - the nuts and bolts of brewing, if you will. Food is prepared, like the beer, in full view of the customers at a copper-hooded exhibition style grill.

Boston Beer Works has earned a well deserved reputation among an eclectic group of patrons. The crowd is primarily the 25-35 year old set, but this place hums with a mix that includes the college types, professionals and Red Sox fans of all persuasions. A wait for a dinner table can last more than an hour on a Friday night or before any game at Fenway. But, what's your hurry when you have such a great selection of brews.

Boston Beer Works was founded by brothers Steve and Joe Slesar and Marc Kadish. Marc has been in the restaurant business for more than fourteen years. In 1987 he opened the Sunset Grill in Allston. Since opening, it has become metropolitan Boston's premier beer bar, offering about 80 beers on tap and 380 bottled beers, including many obscure brands, Belgian ales, and micros. It has won the the Best of Boston Award many times over for extensive collection. At Boston Beer Works Marc is executive chef. Joe, a graduate of the Cornell School of Hotel & Restaurant Administration, as well as Boston University's School of Law and Graduate School of Business, is in charge of overall operations, and expansion plans.

Steve is no stranger to brewing. After graduating from the University of Rochester in 1987 he started working as assistant brewer at Commonwealth Brewing. Within a year he had become head brewer and then left in 1989 to join the brewing staff at Mass. Bay Brewing. He then left Boston on 1989 to take a three-month brewing course at the Siebel Institute in Chicago. When he returned to Boston, Steve became head brewer at Mass. Bay. In 1990, he moved back to Commonwealth, where he became brewmaster again. From there, Steve, his brother Joe, and Marc Kadish planned the creation of the Boston Beer Works. Steve has been head brewer since it opened in April of 1992.

The Brew

If variety is what you like, you have just entered (roll of drums) Beer Nirvana. Brewmaster Steve Slesar, along with assistant brewers Bryan House and Paul Hogan, are keeping an incredible number of beers on tap at any given time. They normally have twelve (count 'em), twelve beers on tap.

Boston Beer Works makes unusually large batches for a brewpub, with three, eighteen-barrel, open fermenters. The malt is milled in-house and they use a mixture of American six-row, Canadian and British two-row, and German malts. The hops are all American pellets. A German alt yeast is used to ferment the ales and a true lager yeast is used for the lagers. All but the stout and the wheat beer are filtered. All beers are dispensed using CO_2 pressure, normally from kegs, although a few beers are dispensed from serving tanks. In 1993, 3,300 barrels were produced. Demand is so high, they are making eighteen barrel batches, five days a week.

Beers are available in twelve-ounce glasses ($2.75), pints ($3.25), 22-oz. glasses ($4.25), and pitchers ($12.95). Four three-ounce samplers can be had for $5.25. They also make Major Root Beer and Turnpike Lemonade and on occasion, house-made hard ciders and meads.

Boston Beer Works offers six regulars at all times; the rest are rotating.

Acme Light - pale gold; fresh hops, crisp and dry; light and refreshing; made with pale and cara-pils malt and flaked maize; hopped with American Tettnang (1.036)

Kenmore Kölsch - bright gold; dry and malty (1.042)

Back Bay IPA - deep gold; bright; fresh hop aroma; strong bitter hop finish; very long; made with pale, wheat, Vienna, cara-pils, and chocolate malts; hopped with Centennial for bittering and Cascades for finishing; dry hopped with Cascades

Boston Red - bright dark copper to amber; light tan head; dry malt aroma; roasted barley, malt flavor; very rich; medium length; bitter, malty finish; slightly nutty; made with pale, wheat, Vienna, caramel, chocolate, and black malts; hopped with Hallertau for bittering and crystal for finishing (1.050)

Buckeye Oatmeal Stout - opaque, dark brown; chocolate-roasted barley flavor; very sweet entry; sweet finish; made with pale, wheat, and chocolate malts, and roasted barley and flaked oats (20%); hopped with Northern Brewer and American Tettnang (1.055)

Hercules Strong Ale - received honorable mention at the Great American Beer Festival, a barley-wine; a sipping beer; made with pale and Munich malts; hopped with Chinooks (dry hopped); sucrose is added to the kettle (1.100)

- - Seasonal - Rotating - -

Bambino Light Ale - not sampled -- **Hub Dry** - blonde ale, not sampled - **Fenway Pale** - dry hopped -- **Muddy River Porter** - not sampled -- **Beer Works Blueberry Ale** - hazy, pinkish gold; slight sour tinge; just like drinking fresh blueberries; what's that left in the bottom your glass? -- why, it's real blueberries!; made with pale lager malt; garnished with blueberries which have been marinated in the Hercules; hopped with American Hallertau -- **Beer Works Raspberry Ale** - bright gold; crisp and fruity; raspberry in the finish; dry malt flavor (1.036) -- **Beer Works Oktoberfest Lager** - reddish amber; malty aroma; sweet, caramelized malt flavor; hoppy, bitter-sweet malt finish; a true lager -- **Bean Town Brown Ale** - light, roasted-barley aroma (slightly chocolatey) -- **Nut Brown** - bright, deep reddish brown color; very sweet, malty entry; fairly sweet, malty finish -- **Great Pumpkin Ale** - made with real pumpkin and pumpkin spices; pale, cloudy, orange looking, peach colored head; an autumn ale -- **Climax Winter Wheat** - dark color; clean and crisp; an American version; made with 66% malted wheat -- **Beer Works Eisbock** - a doppelbock; served in 12-oz. glass for $5.25; not sampled -- **Salute to Summer Watermelon Ale** - fruity and slightly sweet -- **Winter Works** - fresh vanilla bean, whole cinnamon stick, orange peel -- **Beer Works Centennial Alt** - the one hundredth brew of each year; not sampled -- **Smoked Scotch Ale** - brewed with peat-smoked malt; not sampled

Barrel of Miscellany

Address: 61 Brookline Avenue
Boston, MA 02215

Telephone: (617) 536-2337

Hours: 11:30 a.m. - 1:00 a.m. daily

Television: 4 sets

Credit cards: American Express, Carte Blanche, Diners Club, Discover, Mastercard, Visa

Handicapped access -- non-smoking area

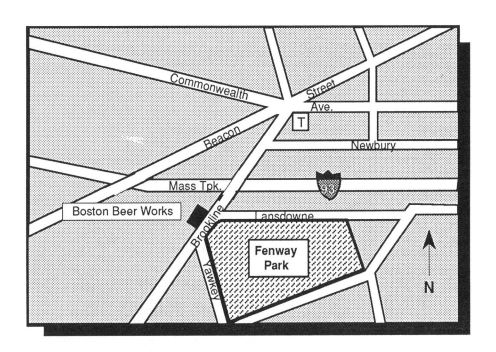

Cambridge Brewing
Cambridge

The Order of the Barstool

At many a tavern, "regulars" have their favorite places where they prefer to perch while enjoying a brew. Norm and Cliff made that perfectly clear to all of us who watched them exercise their territorial behaviors at Cheers. At some watering holes, the regulars can make their mark by hanging a mug inscribed with their name or other distinguishing characteristic - a kind of "I've been here and I'll be back" statement to the other customers. But at Cambridge Brewing Company, a place where serious beer tasting and beer drinking go on seven days a week, the management has taken it upon itself to honor a small number of their regular customers with their very own bar stool. That's right. Since 1990 when Phil Bannatyne and John (J.T.) Tremblay instituted The Order of the Barstool, ten valued customers have been recognized at annual festivities for their demonstrated love of fine beer, good company, good food, and jocularity.

These four loves are, of course, what Cambridge Brewing Company at One Kendall Square is all about--love of beer. Seated at the sleek blonde wood bar in this beautiful conservatory style brewpub you are likely to overhear inquiries to the bartender about the number of bittering units or the kinds of hops used in a particular beer. Sip and enjoy in this pleasant oasis of green and greenery, just steps away from the frenzy of one of Cambridge's hubs of hi-tech business. CBC is housed in a converted 1890s mill building, The Woven Hose Factory, where many a mile of fire hose was manufactured for many a year. The building's origins and character have been preserved in the interior walls of old brick, cement floors, and the exposed ductwork which hangs from high ceilings. This building has a venerable history of firsts, including the development of the first continuous, or seamless bicycle tire. And, would you believe, astro turf? In its second century, this building is still the site of innovation, residence of hi-tech bio-medical firms, software companies and Cambridge Brewing Company, where brewmaster Phil Bannatyne, age 38, is pushing the frontiers of craft brewing.

The old mill building elements are a perfect foil for the contemporary American additions of sunroof and atrium glass which reaches outside the original walls to bring the sunlight in. Potted trees, hanging flower

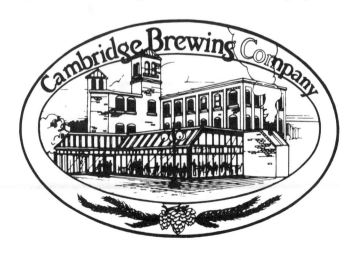

baskets and window boxes lend their touch to the light and airy interior, outfitted with light oak and maple furnishings. On balmy days customers can choose seating on the brick patio which extends out to the sidewalk.

So who comes here to eat and drink? A very Cambridgian crowd, to be sure. Primarily 25-35 year old professionals, particularly those from the surrounding hi-tech firms, as well as a goodly smattering of MIT folks. This is the R &

which never sees its way to the mash tuns at One Kendall Square.

Gentleman farmer, CBC owner, and brewmaster Phil Bannatyne hails from Stratford, Connecticut, but spent the early 1980s in San Francisco where the beer renaissance was emerging. Bit by the homebrewing bug, he went on to take some brewing courses at UC-Davis and began dreaming of owning a brewpub with the ambience of the Triple

The Menu

The menu is about as international a mix of vittles as you can imagine. Traditional fare of burgers, sandwiches and sirloin steak is supplemented by dishes inspired by Southwestern, Cajun, Italian, Greek and Middle-Eastern cuisines. Start a Southwestern meal off with baked Monterey Jack cheese and artichokes served with crustini and red grapes and then choose from enchiladas, chimichangas, or perhaps the cashew encrusted chicken served with a mole sauce and Spanish rice. How about marinated chicken breast grilled with eggplant, tomato and fresh basil served on French bread with an herbed mayonnaise? Or a chick pea salad and grilled smoked shrimp served with tabouli and chillied peanuts? A few of the entrees feature house beers as an ingredient including grilled sirloin tips which have been marinated in porter and "Drunken Pork Chops" (simmered in amber ale and lightly sweetened with brown sugar).

D crowd, well educated, cosmopolitan, but just a little bit funky. Mixing it up with the day-time locals are area artists and a respectable bunch of celebrities from stage and screen. And yes, actor George Wendt, who played Norm, the most regular of tavern regulars on Cheers, has frequented CBC.

An interesting bit of trivia, especially for those who love examples of archaic or anachronistic laws, is that Cambridge Brewing, situated in the heart of a thriving metropolitan center of commerce, education and industry is, in fact, a farm brewery. In order to meet the letter of Massachusetts law, CBC contracts with a Hadley farmer to grow barley--grain

Rock, a West Coast shrine for many a lover of good beer. Phil saved the money he was making in the balloon and greeting card delivery business, borrowed from family, friends and a bank and built his East Coast version of Triple Rock. It was created under the guidance of J.T. Tremblay, 31, a restaurant consultant whom Phil happened upon while working for Balloons Over Boston. The end result is a California-style brewpub set in MIT's backyard.

Cambridge Brewing opened its doors on April 1, 1989, and as April Fool's luck would have it, CBC's beers were not ready for serving. In fact, a whole month passed before they had any beer at all! The rest of that first year was full of adjustments and fine tuning, but by the first anniversary CBC was ready to present brass name plates to two charter members of The Order of the Barstool.

The Brew

Brewmaster Phil Bannatyne and head brewer Darryl Goss, 35, provide a nice cross section of American ales, each delicious in its own way and very distinct from the other (none of the light, amber, dark syndrome, with all three tasting basically the same). They usually have four regulars and a specialty available for your tasting pleasure. The handsome ten-barrel, Pub Brewing System equipment can be seen from the dining room in the rear. Fermenters, conditioning, and serving tanks are located behind the wall. All American, pre-ground, two-row malts and hops are employed. Phil says the city water does a fine job for the darker ales, but he adds gypsum to the water for the lighter ones. The ales are filtered and served under CO_2 pressure. They brew about four times a week and are producing some 2,000 barrels annually, 25% of which is sold to off-site accounts.

Beers are available in a 6-oz. tasting glass ($1.00), 9-oz. servings ($2.25), 16-oz. servings ($2.75), 60-oz. pitchers ($8.75), and glass yards ($9.00).

Regatta Golden - light gold; malty-hoppy nose; off-sweet entry; slightly grainy; fresh hops throughout; nice dry finish; medium body; fruity and a little flowery; very nice; made with pale malt (1.042)

Tall Tale Pale Ale - gold; complex, spicy, and very hoppy; made with pale, crystal, dextrin malt; heavily hopped with Cascades, dry hopped with whole leaf hops; very popular with the patrons (1.058)

Cambridge Amber - amber; nice caramelized malt and toasty barley character; slightly grainy, good balance; sweet up front; fairly dry finish; nice and smooth; made with pale, crystal, and chocolate malt; a favorite with the patrons (1.048)

Charles River Porter - opaque; dark brown and reddish; tan head, roasted barley nose; off-sweet, malty entry; caramelized malt and a little chocolate in the middle; very long, dry, roasted barley finish; made with dry, pale, crystal, chocolate, and black malts, and generous portions of roasted malt; dry hopped with Cascades; Galena hops for bittering; Willamettes, Cascades, Liberty in pellets for flavoring; a very nice and drinkable porter; won a bronze medal at the Great American Beer Festival (1.062)

Triple J's - clear, reddish amber; smooth malt aroma, a little alcoholic; lots of toasty barley, nutty finish; fairly full bodied; nice, off-sweet finish; nice bitterness; very good; 6.2% alcohol by volume; named after the three Cambridge Brewing managers: Joel, John, and John; a big beer, like the guys; the amount of malt is equal to about the combined weight of the three Js

Triple Threat - this gold medal winner at the Great American Beer festival is perhaps the first abbey-style ale brewed in America; Darryl makes it exclusively with pale malt (and lots of it), generous portions of Galena and Cascades for bittering and Liberty for flavoring, and just to make it a little more interesting they use whole oranges and coriander (1.088)

Winter Warmer - mahogany color; spicy; malty flavor; long and complex (1.062)

Wheaten Ale - not sampled (1.036)

Bock - not sampled (1.060)

Barrel of Miscellany

Address: 1 Kendall Square, Bldg. 100
Cambridge, MA 02139

Telephone: (617) 494-1994

Hours: Monday - Saturday: 11:30 a.m. - 1 .am.; Sunday: noon - 1 a.m.

Beer to go: in gallon poly cubes

Music: live music on Saturday (country, rock, and blues); CD juke box

Credit cards: American Express, Diners Club, Visa

TV -- handicapped access -- off-street parking (pay) -- non-smoking area

The works of local artists are displayed on a rotating schedule.

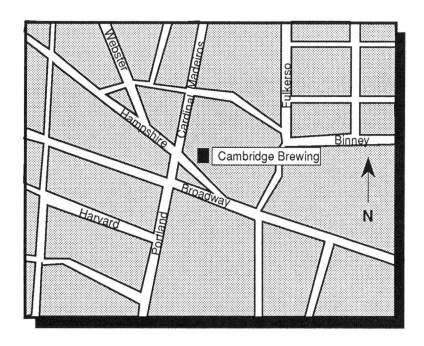

Commonwealth Brewing

Boston

The British Invasion

Well, let's see. There was the invasion of April 1775 marked by one lantern in the spire of the Old North Church and a very famous ride "through every Middlesex village and farm." Not altogether happy with the outcome of the Revolutionary War the British came again in 1812 and trashed our nation's capital. At century's end the British Queen herself took us by storm although she never set foot on our shores. Victoria's sensibilities affected manners, mores and all of the arts in the U.S. for decades. And then it happened again in the 1960's. The landing party was called The Beatles, and they led an army of rock and roll entertainers - the Rolling Stones, Herman's Hermits, and the Monkeys. Twiggy arrived next and we were taken over by the Soho couturiers and hairdressers. We just couldn't seem to get enough of these chaps.

But for the connoisseur of real ale, the most significant British invasion came in the 1980s when the brewers of real ale arrived. Richard Wrigley led the charge, and after establishing Manhattan Brewing Company in the Big Apple, he moved his campaign northward and set up a second outpost in Boston, aided and abetted by two Chinese - Americans. Commonwealth Brewing Company opened its doors in 1986 with the mission of offering Boston's beer drinkers real ales, brewed on the premises using British brewing processes, dispensed by hand pumps, and served at room temperature in British units of sale. The campaign has been a resounding success in spite of some temporary reconnoitering. Wrigley moved on in 1989 to set up another outpost in the far West. Commonwealth Brewing is now run by the team

of Joe Quattrocchi (owner), Bill Goodwin (manager), Tod Mott (brewer), and Larry Kane (executive chef).

Commonwealth is a place with character, lots of it, inside and out. The building itself, located one block from the Boston Garden and surrounded by state and city office buildings, is a five-story, red-brick structure erected in the early part of this century and now on the National Register of Historic Buildings.

Inside Wrigley transformed the cavernous street-level floor, previously used as a furniture warehouse, into an industrial chic brewpub and restaurant. Filtered light pours in from the fourteen foot tall bank of windows which stretches along three outside walls so the place barely dazzles with a mix of highly polished copper and brass fixtures. Five, huge, copper brew kettles dominate the decor, but the bar, table tops, and even the heat and air conditioning ducts glow in their warm copper sheathings. The overhead ductwork glistens against the backdrop of the high, matte-black ceiling. Brass abounds in decorative trim and pipe railings. The black is picked up again in table legs and metal folding chairs, while the bar stools are the most simple of lab stools interpreted in blonde oak. Dark stained wainscotting adorns the face of the serpentine bar and the bases of the huge, faux marble columns which punctuate the space.

On display in the loft above the bar are the Commonwealth's prize possessions, Burton Union casks. For the uninitiated, Burton Unions were a system of linked wooden casks used for fermentation at the famous

Bass Brewery in Burton-on-Trent, England (Bass dismantled the antiquated system in the early 1980s). Other British breweriana decorate the small patches of interior wall space.

A trip downstairs to the TapRoom is a must, even if it's just to view the open fermentation vessels on display behind glass and the bank of secondary tanks. Of course this may be your primary destination if a pint and some darts are what you are in the mood for. The TapRoom, smaller than the upstairs restaurant, is the simplest of English pubs for those who want to focus on the drink at hand and one's companions in conversation or game. On weekend evenings this room livens up considerably, taking on the ambience of a small nightclub with the addition of live reggae music.

The Menu

Commonwealth's slogan, "Let no man thirst for lack of real ale," could just as easily be "let no man (or woman!) go hungry for lack of good food." The name of the place is Commonwealth Brewing Company, but the front of the menu also proudly states that it is Boston's only restaurant brewery. The menu is about no-nonsense eating--8-oz. burgers and french fries, Three-Alarm Chili, beer battered fish and chips, grilled steaks, and carrot cake are representative. Cuisine of the Commonwealth is reflected in the offerings of New England clam chowder, Harvest Pie (ham and turkey pot pie), fresh catch of the day and the Tollhouse Cookie Pie. The house claim to fame, however, is their B.B.Q. babyback ribs plate, voted in 1992 the winner of the Best Damn Yankee Rib Festival Cook-Off Contest.

Commonwealth's executive chef, Larry Kane, and the head brewer put their creative energies together monthly and offer a by-reservation-only Brewer's Banquet featuring complementary dishes and brews. In February, when the snow was piling up all around Bean Town, the Commonwealth Brewery offered a gastronomic escape to the Caribbean. Their "Jamaican Excursion," began with lobster filled pastries served with ginger slaw and pepper relish. Palates were cooled down with a salad made with pimento, wood-smoked chicken, pineapple, scallions, and toasted cashews. The Pepperpot Stew heated things up again in the soup course with smoked ham, okra, and callaloo. Beer-marinated shrimp and beef starred in the Island Jerk Kabobs, served with chutney, plantain, and rice and peas. And finishing it all off, Mango Mousse garnished with fresh raspberries, crystallized ginger, and candied lime zest.

The Brew

Like so many brewmasters, Tod Mott came into the field through the back door. Originally from Greenwich, Connecticut, Tod was schooled as a potter. At the time the brewing revolution was getting under way in Massachusetts, Tod had a studio in Somerville and he and his wife Galen did home restorations on the side. When she gave Tod a homebrew kit as a birthday present, Tod's life took a new direction. After doing a couple of malt extract recipes, he quickly progressed to full-mash brewing and began entering and winning homebrewing competitions. Feeling he had a natural talent for brewing, Tod decided to learn about brewing on a commercial scale. He apprenticed at Catamount Brewing for four months and then began working as an assistant brewer at Mass. Bay Brewing, where he was trained by brewmaster Russ Heisner in 1991. After a year he became head brewer. Tod came to Commonwealth in late 1993.

Tod, assisted by brewer Jim Migliorini, is making 24-barrel batches using a brewing system which was manufactured, for the most part, on site. The cask-conditioned ales are made in the following manner. The grist is sent into the auger, where it is mixed with hot water as it drops into the mash-lauter tun. After a one-hour mash (or sacrification rest), Tod and Jim recirculate the wort through the vessel until it clarifies. The wort is then drained from the vessel for about ten minutes and then the grain is sprayed with hot water (sparged) to rinse the remaining sugars off the grain (mash). The wort is transferred to the kettle where it is heated to a boil using steam heat. Whole-leaf bittering hops are added and the boil continues for one and a quarter hours. If flavoring hops are to be used, they are usually added 15-20 minutes before the end of the boil. After the boil, the wort is transferred back to the mash-lauter tun where a bed of whole-leaf hops has been laid on top of the plates in the false bottom (this arrangement is known as a hop back). The hot wort is recirculated very rapidly through the false bottom. This process imparts hop flavors and aromas to the wort as well as filters out what is known as the hot break (coagulated protein and spent hops, which were put into the kettle). The wort passes through the heat exchanger where it is chilled to 60° F. From there it is oxygenated as it goes into the shallow, open fermenters, where the yeast is pitched. After three days in the primary, the green beer is racked to 12.5-barrel secondary vessels, or conditioning, tanks, where the 50°, ambient temperature slowly cools the beer. The young beer stays here for three days (this is known as the diacetyl rest, where sulfur is volatized and dissipated). The beer is chilled to 38°-40° and remains in the secondary for seven-to-ten more days. If the timing is correct, some young, still-fermenting beer from another batch is added, or some corn sugar is added to naturally condition the beer. From the secondary the beer goes through a coarse filtration at eight microns and is racked either to conditioning tanks or kegs. After seven more days the ale is ready to be served. The entire process takes 21 days.

They are using imported, two-row, pale and specialty malts, which are milled in-house. They also use wheat malt in the Blond Ale, and a very small amount in the Stout. Whole-leaf hops are used, including Cluster (for bittering), Cascade, East Kent Goldings, and Hallertau. Some of the ales are dry hopped with pellet hops.

About 2,000 barrels of ale were produced in 1993. Their Boston Best Burton Ale is available at select Boston area restaurants (call the brewery for locations).

About ten ales are on tap at any given time. They are available in sixteen-oz. glasses for $3.25 for regular ales and $3.50 for specialty-seasonal ales (the latter are also available in ten-oz.

glasses for $2.75).

Blond Ale - gold color; lovely, fresh hop aroma, hoppy palate and finish; their best seller; made with a 25% wheat malt - 75% barley malt mixture and Hallertau hops (1.035)

Golden Ale - clear, bright gold; nice hop aroma; nice fresh hop flavor; very hoppy; very nice; slightly grainy; finished with Cascade hops (1.040)

Best Bitter - copper color, fresh; malt-hop aroma; appetizing, fresh hop palate and malt to balance; rich, caramelized malt; clean, dry, fruity finish; served at the right temperature; their best cask-conditioned seller

Amber Ale - dark, copper-brown color with reddish hue; dry, malt aroma; pleasant, soft, malty character; medium body; has the character of a mild ale (1.045)

Classic Stout - opaque with creamy brown head; burnt, chocolate-malt nose; nice soft palate; burnt-roasted flavor; malty; long finish; very dry, acid, slightly astringent; cask conditioned

Boston Best Burton Ale - fruity aroma; nice, fresh, fruity-flowery flavor; sweet entry, dry finish; medium body; malty; cask conditioned (1.045)

Famous Porter - very dark brown with a creamy, tan head; very fine, roasted barley aroma; on the sweet side; very smooth with a subdued, roasted-barley - chocolate palate; some hop bitterness (1.053)

Special Old Ale - hazy orange; delicious, fruity-malty-alcoholic aroma; very sweet; syrupy body; very, very fruity; a little medicinal; conditioned for 16 months; a barleywine (1.100)

-- seasonal - rotating --

Nut Brown Ale - dark brown with ruby tones; light brown, creamy head; caramelized malt in the aroma; soft palate; dry and malty; fresh and fruity; short finish; served both cask conditioned and under pressure

The following have not been sampled: Imperial Stout, I.P.A., Sullivan's Irish Red Ale, Smoked Dunkelweizen, Heartland, Wheat Beer, Nut Brown Ale, Big Stiche Alt, Joe Q's Uptown Export, 90 Schilling Ale, and E.S.B.

Barrel of Miscellany

Address:	138 Portland Street Boston, MA 02114
Telephone:	(617) 523-8383; fax 523-1037
Hours:	Monday - Thursday: 11:30 a.m. - midnight; Friday - Saturday: 11:30 a.m. - 1:00 a.m.; Sunday: 1:00 p.m. - 10:00 p.m.
Music:	live, reggae music in the TapRoom on Friday and Saturday evenings
Credit cards:	American Express, Diners Club, Visa

TV -- darts -- off-street parking (pay) -- non-smoking area

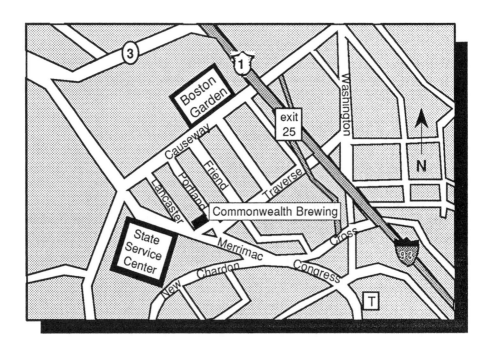

Andy Hazen cracks the grain on his home-made grist mill
Andrews Brewing Co., Lincolnville, Maine

Richard Dube cleans spent grain from the mash tun
Boston Beer Co., Boston, Massachusetts

The
bottling
line
at
Catamount
Brewing
Co.

White
River
Junction
Vermont

photo
by
Roger
Levesque

David Geary
Geary Brewing Co., Portland, Maine

Joe and Pam Rolfe
Ould Newbury Brewing Co., Newbury, Massachusetts

Tod
and
Suzi
Foster

Bar
Harbor
Brewing
Co.

Bar
Harbor
Maine

Ray McNeill
McNeill Brewing Co., Brattleboro, Vermont

Al Marzi and Fitz Granger
Mass. Brewing Co., Boston, Massachusetts

**Kegs,
bright
tanks,
and
fermenters**

**Mass.
Bay
Brewing
Co.**

Portsmouth Brewing, Portsmouth, New Hampshire
Photo by Roger Levesque

Cambridge Brewing Co.
Cambridge, Massachusetts

John Harvard's Brewhouse

Cambridge Mass.

Martha's Exchange
Nashua, New Hampshire

Sea Dog Brewing Co.
Camden, Maine

Beers of the Sea Dog

PENOBSCOT MAINE LAGER
a classic Bohemian Pilsner characterized by a fiery golden color and a clean, creamy mouth feel combined with the floral fragrance and dry finish of the Saaz hop. A select bottom-fermenting yeast and extended cold-conditioning period impart a refined character

WINDJAMMER MAINE ALE
the intense aromatics and full flavor of Cascade hops are balanced by the richness of traditional two-row British malted barley to produce a Blonde Ale of uncompromising perfection. Top-fermented, the fruity palate and crisp finish bespeak its British origins.

OWL'S HEAD LIGHT
an extremely light and flavorful beer brewed in the popular American style but utilizing traditional British two-row barley. Light in color and texture but rich in subtle hop bitterness and mellow in its understated maltiness.

(more...)

Jim Koch
Boston Beer Co., Boston, Massachusetts

Gritty McDuff's
Portland, Maine

The
Mural

Gritty
McDuff's

Portland
Maine

Greg Noonan
Vermont Pub & Brewery of Burlington, Burlington, Vermont

**Northampton Brewing Co.
Northampton, Massachusetts**

**Shawn
Duncan
and
Roger
Normand**

**Lompoc
Café**

**Bar
Harbor
Maine**

Steve Slesar and Marc Kadish
Boston Beer Works
Boston, Massachusetts

Boston Beer Works
Boston, Massachusetts

**Commonwealth
Brewing Co.**

**Boston
Massachusetts**

photo
by
Jamie
Spritzer

Tim Wilson
Jasper Murdock's Alehouse at the Norwich Inn, Norwich, Vermont

Latchis Grille
Brattleboro, Vermont

Norwich
Inn

Norwich
Vermont

Portsmouth Brewing Co., Portsmouth, New Hampshire

**Cape Cod Brew House
Hyannis, Massachusetts**

**Union
Station
Brewing
Co.**

**Providence
Rhode
Island**

Holiday McNeill, McNeill's Brewing Co., Brattleboro, Vermont
photo by Roger Levesque

Sunday River Brewing Co., Bethel, Maine
photo by Roger Levesque

The view from the deck of Federal Jack's

Kennebunk Maine

photo by Roger Levesque

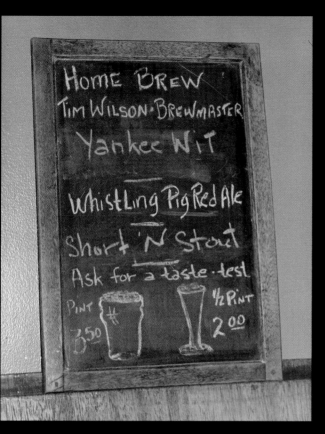

**The chalkboard
Jasper Murdock's Alehouse
at the Norwich Inn
Norwich, Vermont**

Photo by Roger Levesque

**The author
doing research
at
Hartford
Brewing Co.**

**Hartford
Connecticut**

photo by
Roger
Levesque

This FABULOUS Illustration highlighting NEW ENGLAND'S BEST BREWERIES is available as a 100% Cotton T-Shirt ($18.95), a full size poster 24" x 36" ($7.95) and even a 1000 Piece Jig Saw PUZZLE ($14.95). Call White Mountain Graphics @ 1-800-548-8009/Fax 603-383-4572 ORDER TODAY! MC & VISA orders accepted

John Harvard's Brew House
Cambridge

Beer Magna Cum Laude

Quiz time. Did you know our first and most esteemed institution of higher learning, Harvard University in Cambridge, Massachusetts was founded in 1636 as the College in Newtowne? That it's first president and treasurer was dismissed during the first year for misappropriating funds and only serving beer once every two weeks? That the University was named for one John Harvard, London tavern owner and later minister of the Charlestowne Church? That the College at Newtowne's benefactor brewed ale using recipes given him by none other than William Shakespeare?

Tis true, and more. Grenville Byford, co-owner of the John Harvard's Brew House on Dunster Street, just paces away from the gates to Harvard Yard, has done his research and has put together a credible history of the Brew House's namesake. It appears that Robert Harvard, butcher, alderman and widower of Southwark, England, was befriended by the Bard while he was between shows at The Globe Theatre. Shakespeare and wife, Anne Hathaway are credited with introducing Robert to Katherine Rogers, who became his second wife in 1605 and mother to their first-born son, John, in November 1607. Katherine owned The Queens Head Inn at Southwark, so no doubt John learned the art of brewing long before he entered Emmanuel College in Cambridge in 1627.

John spent eight years in Cambridge preparing for the ministry. Back in London his family fought the waves of plague that swept through their city, but with little success. By 1635 all had succumbed to the Black Death save one brother. John's mother left the Queens Head Inn to her eldest son, and the aspiring clergyman found himself once again running a tavern and brewing ales. But not for long. In the spring of 1637 John Harvard set sail for New England and a new life. John the scholar brought a library of more than 300 volumes of history, philosophy, theology and the like. John the brewer, according to Grenville, brought a book of brewing recipes which had been given him by Shakespeare, the writer and homebrewer of the "Dark Lady."

John's new life in America was brief. He died just a year after his arrival, leaving the newly chartered college at Newtowne his collection of books as well as a bequest of almost 800 pounds sterling. The Board of Trustees saw fit to memorialize his contribution by changing the name of the school to Harvard College. And what of the book of brewing recipes? It was lost altogether until the summer of 1992 when it was found buried under the floors of 33 Dunster Street during renovation work. Now the slim volume of the Bard's best is proudly displayed behind glass at John Harvard's Brew House.

Wonderful story, wonderful restaurant-brewery. Grenville and his partner, Gary Gut, have transformed a windowless basement of a former parking garage (the building is known as The Garage) into a sophisticated, yet warm and inviting beer cellar. Dark oak furnishings, including a good many antiques, are set in rooms lined with brick and handsome

The Menu

Gary and Grenville set out to create a comfortable setting in which their customers could enjoy fine beers and fine food at reasonable prices. Chef Joe Kubik came here after serving as chief chef for three years at the Boston Harbor Hotel. The menu is like the decor, traditional, but with just a bit of imaginative extras here and there.

Kubik smokes chicken, ribs and salmon and makes an array of international sausages himself. Sauces, dressings, breads and pastas are also house made. While just a couple of entrees incorporate house brews in the ingredients such as the beer-batter dipped fried fish dishes, the menu includes hearty and well seasoned items which fair well when served with a brew. Try the buttermilk fried chicken served with slaw and spiced cornbread, baked breast of chicken topped with Dijon flavored crumbs, or the Britisher, a grilled sirloin burger served with bacon and cheddar cheese atop an English muffin. To end the meal, the Boston Phoenix food editors commend the "Dessert of the Year," the Maple Pecan Pie served warm with cinnamon whipped cream.

The Brewery Dinner

Kubik's culinary genius is most evident in the monthly creation of the John Harvard Brewery Dinners, featuring ingredients and brews of the season. October's "evening of fresh beers and excellent cuisine," included a first course of maple smoked salmon, served with German potato salad, American caviar, and pumpernickle bread made with dark lager. This was followed by beer steamed wieswurst sausages served with cabbage, roasted shallots and shittake mushrooms and then a strudle filled with lobster, shrimp and scallops served with a Cristal Pilsner butter sauce. Dessert was a variation on the Black Forest Cake theme, this time in the form of a chocolate mousse laced with porter and served with fresh cherries. November's harvest feast included roast pheasant with spinach, acorn squash and huckleberries in a port wine sauce with panchetta, accented with Pilgrim's Porter. And Kubik would certainly have pleased the Bard of England in December with his filet mignon of beef with sauteed potatoes and a rich roasted stout red wine sauce. Understandably, these are not drop-in affairs; reservations and a deposit are required to participate in these gastronomic extravaganzas held midweek during the second week of each month.

paneled walls. Floors are a combination of lovely old pine boards and richly colored oriental carpets. Decorations include paintings, memorabilia from the old Harvard Brewing Company of Lowell, Mass., and a pictorial history of the life of John Harvard.

The bar is a long mahogany affair faced with panels which must have seen a prior life in some old church, pointed arches in deep relief, like the fronts of cathedral choir stalls. The Gothic motif is repeated in the original back-lit stained glass windows which line one wall, depicting a most unlikely group of saints including Spiro Agnew, Humphrey Bogart, Bobby Orr, Germaine Greer and Richard Nixon. To add to the absurdity each is garbed in medieval attire and has been endowed with a halo.

Large brewing vessels of gleaming copper and brass are out in full view, one antique copper brewing kettle sits right in the middle of the main dining room on a platform of brick. The stainless steel serving tanks can be seen behind the bar.

The Brew

Master Brewer Tim Morse, 45, is making a great variety of lagers and ales, using a blend of traditional, imported English, two-row malts and domestic, English, and German hops. The lagers are made using true lager yeasts and are aged longer than the ales. Many of the ales are served both under pressure and cask conditioned (unfiltered, no artificial pressure, and at warmer temperatures). A few of the beers are dry hopped. Tim has demonstrated a combination of creativity and authenticity in his revivalist brewery. The end product is both delicious and true to style.

Tim worked at the renowned Anchor Brewing Co. in San Francisco for nine years, starting as a trainee and working his way up to head brewer. From there he took a three-month course at the Siebel Institute in Chicago, worked for Hope Brewing of Providence, Rhode Island, and then at Commonwealth Brewing, before coming to John Harvard's.

Beers are available in ten-ounce glasses ($2.25-3.25), pints ($2.75-4.00), and 60-ounce pitchers ($7.95-10.95). Bard's Samplers (five beers) are available for $4.95.

All American Light Lager - light gold; grainy, malty taste; light body; medium bitterness in finish, served fairly cold, made with pale malt and Cluster hops (1.034)

Cristal Pilsner - bright gold; fresh, Hallertau nose; very hoppy; nice, fresh hop finish; a very good example; made with pale malt and Hersbrucker and Cluster hops (1.048)

John Harvard Pale Ale (cold draft) - clear copper; fresh hops, dry and bitter; made with pale and caramel malt; hopped with Cluster, Willamette, and Fuggles; served cold draft or cask conditioned (1.048)

John Harvard Pale Ale (cask conditioned) - served at cellar temperature; fine head; nice, fruity and flowery, hop nose; fresh and very hoppy; medium body; very nice indeed!

Old Willy India Pale Ale - light copper; very fine head; much maltier than the other pale ales; medium body; nice bitter finish; good balance, delicious roasted malt flavor; some Belgian lace on glass; made with pale and chocolate malts; hopped with Willamettes and Fuggles; dry hopped (1.064)

Export Stout - opaque and black with a brown head; roasted barley nose; chocolatey; fresh-roasted coffee; heavy on the roasted barley; finish is rich, bitter, and long; dry and complex; made with pale, caramel, and chocolate malts and roasted barley; hopped with Clusters; unfiltered; served cold draft or cask conditioned (1.051)

- - Seasonal - Rotating - -

Amber Bockbier - deep amber; strong and malty; medium to full bodied; try it after dinner; made with pale and caramel malt; hopped with Hersbrucker and Hallertau (1.064)

Bavarian Lager-Weisse - straw gold; lightly hopped; light body; cold and refreshing; enjoy it with a slice of lemon; made with pale and wheat malt; hopped with Clusters and Hersbruckers (1.040)

Black Forest Lager - opaque, dark brown; an appetizing, rich, toasty-malty flavor, a Schwarz bier; made with pale, caramel, and chocolate malt; hopped with Hersbrucker and Hallertau (1.046)

Alt Bamberger Smoked Beer - deep amber; smokey and malty; made with home-smoked pale malt, pale, caramel, and chocolate malt; hopped with Hersbrucker and Hallertau; a rauchbier (1.056)

Oktoberfest Weizenbock - amber; hoppy, tart, and tangy; available both as Hefe (unfiltered, with yeast, and cloudy) and Cristal (filtered and clear); made with wheat (about 60%), pale, and caramel malt; hopped with Hersbrucker and Hallertau (1.064)

Nut Brown Ale - clear brown; nice and malty; very drinkable; made with pale, caramel, and chocolate malt; hopped with Clusters; a northern, dry style (1.045)

Newtown Harvest Ale - amber; malty and spicy; made with pale, caramel, and chocolate malt; hopped with Clusters and Willamettes; whole cinnamon, nutmeg, allspice, cloves, and fresh ginger added in a cheesecloth bag to the boil (1.048)

Pilgrim's Porter - dark and malty (served cold draft or cask conditioned); made with pale, caramel, and chocolate malt; hopped with Willamettes and Fuggles; served cold draft or cask conditioned (1.064)

Harvard Highland Ale (80 shilling) - amber and malty; moderately hopped; a Scotch ale made with pale, caramel, and chocolate malt; hopped with Willamettes and Fuggles (1.047)

Mid-Winter Strong Ale - heavy, malty, and alcoholic; a barleywine; sip this one; made with pale and caramel malt; hopped with Willamettes and Fuggles (1.084)

Barrel of Miscellany

Address: 33 Dunster Street
Cambridge , MA 02138

Telephone: (617) 868-3585

Hours: Monday - Wednesday: 11:30 a.m. - 12:30 a.m.; Thursday - Saturday: 11:30 a.m. - 1:30 a.m.; Sunday: 11:00 a.m. - midnight

Music: Irish music Monday night live acoustic and jazz Tuesday from 8:00 p.m. - midnight

Credit cards: American Express, Diners Club, Discover, Mastercard, Visa

Handicapped access -- non-smoking area -- fireplace

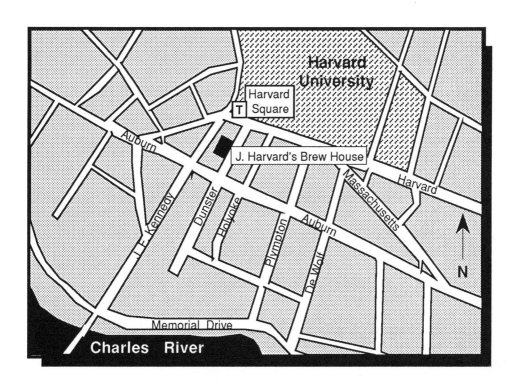

Mass. Bay Brewing
Boston

The Boston Beer Party

Boston is famous for its Tea Party, thrown by its citizens way back in 1773. As a protest against unfair British taxation, the colonials, dressed as Indians, threw tea from three sailing ships into the bay. Down by the harbor side, and just a few blocks away from the original site of this act of rebellion, twentieth century Boston citizens are throwing a new kind of party: a beer party.

It started as an interest in good beer by three college buddies back in the mid-eighties and it is still going strong, only now it is a keg party in and around their brewery, Mass. Bay Brewing.

Party, party, party, mixed with a lot of hard work, seems to be the theme of this talented, youthful, and energetic crew. Let's see, first there are the two big ones: the **Harpoon Beer Invitational** to celebrate their birthday every June, and the **Harpoon Octoberfest**, held the first weekend in October. For each of these celebrations the Harpoon crew cordons off the street in front of the brewery, sets up circus tents outside, and provides live music, dancing, food, and, of course, plenty of Harpoon. The brewery is opened up for visitors. Each of these affairs attracts in excess of 7,000 beer-drinking, fun-loving people who manage to empty more than 180 kegs of Harpoon beers. In addition, the summer festival provides brews from twenty other Northeastern breweries. Each party runs from Friday through Sunday, rain or shine. A modest admission fee is charged.

Then, in December they hold the annual **Harpoon Benefit Party**; this is an indoor affair for the first 400 people who show up. It fea-

tures food from local restaurants, live music, and, of course, Harpoon. In 1993 they raised $4,000 for Rosie's Place, a homeless shelter in Boston. After raising the funds, the Harpoon crew purchased food and made a 4th of July party (in the middle of January) for all of the women at Rosie's Place.

Finally, in March they hold their **Harpoon St. Patrick's Day Benefit**. Again, an indoor party for the first 400 showing up, with food, live music and Harpoon.

But that's not all. One of their most popular events is the **5:30 Club**. Every Tuesday, Wednesday, and Thursday at 5:30 and 7:00 p.m. the Harpoon crew opens the brewery to groups (it can be a company, clubs, or just a group of friends) for a free tour of the brewery and beer tasting in the tap room. This provides a perfect format for an office get-together. This is a very popular program and your group must be scheduled in advance to attend. During the first year, more than 8,000 people from over 300 different companies attended 5:30 Club events. The Harpoon crew can handle up to 80 people at a time.

And finally, they host **brewery tours** every Friday and Saturday at 1:00 p.m., which includes beer samples in the tap room. Large groups may make special arrangements. Call their "Let's Talk Beer" line at 800-666-3496 or (617) 455-1935.

Mass. Bay Brewing Co. was founded by Richard Doyle, age 33, back in 1986 when he was fresh out of college. Richard had traveled the world drinking good beer. When he returned to the States he was surprised at just how difficult it was to find a really good brew. That was when he and Harvard Business School chums Dan Kenery and George Legeti decided to combine their schooling and interest in good beer to form a business. They chose to do a research project on craft breweries in order to find out how to create their company. This included a trip to the Pacific Northwest where they visited several breweries. After graduation, in January of 1986 the trio formed their company and hired Russ Heissner, fresh out of the UC-Davis brewing program, to design their beers and set up the brewery. Incredibly, by June 2, 1987, they had written their business plan, conducted an extensive marketing survey, raised the capital, hired a brewer, installed the brewing equipment, and had their first keg ready to roll.

Finding a location was one of the most difficult tasks. There was little commercial real estate available in Boston. Despite setbacks, they insisted on finding a location within the city limits. They eventually found a warehouse which had been used for ship building down by the bayside. In opening the brewery, they were the first to operate in Boston in decades.

Early on, they did their own distribution, but eventually learned to rely on the distribution network for locations outside of Boston. In 1988 they began bottling, but discontinued that and had their bottled beers made for them by F.X. Matt Brewing in Utica, New York. They have ordered a new bottling line and expect to be bottling again by April 1994.

Brewmaster Al Marzi, age 27, had brewed a few batches at home when he decided he wanted to work in a commercial brewery. He started out as a driver in early 1991 and after only four months became assistant brewer to Todd Mott. When Todd left to go to Commonwealth Brewing in 1993, Al became head brewer.

The Brew

Al is turning out nine products--four all-year beers, four seasonals, and one hard cider, their newest product. Three triple, 20-barrel batches are brewed Monday, Wednesday, and Friday to fill their 60-barrel fermenters (they have a 60-barrel brewhouse planned for the near future). An infusion mash is employed with sparging starting only fifteen minutes into the mash. The beers are made using domestic two-row pale and six-row specialty malts, milled at the brewery. Cluster hops predominate, but they also use Cascades, Fuggles, Kent Goldings, and some Saaz. The IPA is dry hopped. All beers are whirlpooled for clarity, filtered, and kegged under CO_2 pressure.

The brewery places great emphasis on freshness and prides itself on keeping all draft and bottled products no more than two weeks old at the retailers in the Boston area. The draft beer has about a 60-day shelf life and the bottled beer, which is pasteurized, about a 90-day shelf life. Production for 1993 was 7,500 barrels in Boston and another 6,000 barrels at the Utica plant.

Harpoon Light - bright gold; light, dry, and grainy; a refreshing beer; made with pale malt; hopped with Clusters and Cascades; American Pilsner (1.042)

Harpoon Golden Lager - bright gold; fresh, lightly malted, hoppy, and crisp (a little hoppier than the Light); made with pale malt; hopped with Clusters; European Pilsner

Harpoon Ale - bright copper; malty, fruity, hoppy aroma; hoppy, tangy, malty flavor; very dry; made with pale and caramel 40 malts; hopped with Clusters for bittering and flavoring, finished with Cascades; their flagship beer (1.044)

Harpoon Dark - similar to the stout, but with a lighter body; made with two-row pale, caramel 80, and chocolate; hopped with Clusters; available on draft only; frequently sold by accounts under different names; a cross between a nut brown and a porter

Harpoon Hard Cider - bright gold; fruity, appley aroma; off dry finish, sweet with a fresh apple taste (not available to the public at press time)

-- seasonal --

Harpoon IPA - bright, pale amber; fresh and flowery aroma with rich malt and hop accents; very fresh with roasted malt flavor; made with pale and caramel 40 malts; hopped with Clusters and Cascades for bittering and flavoring, dry hopped with whole-leaf Cascades; my favorite Harpoon beer; available in the summer (1.062)

Harpoon Octoberfest - bright reddish amber; very malty with good hop balance; a nice drinking Oktoberfest; made with pale and caramel 80 malt; hopped with Clusters; conditioned for six weeks; availability starts at the end of August (1.058)

Harpoon Stout - dark; malty and dry with a hoppy bitterness; made with two-row pale, caramel 80, chocolate, and black malts, malted wheat, and roasted, unmalted barley; hopped with Clusters, Fuggles, and East Kent Goldings; available in the spring

Harpoon Winter Warmer - clear amber; fresh, spicy, cinnamon nose; predominantly cinnamon flavor with some nutmeg and malt; dry; available in late November - December,

Birthday Reserve - unfiltered, brewed for the Harpoon Beer Invitational

---

Barrel of Miscellany

Address:	306 Northern Avenue
	Boston, MA 02210 (located in the Marine Industrial Park)
Telephone:	(617) 574-9551; (617) 455-1935--voice mail; (800) 666-3496
Tours:	1:00 p.m. on Friday and Saturday. No reservations needed.
Distribution:	draft products--eastern Massachusetts, Rhode Island, and southern New Hampshire

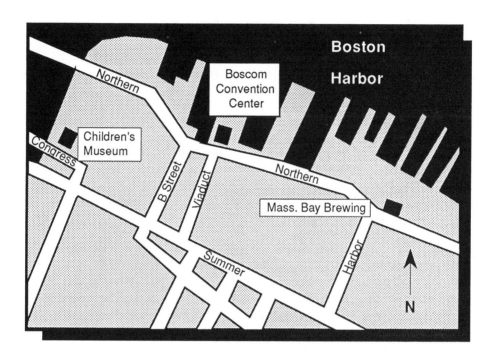

Middlesex Brewing
Burlington

Beer in the Basement

What do you do when you get fed up with your job? Open a brewery! At least that's what Brian Friguliette did, even at the risk of having his friends say he had lost his marbles.

Turning a hobby into a business was not what Brian, age 35, intended to do when he bought his first malt-extract homebrew kit several years ago. Things took place gradually. After the malt-extract phase, Brian began making his beer using malted grain. His beer continued to improve and over time, he developed a skill for duplicating the commercial beers he liked. Finally, with encouragement from his father, Brian began looking into opening his own brewery. First, he and a neighbor homebrewer, who was a welder by trade, made plans to build their own brewery. But as the neighbor's welding business picked up, he had less time to devote to opening a brewery.

So, inspired by other cottage breweries which were springing up in New England, Brian decided to go it alone with a two-barrel brewing system in his own basement. He named the brewery after the county in which he lived: Middlesex. The equipment was custom made for him by Pierre Rajotte of Montreal. Brian measured the width of the basement door very carefully and says the kettles came through with just a little scratching and scraping. Once in, the brewery fit in the basement like a glove, which Brian had converted and reconditioned into a brewing area. He converted a home hot-water heater into a hot liquor tank and made his own heat exchanger out of copper and PVC tubing. At first, in order to conserve on space, he stored his grain in a neighbor's house, where Brian ground it with a hand-operated grain mill.

In May of 1993 Brian came out with his first ale, Middlesex Brown Ale. He began distributing directly to the beer retailers in 22-oz. bottles and in kegs to his one draft account, the Sunset Grill in nearby Allston. Response was immediate and overwhelming. There was no need to market the beer, which is just as well, as Brian says he had no desire nor skill for doing this. News about the ale spread quickly and a waiting list for new accounts grew longer. Brian ordered two four-barrel fermenters, borrowed some money and sold all his worldly possessions, with the exception of his pickup truck, which he needed for beer deliveries, in order to pay for them. Brian also cut back his hours at his regular job as an optician in order to devote more time to brewing. In September he quit his job altogether and now devotes all his waking moments to making beer. At the same time Brian came out with his second ale: Middlesex Oatmeal Stout. Between the two ales, he is producing four to six barrels of ale each week.

At the writing of this book, Brian was looking for another location for his brewery, one which would give him more space and and flexibility. The town of Burlington will currently not allow him to conduct tours of the brewery because it is located in a residential area.

The Brew

Brian is making two-barrel batches of ale using a single-step, infusion mash. He then ferments double batches in four-barrel, closed tanks. He employs imported Canadian and Munich malts which he mills himself. Pelletized Chinook and Willamette hops are used for bittering and flavoring, and Cascades for aroma. The bottles are primed with a small amount of corn sugar. The two ales are unfiltered, nor are any clarifying agents used. They are bottle conditioned in 22-oz. bottles.

Middlesex Brown Ale - deep brown with reddish tint; delicious and malty; the chocolate malt comes through loud and clear; very mild and drinkable (1.044)

Middlesex Oatmeal Stout - opaque and black with a reddish brown, creamy head; rich and appetizing, dry, roasted barley aroma; sweet and malty, but with a rich, drying, burnt malt and coffee finish; wonderful soft, chewy, but tingly mouthfeel; in addition to the malts, Brian uses roasted unmalted barley and flaked oatmeal (1.056)

Barrel of Miscellany

Address:	a secret
Telephone:	(617) 932-8400
Tours:	Sorry, the city does not allow them.
Availability:	At good liquor stores in the Boston area and at the Sunset Grill in Allston
Moving?:	Brian is activily looking for a new location. So, there may be brewery tours in the future. Keep checking the Boston metropolitan yellow pages under "breweries."

Cape Cod Brew House
You're sure to fall in love with the Cape Cod Brew House

"If you're fond of sand dunes and salty air, quaint little villages here and there, you're sure to fall in love with old Cape Cod." Had Patty Page known about the Cape Cod Brew House in Hyannis, she may well have added a verse to the song about the food, brews, and atmosphere of this delightful brewery restaurant. The attractive 225-seat restaurant is really one building to which several additions have been built. The original building, nestled in the middle, is a traditional white, clapboard structure, covered with a red roof, and capped with a cupola. Handsome contemporary additions, including an impressive two-story entry, have been beautifully integrated and the whole complex is tied together by long expanses of dark green awnings. The Brew House is situated on the main street of the Cape's most populace and "year round" town. Hyannis also holds a special place in the hearts and minds of those who remember years of news releases about the activities at the Kennedy compound.

As you enter the front doors of the Brew House, the glass-enclosed brewery is on your right. Tanks of gleaming copper and stainless steel alert all who enter what the first order of business is here. Continue past the brewery and you approach one of the most attractive bars anywhere. The large, four-sided bar is an achievement of light oak cabinetry using traditional, raised panel and molding elements. A brass foot rail runs around the base and the design is repeated in the brass light fixtures on two corner posts and in the handsome overhead storage and display racks for glassware. A mosaic tile floor wraps around the bar, further defining the space.

The main dining room is a warm and welcoming room with cranberry carpeting, paneled walls, booths, and tables set with paper place mats and the ketchup bottle at the ready. Overhead hangs a highly polished, antique rowing shell and one wall displays a set of three beautifully matted and framed nautical maps of the Cape. At one end of the room there is a raised fireplace which also opens up to the adjoining dining room.

The second dining room, a later addition, is more open and airy in feeling with white walls above and green walls below the stained plank chair rail molding. Large windows on two walls invite the sunlight in, and this room is decorated with hanging plants for a garden room effect.

The third dining area is the coziest space of all. This room was once a porch and the low ceiling of white bead board and beams follows the pitch of the roof down to a continuous row of windows. Booths line this outside wall of windows which are capped with a floral valance for a bit of added charm.

The Cape Cod Brew House has a steady clientele of locals who keep the place hopping at lunchtime and at the end of the workday. In addition, the summer crowd and tourists have made the place quite popular in its first year.

The Menu

The Cape Cod Brew House, which opened in July 1993, is housed in what had been the home of two of the Cape's most popular American seafood restaurants, and that fact is stated with pride by the owners Robert Melley and Jack Cunningham. In fact, the Seafood Stew listing on the menu alerts diners that the recipe was "stolen directly from Barbyann's and Shannon's," the Brew House's previous tenants. Seafood is the mainstay of the menu and in addition to the seafood stew, you can choose from clam chowder, gumbo, fried clams, a fried fish sandwich, and a cajun seasoned appetizer, Crab Cakes N'awlins. Fresh scrod is served either with a crumb topping or dipped in beer batter and fried.

Landlubbers should be more than satisfied by the selection of burgers, steak, babyback ribs, and the most popular item served, chicken pot pie. And what kind of brewery restaurant would this be without a pizza menu? The Brew House makes both Chicago style, deep-dish and New York style thin crust with some pretty novel toppings. The Chicago style Da Bears is topped with pepperoni, pepperoncini, red pepper, and provolone while the Wall Street is decked out in broccoli, red pepper, spinach, grated carrot, mushroom, onion, diced tomatoes, basil, and, try this, chopped kale.

The Brew

For its first year, Cape Cod Brew House had its beers made under contract at the Mass. Bay Brewing Co. in Boston. In the spring of 1994, Richard Young came on board as brewmaster. Richard had previously been head brewer at Seabright Brewing in Santa Cruz, California, where his beers had won three gold medals at the Great American Beer Festival. At Cape Cod he will to be using a seven-barrel, JV Northwest system, with fourteen-barrel fermenters. He planned to use imported, two-row malts and primarily domestic hops. He planned to have six brews on tap at one time, plus six beers from other breweries. The beers are served in 10-oz. glasses for $2.00 and a pint for $2.75. A set of six samplers is available for $2.50. Richard's first brews were to be on tap by the end of April 1994.

Barrel of Miscellany

Address: 720 Main Street
                   Hyannis, MA 02601

Telephone: (508) 775-4110

Hours: 11:30 a.m. - 1:00 a.m. daily

Credit cards: American Express, Visa

handicapped access -- non-smoking area -- TV -- free off-street parking -- fireplace

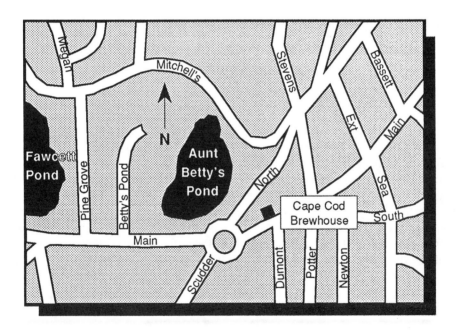

Ipswich Brewing

Real Ale in a Jug

Ipswich Brewing started as a day dream. Jim Beauvais was an industrial engineer by training who had switched to software engineering. During his spare time, Jim tinkered with brewing at home. As the years passed, he began drawing up plans for a small-scale commercial brewery. Then, in the early nineties, he suddenly found himself involuntarily unemployed. Just about that time Paul Sylva learned about Jim's plans and they formed a partnership, Paul as treasurer and distributor/salesperson, Jim is brewer and president. Paul was an entrepreneur from nearby Rockport, where he had started several businesses. He had heard about the craft brewing movement and was eager to be a part of it. Their first barrel of Ipswich Ale rolled out in August of 1992. They began producing Ipswich Dark in the summer of 1993.

Just when the pair got financing from a local bank and licensing in place, Jim was offered a position as a software engineer which he couldn't refuse. But by then he had decided he was going to follow his dreams. So, he worked as an engineer during the week and a brewer on weekends. My visit to the brewery was on a Sunday night and Jim was in a zombie-like state, with blood shot eyes, trying to finish up the brewing before starting his regular job the next morning. Since then, he has been able to resign his job and devote his full attention to his true calling, brewing.

In order to save money, Jim did some of the renovation and equipment modification himself. Inside their rented metal warehouse I could see equipment he pieced together from various sources. The seven-barrel mash tun was originally a dairy tank which Jim was able to buy from someone before it was to be converted to a tank for live lobsters. He made the sparge arm and mesh himself. They began making seven-barrel batches. Since then they have added four, fifteen-barrel, primary fermenters and in the spring of 1994 converted to a thirty-barrel mash-brew system with six, thirty-barrel fermenters. They use a three-vessel brewhouse: mash tun, brew kettle, and whirlpool.

The Brew

Brewer Jim Beauvais is making two delightfully fruity and mouth-watering ales: Ipswich Ale and Ipswich Dark. These ales can only be found in the Boston and North Shore areas. To ensure freshness, Ipswich distributes its products directly to the retailers on a weekly basis. A trip to eastern Massachusetts is warranted for these ales alone; forget about the Red Sox, Faneiul Hall, and Old Ironsides--just go for the ale. Any brew pilgrim lucky enough to happen across either of the Ipswich products should snatch them up quickly and consume them while still fresh. They can also be found on tap in the better beer bars in the area.

The unusual fresh and fruity character, the cloudy, light orange-brownish color of the Ipswich Ale, and cider-looking 64-oz. jugs conjure up pleasant memories of fresh, New England apple cider. But make no mistake, this is ale.

Jim makes his beers using pre-ground, domestic, two-row pale malt and six-row specialty malts from Briess. He employs domestic, pelletized hops as well. Finishing hops are added in the whirlpool, after the brew is complete. The ales are naturally conditioned for two weeks and are unfiltered. About half of their production goes into 64-oz. growlers; the rest is sold in kegs to restaurants and bars.

Ipswich Ale - hazy copper with an orange tint; fresh, fruity aroma with light hops; very malty, very fresh, and especially very fruity; delicious fruity-hoppy character; made with two-row pale malt and six-row, 40 luvabond caramel malt; Galena for bittering, Willamette for finishing; a pale ale (1.045)

Ipswich Dark - dark, hazy brown; creamy, tan head; very fresh, fruity, malty nose; sweet malt entry; rich, sweet malt finish; moderately bitter; richly endowed with roasted barley a little coffee flavor; nice and fruity and fresh, complex, yet very drinkable; made with two-row pale, 40 luvabond caramel malt, and roasted barley; Galena for bittering, domestic Tettnang and Cascades for finishing -- (1.060)

Barrel of Miscellany

Address:	25 Hayward Street Ipswich, MA 01938
Telephone:	(508) 356-3329
Tours:	Saturday at 1:00 and 3:00 p.m. Samples are given.
Take out:	64 oz. growlers at the brewery to go
Other Products:	Pilgrim Ale, Old Harbor Brewing

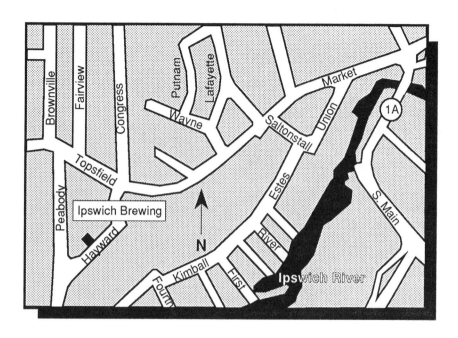

Lowell Brewing
The Brewery Pub & Restaurant
Down by the Old Mill Stream

For more than a half century, Wannalancit was Lowell's famous textile mill. Each year, tens of thousands of yards of textiles were produced in the mills, using water-powered turbines to drive the machinery. The mills have stood idle for many years, ever since the textile industry migrated from Massachusetts (the old water turbines can still bee seen in a museum operated by the National Park Service).

However, the red brick walls are echoing again to the sound of industry, this time it is the craft brewing industry. At press time the Lowell Brewing Co. was producing beer and the restaurant adjacent to it was rapidly taking shape.

Although not involved in the restaurant, brewery owner Guy Haas, planned the brewery so that diners would get a magnificent view of the brewing process. The brewery is completely enclosed in glass on the first floor and diners in the cafe and game-room occupants will get a birds-eye view from the second and third floors. The second floor was to offer pool, billiards, darts, and a dance floor with either a live band or DJ. The third floor was to have a game room for the younger set, offering a video arcade, indoor miniature golf, indoor basketball, foosball, and soft drinks. To make the entertainment complex complete, close-by there is movie theater called the Lowell Flick.

The Brew

Brewer Paul McErlean is making 20-barrel batches using a new, custom-built, Pub Brewing system, with four, forty-barrel and two sixty barrel fermenters. He uses domestic, two- and six-row pale and caramel malts and three different domestic hops to make his first product, Mill City Amber Ale. The ale is being packaged in kegs and 12-oz. bottles. A Classic Pilsner was to be released soon after, and other brands were to follow.

Mill City Amber Ale - amber color with a creamy head; very clean and well balanced; fresh and robust with nice roasted maltiness; plenty of bitterness--more of a bitter than a hoppy flavor

Barrel of Miscellany

Address: 199 Cabot Street
Lowell, MA 01854

Telephone: (508) 937-1212

Tours: Thursday at 4:00 and 8:00 p.m. and Saturday at 2:00
and 4:00 p.m.

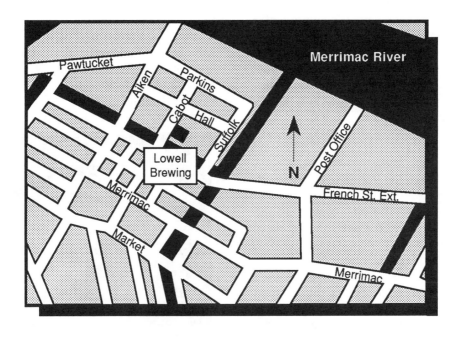

Ould Newbury Brewing

Honey, I brewed some beer!

For Joe and Pam Rolfe, brewing is a family affair. You see, their brewery is located in the cellar of their Newbury home. Joe, 35, does the brewing and Pam labels the bottles, does the marketing, and the paperwork. They share the bottling and delivery responsibilities.

I visited the Rolfe's in their home on a Sunday evening. The kids were just being tucked into bed and Joe was settled at the kitchen table for a glass of, what else, Ould Newbury Porter. But first, he took me to the cellar for a tour of the brewery. It was then and there I came to understand what the term "cottage brewery" really meant. We were really talking small here--a two barrel mash tun; a two-barrel brew kettle; a two-barrel fermenter; four, four-barrel fermenters; a small, six-bottle, bottle filler, a keg filler, a hand-operated bottle capper, and bottles, bottles everywhere. Since then, Joe has upgraded to a 5.25-barrel kettle and has also added several Grundy fermenters.

Although small, their brewery has been more successful than the Rolfe's ever dreamed. They have not had to push their product at all. After landing their first account at the Thirsty Whale in Newburyport, the retailers and bar and restaurant owners started showing up at the Rolfe's door. They now have a waiting list for new accounts. And since there is such a high demand at their existing accounts, they have been able to negotiate delivery schedules which ensure that only fresh ale reaches the consumers. The Rolfes will only deliver what will be sold in one to two weeks. Even though this means more work for them, protecting the quality of their product is a major commitment at Ould Newbury.

The biggest hang-up has been lack of storage space. Joe and Pam had planned the brewery very carefully, but did not anticipate the enthusiastic demand for their product. Joe insisted that no beer go out the door before it had been bottle conditioned for three weeks. Oops!--no space for all those bottles. The solution was to move the milling and bottling operations from the garage (their cars have already forgotten what the inside of the garage even looks like), and use it for a new bottle and grain storage room.

The antecedents to Ould Newbury Brewing go back several years, when Joe was working as a software engineer at the Wang Laboratories in Lowell. He overheard some of his co-workers talking about making beer at home, and he decided to try it. He received a very favorable response when he brought them some of his beer to try. When he

revealed that this was his first batch, they told him he was a natural.

Joe's homebrew got better and better. Then, on a trip to California, he and Pam experienced their first brewpubs--Tied House in Mountain View and Santa Cruz Brewing and Seabright Brewing in Santa Cruz. They were inspired. When they returned to Massachusetts, Joe began investigating the possibilities of opening a brewpub in Newburyport. But, he found, the investment would be more than they could afford. Then the computer industry in New England began to slump, and Joe could see the handwriting on the wall. This gave him a new impetus to start a brewery.

His next inspiration was to start a craft brewery--the investment would be much smaller than a brewpub. But, what they could afford, a two-barrel, extract brewhouse, was regarded by those in the know as, well, laughably small. Joe ran the numbers on his Wang computer and felt that his dream was doable. The trick was to do all the work themselves and economize any way they could. Joe and Pam would have to make, package, market, and distribute the beer themselves, with no paid employees. And they would have to do it in their own home, to avoid any additional lease.

Joe learned about a manufacturer in Montreal by the name of Pierre Rajotte who would design and build a tiny brewery which would just fit the confines of their basement. He visited Pierre and was sold on the idea. He could purchase the equipment and have it installed for under $50,000.

The first keg of Yankee Ale rolled out the door of the Rolfe residence in September 1992. Since then they have begun to bottle their beer in 22-oz. bottles and later developed the Porter. Now 90% of their product is bottled. Pam says the unusual bottle size and distinctive label have been a very important aspect of marketing the beer.

Since the brewery opened, Joe, along with a lot of fellow Wang employees, received his pink slip. However, the brewery is producing a positive cash flow and at a two-to-three batch per week clip, the Rolfes produced about 250 barrels during 1993. And, they are considering moving to another house, which would give them space for more brewing equipment and storage space.

The Brew

Joe Rolfe is making two ales, using Canadian two-row pale malt, crystal, amber, and chocolate malts, and American, pelletized hops. He began with a malt extract brewery, but quickly progressed to all grain. He primes the bottles with a small amount of corn sugar. Joe mills his own malt. The ales are unfiltered and are bottle conditioned. He is brewing about two batches per week.

Yankee Ale - hazy copper; pungent, fruity malt aroma; fresh, malty-bitter taste; soft mouthfeel; made with Canadian, two-row pale and crystal malts; hopped with Cascades for bittering, Willamette and Tettnang for flavoring and aroma; a pale ale (1.045)

Ould Newbury Porter - dark brown; cloudy; deliciously rich, sweet malt-toffee-estery-fruity aroma; very fresh and malty palate; sweet, bitter, malty finish; full body; very drinkable; made with Canadian, two-row pale malt, as well as crystal, chocolate, and amber malts and roasted, unmalted barley; hopped with Perle (bittering) and Cascades (flavoring-aroma) (1.050)

Barrel of Miscellany

Address:	227 High Road Newbury, MA 01951 (this address will probably change in the near future)
Telephone:	(508) 462-1980
Tours:	Call for information and please do not show up unannounced, as the brewery is located in their basement.
Availability:	at good liquor stores in the Boston area and at the Sunset Grill in Allston

Northampton Brewery
Brewster Court Bar & Grill

Brewster on Brewster Court

The temptation was just too much. Janet Egelston and business partner Mark Metzger had been to California and had visited the Santa Cruz Brewing Co. They had worked as promoters of rock band paraphernalia and had come east to start something new. And then, there it was. A "For Sale" sign hanging on what had once been a livery stable and carriage house for the Brewster mansion, but had served more recently as the offices for a fuel company. The address: Brewster Court. Brewster: female brewer. She tried, but Janet could not resist. Janet gathered her family and friends, convinced them that this was their collective karma, and they bought the place. Hello new life!

Janet's brother, Peter Egelston, was a schoolteacher, but he'd been homebrewing for a while, so he signed on as brewer. Cora, Peter's wife was a commercial artist and she too joined the great entrepreneurial adventure. Between December 1986 and its opening nine months later, a lot was done to transform a garage into a modern brewery restaurant. Outside, the brick walls were painted white and hop vines were planted to climb the walls. The structure has a slate roof, a cupola and a large circular window above the entry which altogether gives the appearance of a church building.

Inside is a very contemporary, California-style, two-story room of gray stucco walls and exposed beams. An open loft provides a second tier of seating. The indus-

trial-style railing that defines the loft area traces the arc shape of the sleek, semicircular bar below. The circular window above the entry is no cathedral rose window, but rather a striking design element which is beautifully repeated elsewhere in the interior design, most notably in the shape of the bar and in the set of mirrors behind the bar. The brewpub's logo and sign also repeat the circle motif.

A beer garden was added in 1988 and is a jewel of a courtyard patio surrounded by a tall wooden fence which serves as a backdrop for a

profusion of flowers. This is a world away from it all where you can sit beneath an umbrella and enjoy a relaxing meal in the middle of a garden.

On July 24, 1993, Janet and Peter Egelston, along with a long-time friend and Northampton Brewery's off-premises sales manager, hosted the first annual Great New England Brewer's Festival. The event was a big hit, attracting participation by 23 regional brewpubs and micros, and attendance of 4,800 paying guests in just seven hours. Plans for July 1994 are scheduled for two days and will include thirty breweries, plus food and entertainment.

The Menu

Fresh, California fare with lots of color and flavor. Appetizers include an assortment of Tex-Mex items to munch on, but there is more. Amber beer is featured in the cheese and ale spread which is served with crackers and veggie sticks. There is a soup of the day and an assortment of salads with and without meat, served with housemade dressings. The sandwiches have imaginative names and ingredients to match. For example, the Basil's Rathbone is a combination of basil leaves, sliced tomatoes, roasted red peppers, red onions, provolone, and garlic mayonnaise; baked and served open-faced on a baguette. The Bohemian Rhapsody is ham and brie with pesto mayonnaise on grilled sourdough bread. Pizza aficionados will be pleased with the choice of white or red pizzas with a large selection of traditional and not-so-traditional toppings. Or, how about the special white pizza topped with grilled eggplant, goat cheese, and sun-dried tomatoes with roasted garlic and jack cheese?

Northampton is known for its sizzling platters of fajitas, but you can also choose from a number of other entrees, including grilled steak and chicken items made with a choice of spicy marinades and sauces. All of the spicy dishes, whether made with the house BBQ suace, a hot chili oil sauce, Jamaican jerk spices or fresh ginger, are rated on a three-star scale, with the hottest dishes carrying the additional advisory, "we warned you!"

The Brew

Northampton's beers are made by head brewer Rick Quackenbush and assistant brewer Kevin Kittredge. Many of the recipes were originally formulated by Peter Egelston, however, over the years Rick has modified several of them. Rick has a solid background in brewing, making beers with Peter for more than five years. Before coming here he had made beer at home for almost twenty years, and also worked for a year at Payne & Co., a small brewery in Cambridgeshire, England.

They brew with a ten-barrel, JV Northwest system, featuring one 10-barrel, two 20-barrel, and one 30-barrel, closed fermenters. They are brewing three-to-four times a week and usually have five beers on tap in the winter and three in the summer. They made 900 barrels during 1993.

They mill their own malt and use exclusively two-row, imported malts. They use both pellet and whole leaf domestic and imported hops. The ales are unfiltered, the lagers are filtered and made with a true lager yeast. The beers are dispensed from either serving tanks or kegs, using CO_2 pressure.

The beers are available in seven-oz. glasses ($1.75), twelve-oz. glasses ($2.50), and pints ($2.90). They also have two-oz. samplers for a minimal charge.

Golden Pilsner - bright, pale gold; very light malt taste; nice malt and Saaz hop finish; made with imported 98% two-row lager malt and a touch of crystal; Cluster for bittering, Cascade for flavoring, finished with Saaz (1.048)

Amber - bright, light amber; sweet, malty entry; crisp-hoppy-bitter finish; made with two-row lager malt, crystal, Munich, and cara-pils malt; Clusters for bittering, Cascades for finishing; American-Vienna style; their best seller (1.048)

-- Seasonal - rotating --

Oktoberfest - good looking, deep copper-to-orange; beautiful, creamy head; great mouthfeel; off-sweet, malty; short, but delicious hop finish; very tasty; hopped with Mt. Hood (1.052)

Black Cat Stout - hazy, dark brown-to-black; delicious roasted coffee aroma; chocolate-coffee taste, (1.060)

Pale Ale - made with two row pale malt; hopped with Crystal and Cascade for bittering, Willamette for finish; not sampled (1.055)

Old Brown Dog - won a silvermedal at the 1988 Great American Beer Festival, not sampled (1.055)

Daniel Shays - Perle for bittering, whole Cascades for finish, named after farmer who started Shays rebellion and attacked the Springfield Armory; a special bitter; not sampled

Pumpkin Ale - made with fresh pumpkin and pumpkin spices; not sampled (1.045)

Steamer - dry hop with pellets; California common; not sampled (1.050)

Hoover's Porter - not sampled (1.050)

Weizenheimer - not sampled (1.044)

Spiced Cranberry - holiday beer, not sampled (1.064)

Smoked Brown Ale -holiday beer, not sampled (1.060)

Snow Shovel E.S.B. - not sampled (1.050)

Dunkleweisen - not sampled (1.044)

Wally's Special Mild - not sampled (1.038)

Johann's Bock - not sampled (1.067)

Maggies Wee Heavy - not sampled (1.072)

Barrel of Miscellany

Address:	11 Brewster Court Northampton, MA 01060
Telephone:	(413) 584-9903
Hours:	Monday - Saturday: 11:30 a.m. - 1:00 a.m.; Sunday: 1:00 pm - 1:00 a.m.
Tours:	Saturday at 2:00 p.m.; they will arrange private dinner or luncheon tours Monday-Wednesday for parties of 15-45
Credit cards:	American Express, MasterCard, Discover, Visa
Events:	Halloween Charity Ball, Anniversary Charity Bash in August, Taste of Northampton Festival in August, Great New England Brewers Festival in July

non-smoking area -- handicapped access -- TV -- free off-street parking in the evening

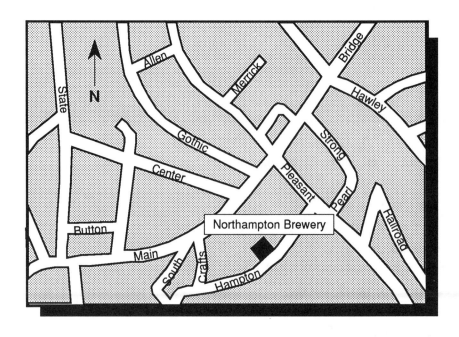

The Brewery on Martha's Vineyard

Ma'tha Would Have Approved

Now here's a bit of trivia. Explorer Bartholomew Gosnold named the island of Martha's Vineyard for his daughter and the wild grapes that grow here. I hope Martha would have approved of having a brewery in her vineyard, because that's what is about to happen.

As *On Tap New England* went to press, Fred Roven, one of the owners of the Brewery on Martha's Vineyard reported the equipment was being installed and brewing was to begin in earnest by the late spring of 1994. Fred said the brewery occupies a forgotten, but historic, landmark on the island: the Dreamland Garage. This was a very popular, turn-of-the-century dance hall which featured some prominent bands of the time.

Fred's inspiration for opening a craft brewery came from homebrewing and from watching Michael Jackson's "The Beer Hunter" series, which he happened to tune into by accident on his TV. He was particularly interested in the tour of Anchor Brewing in San Francisco, California, and the interview with its owner, Fritz Maytag.

At press time, Fred and his associates had secured the financing, location, and licensing and were almost ready to "rock and roll" with their brewery. They purchased a new fifteen-barrel brewing system from JV Northwest and had hired Russell Garet as their brewmaster. Russell came from the Pacific Northwest Brewing Co. in Seattle, Washington, where he was head brewer. Prior to that he had worked at The Lion Brewery in Wilkes Barre, Pennsylvania, and the Manhattan Brewing Co. in New York City. To begin, Russell will be making three ales: Gay Head Light, Menensha Golden Ale, and Oak Bluffs Amber Ale. Their initial brews will be kegged for restaurants and bars on the island, to be followed soon after by 22-oz. bottles. They also plan to make their own soda, the first of which will be Fred's Root Beer.

Barrel of Miscellany

Address:	43 Oak Bluffs Avenue (P.O. Box 1076) Oak Bluffs, MA 02557
Telephone:	(508) 696-8400
Tours:	Please call to tell them when you would like to visit.
Availability:	on Martha's Vineyard and Nantucket

New Hampshire

New Hampshire can boast the third brewery to have opened in New England. This was Henry Sherburne Brewing which opened in Portsmouth in 1640. Over the years the state has been known for two breweries: Frank Jones Brewing of Portsmouth and Anheuser-Busch Brewing in Merrimack. Frank Jones first opened in 1859 and remained open until 1918. It reopened briefly during the 1940s, but closed for good in 1950. Anheuser-Busch of St. Louis, Missouri, opened a large plant in Merrimack in 1970.

In 1988 Don Jones, great, great, great, great grand nephew of the original Frank Jones, acquired the Frank Jones trademark and began distributing Frank Jones beers, brewed at the Catamount Brewing Co. in White River Junction, Vermont. Brewing operations commenced in Portsmouth in March of 1992, but the brewery was only able to stay open for about one year. In 1994 the Frank Jones Brewery was purchased by a joint-venture enterprise and was scheduled to reopen later in the year as the Smuttynose Brewing Co.

In June of 1991 the first brewpub opened in Portsmouth, called appropriately enough, Portsmouth Brewing. The second brewpub, Martha's Exchange, opened in the fall of 1993 in Nashua. At press time, Greg Noonan of the Vermont Pub and Brewery of Burlington was planning to open a brewpub in West Lebanon, called Seven Barrel Brewing Co. Another brewpub was scheduled to open in Manchester in late 1994 or early 1995.

Martha's Exchange Restaurant & Brewing

What it'll be - an ice cream soda or an I.P.A.?

What do ice cream and beer have in common? Well, for one thing, they are traditionally served at a bar. But at the same bar? Well, why not? With this kind of attitude, Bill and Chris Fokas added a whole new dimension to what had been the family luncheonette business in downtown Nashua. They did it with a magnificent horseshoe shaped mahogany bar which they bought at an auction. In its earlier life the bar was the centerpiece of a speakeasy owned by Al Capone.

They took that beautiful bar and installed it so that one side would sit right where the old lunch counter had been. Locals can still come in and sit on their favorite swivel stool at the bar and order a burger and a frappe. But now, they can also sit on the other side of the horseshoe on an oak bar stool and sip an ale brewed in the copper kettles lined up along a nearby wall. Now is that progress, or what?

Back to the beginning. Martha's Exchange started out as Martha's Sweet Shop way back in 1955, when Mitch and Ethel Fokas began making and selling candies and other confections in a small storefront nestled in a three-story, red-brick building, constructed in the 1870s as the Merchant's Exchange Building and renamed Martha's Merchants Exchange during the 1930s. Who old Martha was and why the building was graced with her name remains a mystery, but the Fokases thought it a fine identity for their sweet shop. Then, in the 1960s, Mitch decided to expand the business and set up a lunch counter across from the candy

counter. The sign out front was amended to read "Martha's Sweet Shop and Luncheonette" and a local institution was born.

Success breeds success and in 1988 the Fokas' sons, Bill and Chris, who had assumed the family business, decided it was time once again to expand, this time in a very big way. They acquired adjacent space and built a restaurant dining room, added Al Capone's bar, restored the exterior of the building from the ravages of one too many "facelifts," expanded the menu, and changed the name once more in 1990. "Martha's Exchange" awaited one last addition, however, to complete the transformation: the installation of

The Menu

The menu is American eclectic, a veritable pot pouri of favorite dishes from many cuisines including Greek salads and lamb shish-kebab, several South-of-the-Border dishes, teriyaki and tempura items and a selection of Italian pasta dishes. Steaks and fresh seafood entrees are here and please note that the New England clam chowder is listed in the local dialect as clam "chowda." The luncheonette menu has been preserved in the long list of burger and sandwich offerings as well as the dessert list. Simply put, there is plenty to choose from.

Be sure to check out the sweet shop as you exit--they still make homemade chocolates.

a brewery. In September of 1993 the first house brews were served and the place was all that its new name implied, "Martha's Exchange, Restaurant and Brewing Co."

Enter the front door of this colonnaded Victorian storefront and you step into a bright and pleasant restaurant which was the luncheonette. The original green and white mosaic tile floor is in beautiful condition and sets the mood for this space. The old swivel stool seats have been reupholstered in a soft mauve color, but they haven't moved an inch. Booth seating in oak wood and mauve vinyl upholstery also helps to maintain the character of the luncheonette and you can still get a high chair for the little ones. Martha's remains a place for family dining.

The ice cream parlor gives way to the speakeasy as you round the end of the U-shaped bar, where the swivel stools end and the bar stools begin, where the tile turns to hard wood floor boards, and where the ceiling is painted a deep mauve and decorated with elaborate stamped tin panels from which brass ceiling fans and old fashioned lamps hang. A brick

wall serves as a gallery for photos of Nashua at the turn of the century, lit by two ornate gas lamps which once hung in New York's Grand Central Station. Other prized antiques include a paneled wall from a Midwest bank, complete with teller stalls and a handsome mirror circa 1880. Marble top tables and bentwood chairs complete the speak -easy decorating scheme.

Martha's has been, is now, and intends to be a family restaurant where the good folks of Nashua of all ages can enjoy themselves in comfortable surroundings. Three nights a week the place is jumping with the younger set, drawn in by rock 'n roll and R & B music groups. And now the employees of the local Anheuser-Busch plant can come in after a hard day of brewing a jillion gallons of Bud and Bud Light and relax with one of the handcrafted brews made on the premises.

Al Capone supplied not only the intricately carved mahogany bar, but the inspiration for the names of the house beers: Ale Capone I.P.A., "Untouchable" Scotch Ale, and Volstead '33.

The Brew

Brewer Dean Jones, 29, graduated from the Siebel Institute in Chicago in October 1992. He apprenticed at the now defunct Happy Valley Brewing Co. in State College, Pennsylvania, and from there went to Kidder's (now part of the Hops chain) in Ft. Myers, Florida. Before coming to Nashua, Dean worked at the Florida Brewing Co. in Auburndale, Florida.

Dean is making beer in a beautiful, new, copper-clad, seven-barrel DME system. There are three closed fermenters (one, fourteen-barrel and four, seven-barrel tanks). There are eleven converted Grundies downstairs for storage tanks (six conditioning and five serving tanks). He uses two-row, preground American malts and a combination of pelletized American and imported hops. Dean said the three lighter beers were the best sellers for the first month, then the I.P.A. and Scotch Ale picked up and now the customers are moving on to the heavier beers. He is trying to maintain five regulars and one specialty on tap at all times.

Scotch Ale - sweet and malty; Fuggles are used for bittering and Cascades for aroma; lightly hopped (1.074)

Ale Capone I.P.A. - clear; light copper; fresh, hoppy aroma; fairly long and bitter; good balance; fairly bitter; hopped with Bullion for bittering, Hallertau for flavoring and dry hopped with Cascades; a very drinkable IPA

Volstead - dark gold; fresh Saaz aroma; clean tasting; made exclusively with Saaz; made with two-row pale, a touch of caramel 20, and a little bit of Munich and cara-pils malt; a lager

White Mountain Wheat - a very light wheat beer; made with half two-row barley malt and half wheat malt; Hallertau for bittering and aroma

Bull Frog Stout - made with two-row Munich 20, caramel 40, and chocolate malts, roasted black barley and Bullion, Tettnang, and Cascade hops; not sampled

Old-Time Rootbeer - very good; reminded me of old fashioned root beer barrels; made with extract, Dean tried 120 batches before he found exactly what he liked; added some vanilla and other flavorings; he made it for his dad, who loves root beer

-- Seasonal - rotating --

Indian Head Red - not sampled

Barrel of Miscellany

Address: Martha's Exchange
                185 Main Street
                Nashua, NH 03060

Telephone: (603) 883-8781

Hours: Tuesday - Sunday: 7:00 a.m. - 1:00 a.m.
                Monday: 7:00 a.m. - midnight

Music: live rock 'n' roll and rhythm 'n' blues Wednesday - Saturday
                evenings

Credit cards: American Express, MasterCard, Visa

handicapped access -- non-smoking area

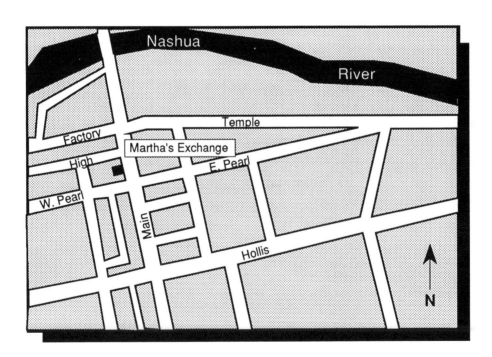

Portsmouth Brewery

Mugs Away in the Old Port

Portsmouth Brewery is located in the Old Harbor historic district, a section of town which bustled during the 18th and 19th centuries with the trade of shipbuilders, riggers and outfitters. It was founded as Strawbery Banke because of the masses of wild strawberries which greeted the first settlers in 1630 as they set foot on dry land. The original fishing and farming village quickly grew into a seaport and shipbuilding town and by 1653 Strawbery Banke was renamed Portsmouth in recognition of its significance as a deep water port at the mouth of the Piscataqua River and shipbuilding began in earnest using the fine and abundant local timber. Portsmouth reached its zenith in the early 1800s when it became renowned for its magnificent clipper ships.

Where once ship chandleries and warehouses operated, Old Harbor is now a mecca for history buffs and tourists who find plenty to look at and enjoy in the old architecture, historic sites, and numerous shops, galleries, boutiques, and restaurants. Where shipbuilders and sailors once lifted a pint or two of hearty ale, we too can indulge in an ale or lager made by the local tavern keeper.

That local brewer is Peter Egelston, a native Californian who "did time" as a high school English teacher in Brooklyn, New York before heading north to New Hampshire and a new life. Portsmouth Brewery opened in 1991 on Market Street in an old three-story brick structure. At street level the facade is a classic shop front with the entryway recessed between large expanses of glass panels. At the top of those windows the brewery name is artfully written in gilt lettering. At eye level the

windows are more humbly decorated with posters announcing local events as well as a succinct statement of the Brewery's mission, "Beer, we like it, we brew it, [we drink it,] we sell what's left over." What is most distinctive, however, about the exterior is the large tankard of frothy beer which hangs above the entryway, visible for a block in either direction.

Inside, Portsmouth is a handsome blending of old and new architectural elements. The walls of mis-matched brick have been left exposed and the original stamped tin ceiling has been retained. Tall slender columns painted in deep green and capped with gilt Corinthian capitals punctuate the front half of the first floor space. All that has been added--booths, room dividers and stairwells--have been done in a contemporary mix of sleek, warm colored woods, white walls, and green table tops. While the front of the brewpub is lit from the tall windows that look out

The Menu

In a word: fresh. The management is committed to the proposition that fresh beer should only be served with freshly prepared foods. The basic menu is not huge, but there appears to be something for everyone and the sauces, dressings and condiments often offer a just bit of a twist on the usual. Take for instance the fried zucchini circles which at Portsmouth Brewery are served with an apricot dipping sauce. The chef's creativity is best sampled, however, by ordering from the monthly specials menu. Recently the entrees included Baked Stuffed Eggplant Rolls which were described as "couscous, feta cheese and spinach rolled in thin slices of fresh eggplant and baked, then topped with fresh roasted tomato sauce." Portsmouth's real claim to local gastronomic fame goes, however, to its pizzas assembled on either a white grilled crust or a thin stone-ground whole wheat crust. From there you choose a tomato or garlic-olive oil sauce and select toppings from a list of standard and some not so standard items.

onto Market Street, the rear area receives daylight from a lovely octagonal skylight. Large panels of a three-dimensional collage depicting food and drink and even a guitar decorate a long brick wall. The first floor has a very high ceiling and the designers have taken good advantage of it by placing the bar up on a two step platform and by creating a small balcony for diners in the rear, right corner of the room.

Downstairs, the space has been transformed into a tavern with stone walls, televisions, game tables and dart boards. Here is where the familiar dart term "mugs away" can be heard, meaning the loser of the last game gets to start the next one.

Several nights a week, the downstairs is alive and pumping to the rythms of bands with bizarre names such as Jabbering Trout, Say Zuzu, Next to Gravity, and Spinach Fly. A special buffet is served during band nights and this is also the place to indulge in Sunday buffet sans music.

The clientele at Portsmouth includes lots of locals, but situated as it is in the heart of the historical district, the brewery-restaurant also attracts a lot of tourists.

The Brew

Owner/brewmaster Peter Egelston, formulates the recipes, while head brewer Paul Murphy, a chef by trade, actually makes the beer. The brewhouse and fermenters came from JV Northwest and conditioning and serving tanks are Grundies from Great Britain. There are two, open, fourteen barrel fermenters. They uses English, two-row malts, which are milled in house. The beers are served under CO_2 pressure from serving tanks. The lagers, the Brown Dog, and the Blonde are filtered. The lagers are made with a true lager yeast.

They try to maintain six beers on tap at all times, but frequently run low during the busy summer months. The lagers, which take longer to make, are especially on short supply during the summer. They brew four to five times a week during the summer and three to four times during the winter months.

Golden Lager - a Pilsner; made with two-row pale malt; hopped with Saaz (not sampled)

Amber Lager - copper color; malty with a dry finish; hopped with Mt. Hoods; Vienna style

Oktoberfest - dark, hazy copper with reddish hue; sweet malt entry; dry finish; rich and malty; made with sixty-forty ratio of two-row pale and Munich malts; hopped with Mt. Hoods; unfiltered; my favorite

Weizenheimer Wheat - clear, deep gold; mostly malty, not too hoppy; made with sixty-forty ratio of wheat malt and two-row pale barley malt; served with a slice of lemon

Blonde Ale - hazy gold; fresh, toasty-malty-buttery flavor; nice finish with caramelized malt and hop bitterness; made with two-row pale and caramel malts; hopped with Pearls for bittering and finished with Cascades

Pale Ale - hazy copper; earthy and fruity; similar to the Blonde Ale, but drier; bittered with Cascades and finished with Willamette

Old Brown Dog - hazy brown; nutty, malty flavor; fresh, hoppy finish; bittered with Cascades and finished with Willamette; a brown ale; winner of a silver medal at the Great American Beer Festival

Pumpkin Ale - (not sampled)

Murphy's Law Ale - clear, deep, dark, and reddish; light earthy, fruity-malty aroma; medium body; nice hop-malt balance; named after the brewer

Black Cat Stout - dark brown; dry, long, roasty, barley flavor; made with two-row pale, caramel, and chocolate malts and roasted, unmalted barley; hopped with whole Chinooks

---

Barrel of Miscellany

Address:	56 Market Street Portsmouth, NH 03801
Telephone:	(603) 431-1115
Hours:	11:30 a.m. - 1:00 a.m. daily
Music:	live music downstairs five nights weekly, acoustic, folk, alternative, rock and roll rhythm and blues
Credit cards:	American Express, Discover, MasterCard, Visa

Non-smoking area -- darts and cribbage downstairs -- off-street parking (pay)

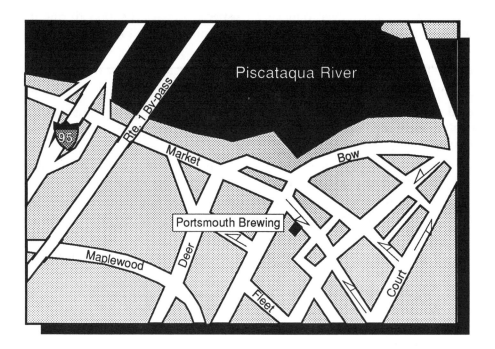

Smuttynose Brewing

What's in a Name?

A little known fact: the name of one of the Isles of Shoals, a minute cluster of islands a few miles off the coast of New Hampshire, is Smuttynose. Apparently someone at the new brewery in Portsmouth is familiar with this island because they have opted to name their brewery Smuttynose. Originally, called Hog Island, sailors used to say it resembled a pig with its nose in the ground. In the nineteenth century there was a famous murder on the island. Four women were attacked by a man who killed three of them. The fourth managed to survive by hiding in a cave. She later fingered the villain in a celebrated murder trial. With a name and a history like this, Smuttynose beers will probably develop a cult following.

Smuttynose Brewing is a joint venture between Janet and Peter Egelston of the Northampton and Portsmouth breweries and Paul Sylva and Jim Beauvais of Ipswich Brewing. They purchased the brewery from Don Jones, who's Frank Jones Brewing Co. had closed during the summer of 1993.

At press time they were not yet brewing, but planned to brew a non-alcoholic root beer and contract some beers for the Northampton Brewery in the near future.

Head brewer Paul Murphy said the equipment originally came from the Renegade Brewery in Thunder Bay, Canada. Some beers will be filtered, others unfiltered. They will be making 21-barrel batches using primarily English malts and domestic hops. The beers will be both kegged and bottled. They plan to offer tours.

Barrel of Miscellany

Address:	25 Heritage Avenue Portsmouth, NH 03801
Telephone:	none at press time
Tours:	call for information, once they have a phone

Seven Barrel Brewery

Lunch Stop on Your Brew Tour

At press time, Greg Noonan was scheduled to open his second brewpub, his first being the Vermont Pub and Brewery of Burlington. Fortunately, the name of his second brewing venture is less of a mouthful; simply, the Seven Barrel Brewery. The name refers to the equipment, all components of which are seven barrels in size--mash tun, brew kettle, fermenters, conditioning tanks, and serving tanks.

The opening of the Seven Barrel Brewery adds a fourth brewery to the Lebanon, New Hampshire-White River Junction, Vermont, area, and provides a unique opportunity for brew pilgrims to spend a day tasting beer, enjoying the local scenery, and shopping for New England-made hand-crafted items. Spend the night at the old Coolidge Hotel in downtown White River Junction. After breakfast you can take a tour of Catamount Brewing which is within an easy walk of the hotel. Next, drive across the Connecticut River to Lebanon where you can tour the lovely Dartmouth College campus. After that, have lunch at the Seven Barrel Brewery in West Lebanon. Next on the itinerary is the Queechee Gorge across the river in Vermont. From there continue up the Queechee River to Bridgewater Mills, where you can spend some time in the craft and gift shops, and trying out the beers in the basement at the Mountain Brewers tasting room. Next, retrace your steps on Route 4 to White River Junction, and then up I-91 to Norwich, where

you can walk around the town green and window shop. Finally, refreshments at Jasper Murdock's Alehouse, and victuals and lodging at the quaint Norwich Inn. End of a perfect day. Tomorrow you can head on down to Brattleboro where there is one of New England's two authentic brewpubs, as well as the region's other brewery inn, the Latchis Hotel/Grille. Or head on up to Middlebury where you can get some Otter Creek Brewing products to go, and then on to Burlington, where you can have some wonderful beer at Greg's other brewery restaurant.

When you find the Seven Barrel Brewery it will be unmistakable, it is housed in a rustic-looking building with stained-wood barn siding, surrounded by shopping centers and strip malls. The brewhouse is located in a new post-and-beam and glass, two story tower in front of the brewery. During the summer there is a small beer garden out front, with tables and umbrellas.

As you enter you will face a large, horseshoe-shaped bar with eight, copper-clad serving tanks (you needn't ask how many barrels of beer each holds) behind the bar. To the left is a rustic-looking dining area. The menu being planned was to be basic pub grub with burgers, sandwiches, bangers and mash, and fries. It was to be similar to the menu at the brewpub in Burlington.

The Brew

As the name of the brewery implies, Greg is using a seven-barrel system, including mash tun; kettle; conical, closed fermenters; conditioning tanks; and serving tanks. He planned to use an infusion mash for the ales and a decoction mash for the lagers. He will use two-row, imported barley malt and imported hops, such as East Kent Goldings and Fuggles, and domestic Saaz. All the beers will be unfiltered. For the most part, the beers will not be copies of those brewed in Burlington, as Greg plans to do a whole new range of beers. The beers will be served using a CO_2-nitrogen mix. By summer '94 they plan to have seven draft beers on tap at all times, four of which will be cask-conditioned ales.

Barrel of Miscellany

Address: Plainfield Road (Colonial Plaza, Route 12-A)
             West Lebanon, NH 03784 (from I-89, take exit 20)

Telephone: (603) 298-5566

Hours: 11:00 a.m. - 1:00 a.m. daily

Credit cards: American Express, MasterCard, Discover, Visa

Non-smoking area--handicapped access--off-street parking

Rhode Island

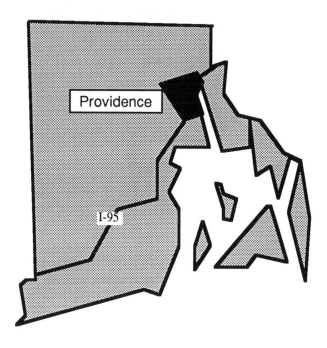

Rhode Island has had a very active brewing history, much more so than one might suspect from its small size. The first brewery was opened in Providence by Sargeant Baulston in 1639 (the same person who operated a brewery in New Haven the previous year). The Otis Holmes Brewery (founded in 1835) was the only other brewery to operate in the state until after the Civil War. A brewing boom took place beginning in the mid-1870s and lasting until the mid-1880s, at which time the smaller and weaker breweries began to close. In 1877, the peak year, there were twelve breweries registered in the state.

By far the largest and best known brewery to operate in Rhode Island was the Narragansett Brewing Co. of Cranston. It operated as an independent brewery from 1890 until 1965, when it was acquired by Falstaff Brewing. Narragansett was one of the only breweries to survive after the repeal of Prohibition, primarily through its sponsorship of the Boston Red Sox. Each radio and television broadcast of a Sox game was started with the phrase, "Hi, neighbor, have a 'Gansett."

Brewpubs were legalized in Rhode Island in 1992 and Union Station Brewing of Providence was the first to open, in December of the following year. It is rumored that breweries will open soon in Kingston and Newport.

Union Station Brewing
Brewing Returns to Rhode Island

On December 28, 1993, the long drought ended in Rhode Island. This date marked the opening of the first brewery in the state since the Narragansett Brewing Co. closed its doors in 1981. Actually, Narragansett was bought by Falstaff Brewing in 1965, at which time it could no longer be considered a New England brewery, but rather a branch of a national brewery.

Union Station Brewing is located in the old Union Railway Station, in the heart of the Providence financial district and directly across the street from the Omni Biltmore Hotel. Owners Joe Gately and Frank Hennessey have done a nice job of restoring the station to its former splendor and creating an attractive surrounding in which to dine or simply enjoy a brew. The old station is red brick and granite inside and out, with arched doorways and windows. Inside, there are two levels, the lower level has the bar and limited dining space. The main dining area is on the upper level, just two steps up from the bar. The entire complex has a seating capacity for 153 people.

The attractive copper brewhouse and stainless steel fermenting and serving tanks are directly behind the bar as you come in, and are plainly visible from the main dining-room as well. The red brick and granite walls are accented throughout the restaurant with dark mahogany, brass, and hardwood floors. The walls are adorned with many artifacts and pictures of the old Narragansett Brewery. Track lighting illuminates the restaurant from high ceilings, from which hang ceiling fans and exposed piping and ductwork.

This is definitely a restaurant brewery, not a brewpub. Most of the lunchtime customers are professionals and office workers from the surrounding offices and businesses. They also do a substantial dinner and weekend business.

The Menu

Unique. Wonderful combinations of flavors, textures, and colors await you. Every item is made or served with some special extra. Take for instance the humble chicken pot pie. At the Union Station the pot pie is made with an herbed biscuit crust and served with a cranberry/orange relish. The spit-roasted smoked pork chops are glazed with a sauce made with hard cider, apples and mushrooms, and then served with pureed sweet potatoes and warm mustard greens. Cod is available fried in beer batter, but wouldn't you like to try the corn crusted cod served on a stew of white beans, tomatoes, and spinach with crispy fried leeks and lemon/basil butter? There is much to choose from.

The sandwiches are just as interesting with the half-pound cheese burger vying for attention with sandwich combinations as original as the grilled yellow fin tuna fillet served with a chunky avocado mayonnaise and bacon on focaccia.

The Brew

Brewer Mark Hamon got his start in the brewing business working at the Modern Brewer Homebrew Supply Store in Cambridge, Massachusetts, where he acquired and devoured all the books he could about brewing. His first attempt at commercial brewing has been an unqualified success. His ales are all clean, well-balanced and quite tasty. On my visit to the pub I grew particularly fond of the half-and-half made from the Pale Ale and the Imperial Stout.

Mark is brewing with a ten-barrel Bohemian Brewing system in rather cramped quarters. There are four, ten-barrel and one twenty-barrel, closed fermenters. After fermentation, the beers are filtered and dispensed from serving tanks. Mark is averaging three-to-five batches per week. He is using a mixture of two-row, pre-milled Canadian malts. The hops are Canadian and American pellet hops.

Golden Ale - dry and malty with bitterness in the background; good body; very pleasant and well balanced; a light ale; their best seller (1.040)

Amber Ale - nice roasted malt; smooth; American brown ale

Pale Ale - very fresh with a crisp hoppiness; very long and very hoppy

Porter - robust; toward the dry side

-- Rotating --

Imperial Stout - black; a very tasty brew with sweet maltiness up front and a long, rich, bittersweet finish

Irish Red - amber; slightly perfumy aroma; pleasant malt flavor

India Pale Ale - not sampled

Scotch Ale - not sampled

Munich Dopple (lager) - not sampled

Barrel of Miscellany

Address:　　　　36 Exchange Terrace
　　　　　　　　　Providence, RI 02903

Telephone:　　 (401) 274--BREW

Hours:　　　　　Monday - Friday 11:30 a.m. - 2:00 a.m.
　　　　　　　　　Saturday & Sunday: 5:00 p.m. - 2:00 a.m.

Music:　　　　　live music on Saturday (country, rock, and blues); CD juke box

Credit cards:　 American Express, MasterCard, Visa

TV -- handicapped access -- validated parking for lunch & dinner patrons ($20 minimum)
　　　　　　　non-smoking area -- beer garden

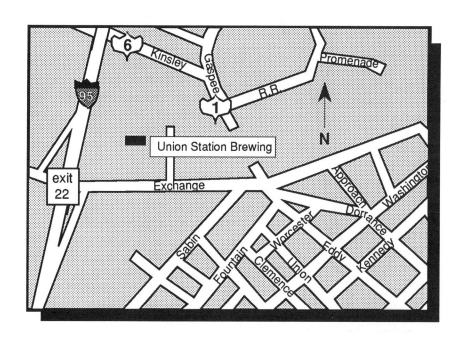

Vermont

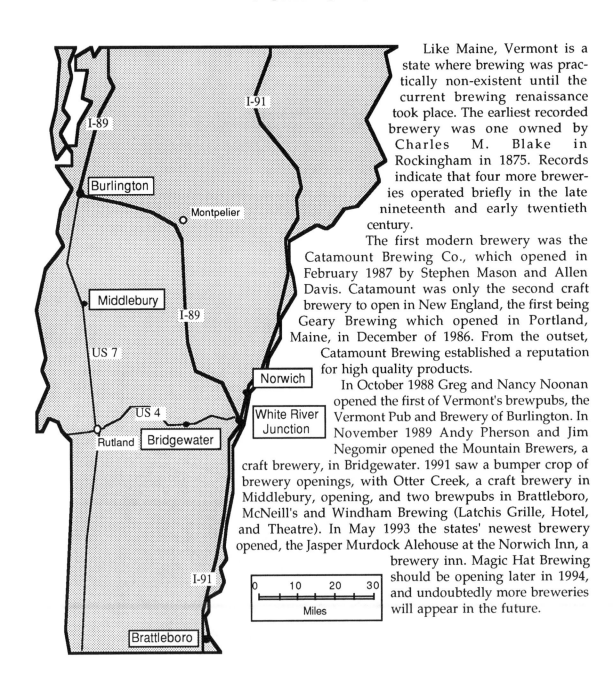

Like Maine, Vermont is a state where brewing was practically non-existent until the current brewing renaissance took place. The earliest recorded brewery was one owned by Charles M. Blake in Rockingham in 1875. Records indicate that four more breweries operated briefly in the late nineteenth and early twentieth century.

The first modern brewery was the Catamount Brewing Co., which opened in February 1987 by Stephen Mason and Allen Davis. Catamount was only the second craft brewery to open in New England, the first being Geary Brewing which opened in Portland, Maine, in December of 1986. From the outset, Catamount Brewing established a reputation for high quality products.

In October 1988 Greg and Nancy Noonan opened the first of Vermont's brewpubs, the Vermont Pub and Brewery of Burlington. In November 1989 Andy Pherson and Jim Negomir opened the Mountain Brewers, a craft brewery, in Bridgewater. 1991 saw a bumper crop of brewery openings, with Otter Creek, a craft brewery in Middlebury, opening, and two brewpubs in Brattleboro, McNeill's and Windham Brewing (Latchis Grille, Hotel, and Theatre). In May 1993 the states' newest brewery opened, the Jasper Murdock Alehouse at the Norwich Inn, a brewery inn. Magic Hat Brewing should be opening later in 1994, and undoubtedly more breweries will appear in the future.

Latchis Grille, Hotel, & Theatre Windham Brewery
The Rockefeller Center of Restaurant Breweries

What do you get when you cross a hotel with a movie theater and a restaurant and a cocktail lounge? Well, when Peter Latchis put all of this together in the late 1930s in Brattleboro he came up with Vermont's answer to Rockefeller Center. The Latchis Memorial Building was THE center of Brattleboro for an era which catered to elegant evenings out with cocktails in the lounge, followed by dinner in the hotel dining room, and then a romantic comedy or musical. The perfect evening would be complete after dancing to the strains of the Latchis Orchestra in the ballroom.

Their architects may have been different, but John D. Rockefeller and Peter Latchis both wanted to create something grand for their cities and their people and they chose art deco as their style. The exterior of the four-story Latchis complex is a monument to the style which stressed simple planes of granite, delineated with strong, vertical lines and bas relief decorations. This particular structure has endured the changes of time and taste and has been recognized as a significant piece of Vermont's heritage by its inclusion on the National Register of Historic Places.

There are now three theaters in the movie complex, but you can still enjoy a first run movie in the original 600-seat theater which has been faithfully restored to its 1938 grandeur. The goddess Athena keeps watch in the lobby as you enter. Inside the theater you are surrounded by murals of Greek myths, figures of the zodiac decorate the ceiling above your head, and your feet are resting on a one-of-a-kind terrazzo floor. Peter's father, Demetrius, for whom the complex was named, was born in Greece and came to the United States in 1901. He started out as a fruit vendor, selling his produce from a horse-drawn cart, but died owning fifteen movie houses and several hotels. The Latchis Memorial Building is indeed a fitting tribute to the patriarch and the family's roots.

Spero Latchis, Peter's great nephew, is the current owner and manager of the hotel and restaurant. In 1988 he decided to open a restaurant and pub in the basement of the hotel with an outside entrance on Flat Street. Access to the Latchis Grille is by way of an interior stair and hallway which passes the glass enclosed brewery. The room which seats 160 is a mix of exposed brick walls, cream colored plaster walls, and lots of windows. Along the length of the restaurant and bar area is a row of windows which look out onto the picturesque Whetstone Brook. Windows are a predominate feature of the interior walls also, helping to create cozy spaces, but without basement claustrophobia.

The bar area is at the far end of the restaurant and features a small, but very attractive curved bar, constructed of four large panels of richly grained walnut and cherry which have been trimmed out in a contrasting raised molding.

Brattleboro, population 12,200, is a small city by anyone's standards, but it is, in fact, Vermont's most industrialized city. It was also Vermont's first, founded in 1724. Despite it's industrial identity, Brattleboro's real character is much more of a college town than a manufacturing center, and has been characterized as a college town without the college.

The Latchis Building sits above the Whetstone Brook, a salt-rich tributary that joins the Connecticut River just a few blocks east. The waters were once thought to be restorative, and Harriet Beecher Stowe and Henry Wadsworth Longfellow were two of the most famous New Englanders who took the water cure developed by Brattleboro's Dr. Robert Wesselhoeft. Another literary figure with connections to Brattleboro is Rudyard Kipling who wrote Captains Courageous as well as his two Jungle Books while in residence in Dummerston, just a few miles outside of Brattleboro.

The Menu

The cuisine is definitely nouveau California, with lots of fresh ingredients, herbs, sun-dried tomatoes, avocados, flavored pastas and marinades from many cultures. Appetizers include spicy potato pancakes with cilantro pesto and chipotle cream, and smoked fish served with horseradish dressing, grilled rosemary bread and assorted garnishes. The fettucine dish is a combination of three pastas with a roasted eggplant and tomato sauce. Lamb chops are grilled and topped with a Port wine demi glace. There are several fresh seafood entrees including a scallop, shrimp and salmon quesadilla.

In addition to the regular menu, the Latchis Grille also serves from a cafe menu which includes soups, salads, burgers and two pub standbys: fish and chips fried in a lime brew-batter and a Bavarian platter of beer-steamed wurst and sauerkraut. The Nachos Grande are made with black beans for a delightful change of pace, and cajun spices are featured in a Louisiana meat loaf. Chicken satay is another specialty served with peanut dipping sauce, rice and vegetables. Most of the items on the cafe menu are designed to complement the Windham brews.

The Brew

Spero Latchis needed both a brewer and a carpenter to help him remodel the basement for the new brewing equipment and then to begin making the beer. So, he took out an ad in the local newpaper for an experienced homebrewer and carpenter. Now this seemed like one really stupid idea--after all, how many carpenter-homebrewers could there be in the Brattleboro area? Not such a bad idea after all--Spero received 60 inquiries from qualified applicants. He settled on John Korpita, a homebrewing fanatic (he even grows his own hops) and experienced carpenter. John has have a 40-mile commute, but remember, he is a fanatic.

Spero and John spent long hours installing the brewery, which consisted of used Grundy tanks, an old Campbell's soup tank for the kettle, and an old dairy tank for the mash tun. Greg Noonan of the Vermont Pub and Brewery came down for a couple of weeks to help them get started. John is making seven-barrel batches of unfiltered beers. He is using imported, two-row malts and a combination of domestic and imported, whole-leaf hops. The beers are dispensed from kegs under CO_2

pressure. John keeps four to five beers on tap at all times, as well as a home-made root beer.

Whetstone Golden Lager - hazy, dark gold; slightly sweet, malty entry; dry finish; well balanced and smooth; very drinkable; made with 20% malted wheat and 60 pounds of honey, and the rest a mixture of pale and crystal malt; hopped with Cascade and Tettnang

Moonbeam Ale - hazy, copper; fruity and malty aroma, slightly sweet entry, finishes on the dry side; lightly hopped; slightly tart finish; clean tasting; made with pale and crystal malt, Cascade and Tettnang hops for bittering

Dynosteam - hazy, nice reddish amber; sweet malt entry; dry finish; lightly hopped; made with all English pale and caramel malt; Liberty hops; a summer seasonal; named after Jurasic Park, California common style

Ruby Brown Ale - not sampled

Raspberry Amber Lager - slighlty hazy, reddish copper; raspberry nose; raspberry flavor; light malt and hops; dry finish; similar recipe to Dynosteam, but with raspberry extrac added

Strawberry Whetstone - not sampled; made with 100 pounds of real strawberries

---

Barrel of Miscellany

Address:	6 Flat Street
	Brattleboro, VT 053301
Telephone:	(802) 254-4747
Hours:	11:30 a.m. - 11:30 p.m. daily
Tours:	Thursday at 6:00 p.m.
Deli:	beer to go in 2.2 gallon globes; T-shirts and glasses for sale
Music:	live jazz Thursday and Friday nights
Credit cards:	American Expresss, Discover, MasterCard, Visa

the dining room is non-smoking

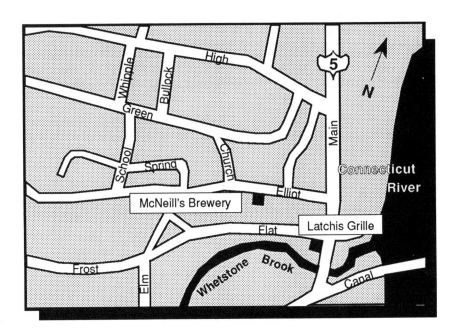

McNeill's Brewery
The Bohemian Brewer of Brattleboro

Brattleboro has been dubbed a college town without the college, in spite of its real position as Vermont's most industrialized city. Perhaps the small town population of just a little over 12,000 has something to do with it. Regardless, Brattleboro is a small, but vital center for the arts and its citizens support the same kinds of businesses and activities you see in Middlebury or Northampton, or any number of other New England academic communities. One of those businesses would be a college bar, one that attracts both students and faculty; nonconformist, but not chic; homey, but not staid. McNeill's then, is the Brattleboro brewpub for those who like their surroundings on the Bohemian side.

McNeill's has been doing business in Brattleboro for nine years, but moved to its current location on Elliott Street in 1990. The building, a five-story, red, clapboard structure was erected in 1872 as the town's fire station and later served as the Brattleboro police station and city jail. The extra room was just what owner and brewer Ray McNeill wanted in order to brew his own ales and lagers.

McNeill's customers are greeted at the entrance by a painting of a handlebar mustached waiter carrying a tray of beers. He gestures to the latch on the brewpub's front door as if to say, "Come on in." Inside, the room has high ceilings and bare wood floors. The oak paneled walls serve as a gallery for local artists. The furnishings are simple, just trestle tables where you can hunker down with your beer, elbows on the table. The bar, which runs along one wall is most notable for its beer taps. Ray has a sense of humor and he has customized the handle of his Duck's Breath Bitter tap with a yellow rubber duckie and the Big Nose Blond tap handle is topped with a Barbie Doll. The Catamount ales come out of a large ceramic cat.

The Barbie Doll behind the bar is not the only child's toy at McNeill's. Ray and his wife Holiday, want their brewpub to be a place where families can congregate as they do in the British Isles, so there are toys for the little ones. And darts and board games for the bigger ones. Ray and Holiday have been told that McNeill's feels like a British pub, and while Ray believes you can't have true English character without British patrons, they have created a neighborhood gathering place for folks to meet and visit at the end of day. In fact, McNeill's doesn't open until four in the afternoon. There is no television and no juke box (hooray!). This place is for people who like people, all kinds of people.

Ray, himself is a self-cast Bohemian brewer, wearing a tie-died lab coat over the

The Menu

McNeill's is a true brewpub, so the emphasis is on the brew rather than the vittles. The menu is limited to munchies, nachos, corn chips and guacamole or salsa, a few sandwiches, and their very special house-made chili.

wildest pants you have ever seen. But he is a philosophical Bohemian who believes that suburbanization and the decline of the neighborhood tavern have taken too big a toll on our society. He wants to bring folks together again to talk and enjoy themselves - over his ales and lagers.

The Brew

Ray McNeill provides the greatest variety of authentic beer styles in New England. So, if you are choosing a brewpub for the beer, McNeill's is an excellent place to visit. True, the Boston Beer Works comes close, but I have to tip my hat to Ray McNeill. He has a minimum of twelve beers on tap at all times, and sometimes as many as fifteen. The amazing thing is that until recently, he was doing all of the work himself.

Ray started as just another beer enthusiast. His first batches didn't turn out particularly well. But, with the zeal of the true fanatic and an uncompromising dedication to perfection, Ray stuck to it, reading, experimenting, and striving for the perfect brew. His brews are not quite heavenly, but close enough to it that you might hear a harp playing in the background when you sip one of his brews.

For each beer style, Ray tries to duplicate the brewing ingredients and method of only the truly great beers of the world. None of the beers are filtered and three are served under only a three p.s.i blanket of CO_2 pressure. The ales are all dry hopped, with the exception of the English-style brown ale and stout. For the the lagers Ray uses the German decoction method of mashing. He grinds his own malt and uses only two-row malts. In the lagers he uses domestic Herrington and Klages and imported Moravian malt. With only two exceptions, the ales are all made with imported malt, including the hard-to-find and highly prized Maris Otter, which he uses in the IPA. The exceptions are the Big Nose Blond and the Fire House, which are made with U.S. Harrington and Klages malts. About ten different hop varieties are employed, all whole-leaf hops, with the exception of the Bullion hops, which Ray uses in the pellet form because they are so perishable. Other hops include East Kent Goldings, Fuggles, Saaz, Tettnang, Hallertau, Chinook, Cascade, Northern Brewer, and Mt. Hood.

Ray makes five barrel batches which are initially dispensed from Grundies. Three batches are made every five days. In order to conserve space and to keep as many beers on tap at once, as the beer in the Grundies gets low, Ray racks the remaining beer to kegs in order to make way for the next batch to come on line.

Four-ounce samples sell for 60¢ and $1.00 each, depending on the strength of the beer. Ten-ounce glasses sell for $1.65-1.75, pints for $1.75-2.00 (strong beers sell for $3.00-3.25).

The exciting news is that by late summer of 1994 Ray will begin distributing many of his beers in 22-oz. bottles. He intends to distribute throughout Vermont.

When visiting the pub, be sure and meet Ray if at all possible--he is as colorful as the names he has chosen for his brews.

Bohemian Pils - hazy, dark amber; a little perfumy; fruity; sweet and very malty and rich; made with 90% Bohemian malts, hopped with Saaz

Big Nose Blond - deep gold; off-dry; medium body; short and smooth finish; very lightly hopped; notice the tap handle, it has a Barbie Doll on it

Fire House North American Style Pale Ale - hazy red-amber; nice, caramelized maltiness; very smooth and well balanced; bittered with Northern Brewer and Cascades to finish; tastes like a classic California red

Dead Horse IPA - clear, reddish amber, a good example of an ale which is very hoppy, but not too bitter; nice marriage of hops and malts in the finish; outstanding; hopped with lots of East Kent Goldings

Pullman's Porter - opaque, very dark brown; dry and bitter with a nice roasted maltiness; made with pale, chocolate, and black malt and a tiny bit of roasted barley; delicious and very drinkable

Slopbucket Double Brown - attractive, deep brown with reddish tint; very malty with nice caramelized malt character; slightly sweet; light hops, yummy

Duck's Breath Bitter - rubber duckie on the tap handle, not sampled

Oatmeal Stout - opaque, ebony; acidic; lots of toffee a little licorice taste; very dry; delicious; flaked oats are used

McNeill's Extra Special Bitter - reddish; very bitter, citrusy, piney, very dry; 55 IBUs; reminds me of Red Seal Ale (North Coast Brewing)

Dopplebock - malty and rich; nice, well-balanced, smooth finish, medium-to-full body

---

Barrel of Miscellany

Address:	90 Elliot Street Brattleboro, VT 05301
Telephone:	(802)254-2553
Hours:	Sunday - Friday: 4:00 p.m. - 2:00 a.m.; Saturday: 4:00 p.m. - 1:00 a.m.
Credit cards:	MasterCard, Visa
	darts -- board games -- toys for the wee ones

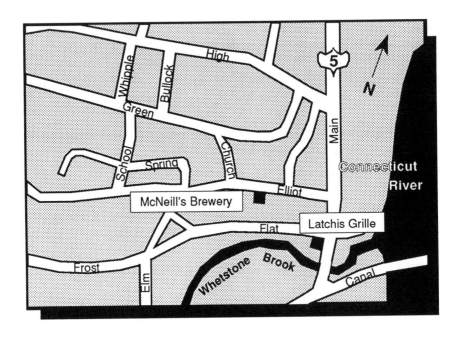

Mountain Brewers

Urban Refugees

Escaping from the city? This is the place to do it. After shopping the craft stores and outlets upstairs at the Marketplace at Bridgewater Mill, a woolen mill dating to 1825, descend to the basement where between noon and 5:00 p.m. you can go on a self-guided tour of the brewery and sit at the bar in the hospitality room to have some free beer. Be sure to examine the antique beer can collection before you leave. You may purchase some souvenir T-shirts, hats, etc. before you leave. If you haven't had your fill of this tasty brew, then drive a few miles East on U.S. 4 to the Queechee Gin Mill where you can drink Long Trail ales to your heart's content.

The Mountain Brewers was founded in 1989 by Andy Pherson and Jim Negomir. Andy had been working as an electrical engineer in Boston in the early 1980s and spent many weekends enjoying the outdoors in Vermont. While on temporary assignment in California he discovered craft brewing. He realized that by introducing the craft brewing business to New England he could follow his dream of escaping the big city and living in the state he loved most, Vermont. Appropriately enough, he named their ales for the Long Trail, which runs the length of the state and predates the Appalachian Trail.

Andy purchased a fifteen-barrel Peter Austin brewing system. However, in order to economize he did much of the installation, as well as expansion and upgrading himself. Brewing the beer and installing the equipment has been a lot of of hard, dirty work, and the brewery workers jokingly refer to themselves as the "leather-handed, squinty-eyed, rubber-footed, cellar dwellers."

The first keg rolled off the line on November 7, 1989. By the next summer they began bottling in twelve-ounce bottles. All the hard work has paid off, with demand far outstripping production. And the Long Trail ales have garnered several awards at the Great American Beer Festival. It started with the silver medal for the Long Trail Ale in the alt category in 1990. Then, in 1991 the same beer took the gold in the Dusseldorf style altbier category, and their Northern Light took the silver in the American lager-ale category. In the 1992 festival the Bicentennial Ale took the bronze medal in the blonde ale category.

The Brew

Andy Pherson and assistant brewer Paul Kowalski are making 30-barrel batches in their Peter Austin brew system. They have eight open fermenters. They are using two-row American malt and both pellet and whole leaf American hops. The ales are filtered with diatomaceous earth, and cold filtered as well. The ales are cold conditioned in the lager fashion. They are making two batches daily, and produce about 14,000 barrels annually. The ales are packaged in kegs and 12-oz. bottles.

Long Trail Light - bright gold; very dry and crisp; slightly astringent

Long Trail Kolsch - bright gold; crisp; dry malt; hoppy finish; very long and bitter

Long Trail India Pale Ale - bright, light amber; fruity, malty aroma; dry; very long and bitter; finished with Cascades

Long Trail Ale - bright copper; dry, slightly sour or tart; very drinkable; finished with Cascades; won a silver in its category at the 1990 Great American Beer Festival, an alt

Bicentennial Ale - bright, dark gold; dry malt; tart; smooth; finished with Cascades

Long Trail Stout - opaque, dark brown with a ruby hue; light brown head; roasted barley; dry; complex flavor; light-medium body; creamy mouthfeel, very nice; pushed with nitrogen-CO_2 mix

Barrel of Miscellany

Address:	Box 140, Route 4, The Marketplace Bridgewater, VT 05034
Telephone:	(802) 672-5011
Tours:	self-guided tours from noon - 5:00 p.m. daily
Beer to go:	12-oz. bottles, singles, six packs, and cases
Availability:	Throughout New England

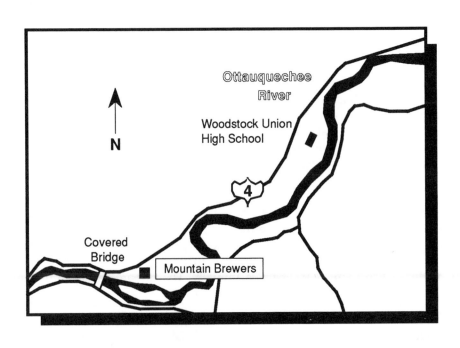

Magic Hat Brewing

Beer Sorcerers

As *On Tap New England* went to press partners Alan Newman and Bob Johnson had surprised everyone by having their beer on the market, even though renovation of the building and installation of the brewing equipment for Magic Hat Brewing hadn't been completed yet. Sound like magic? It's all done with mirrors. Until they have their brewery up and running their brews were being done for them at the Kennebunkport Brewing Co. in Maine. This way they will already have their market and distribution network partially developed when their first keg roles off the line. Neat trick.

Bob and Alan always told themselves, if they could ever actually open their own brewery, it would be like magic. Hence, the name, Magic Hat. The brewery is located about five minutes south of downtown Burlington. It is in a red brick, turn-of-the-century building which was once a mule stable and later a steam plant. When the equipment arrives they will have a fifteen-barrel Peter Austin system, with open fermenters for the ales, and closed fermenters for lagers. Brewer Bob Johnson has quite a bit of brewing experience under his belt. He brewed at home for ten years and has also brewed for one year at Otter Creek Brewing in Middlebury. He will be using imported, two-row malt and roasted barley and domestic pellet and whole-leaf hops. Bob plans to start by making Magic Hat Ale, an Irish red ale (1.049). Several seasonals will follow, including Espresso Stout (dry stout, 1.050), Nit-wit Wheat (Belgian wit style, 1.047), Raj-Ma-Taj IPA (cask conditioned IPA, 1.057), and Virginia's Brown Ale (1.047). Once Bob gets the draft products going, he plans to bottle in 22-oz. bottles.

Barrel of Miscellany

Address:	180 Flynn Avenue Burlington, VT 05401
Telephone:	(802) 658-BREW
Tours:	The owners were uncertain at press time whether they would offer tours.

Vermont Pub and Brewery of Burlington

The Champlagne of Beer

Vermont Pub and Brewery is the result of one man's appreciation for European beers, which inspired a hobby, which turned into an obsession, which begat a research project, which resulted in a manuscript and then into a publication. Once *Brewing Lager Beer* went to press in 1986, the author turned his attention to making his avocation a full-time vocation. By 1988 he had opened his brewpub in Burlington, Vermont. It was born after a very long gestation period and a very difficult labor.

Vermont Pub and Brewery is the offspring of Greg Noonan, one time carpenter, building contractor, manufacturer of paper and wood products, who got hooked on homebrewing in spite of a most inauspicious start. The now renowned expert on the art and science of brewing lager beers, made his very first batch of homebrew with malted barley, a neighbor's electric coffee grinder, a bag full of hops, some yeast, four large pots, and a homebrewer's guide for making beer with malt extract syrup. The resulting brew was barely drinkable, according to Greg, but the challenge had now taken hold: to brew all-grain beers of the highest quality on a consistent basis. What Greg needed more than anything else was how-to information which he could not find in his little burg of Charlemont in the Berkshire Mountains of Massachusetts. Greg hit the road, visiting homebrew supply stores where he bought every guide he could get his hands on. He went to libraries and borrowed whatever he could and ordered more through interlibrary loans.

Greg's homebrew improved steadily, but what was becoming even clearer was the lack of a compendium of reliable and readable information about brewing for homebrewers and craft brewers; the do's, and perhaps more importantly, the don'ts. Greg saw the gap and set his sights on filling it. It took him five years to research, write, and illustrate *Brewing Lager Beer*. The back cover of the 293-page volume says it all, "Warning: This book is for serious brewers only." In this case, serious can be described as one who wants to understand the chemistry of brewing and remove the guesswork out of homebrewing.

When the book was finally published in 1986, Noonan turned his sights to brewing full-time at a brewpub, a place where people would come to relax, socialize, drink distinctive brews, and enjoy a good meal without spending a king's ransom. He wanted a partner, and he found one in Nancy Noonan, his wife. Greg's the brewer, Nancy's the chef. A gourmet cook, she tackled the management of a restaurant kitchen with a determination which matched Greg's passion for excellence as he designed his brewery.

Charlemont, Massachusetts, was a lovely little town, but was not ready for a brewpub. Step one was to find the perfect location for their dream. Burlington, Vermont, a city of 40,000 and home to the University of Vermont, struck them as a New England equivalent of Boulder, Colorado, a preeminent center for craft brewing in the West. Burlington was, in Greg's words, ". . . artistic, progressive, fairly well-heeled, with a taste for good brew." Having selected their city, the Noonans began the trek through the bureaucratic obstacle course of zoning regulations, sewage discharge permits, and the monumental hurdle of obtaining licensing in a

The Menu

The menu at the Vermont Pub and Brewery is pubfare--made-from-scratch, hearty, wholesome, and moderately priced. Soups include a daily special to supplement the New England seafood chowder. The appetizers run from nacho items, cheese sticks, and veggies & dip to cajun-fried calamari and smoked salmon. There is a selection of cold and hot sandwiches and seven different kinds of char-broiled burgers. The English pub grub includes Toad-in-the-Hole, apple sausage and cheddar cheese baked in bread dough; Cornish pasties; Welsh rarebit; Mulligan stew; bangers & mash; and the most popular item, the house-ale battered fish & chips, served with Dublin fries. House brews are also featured in the Welsh rarebit and for steaming the sausages for the bangers & mash. Dinner entrees include two fresh seafood selections broiled in variations of a lemon-sherry-butter sauce, two char-grilled chicken items, and a savory roasted chicken entree. Pasta dishes include a smoked salmon Alfredo and a vegetarian pasta dish served with either Alfredo or marinara sauce over spinach fettucine.

Nancy and Greg are Vermont boosters - the breads are made by a local bakery, the beef is locally raised Black Angus beef certified free of growth hormones or pestisides, and the ice cream is made by, who else, Ben & Jerry. In season, the herbs come from the Noonan's herb garden.

---

state which forbade breweries from selling their products on their own premises. Armed with statistics, aided and abetted by "well placed" homebrewers in the city zoning office, as well as the Vermont legislature, Greg and Nancy emerged from the obstacle course ready to open the brewery door to anxious crowds in just two years!

Vermont Pub and Brewery is located in downtown Burlington, in a contemporary red brick structure. The space was formerly occupied by a restaurant, so Nancy's kitchen was in place. Running the entire length of the front is a glass solarium or conservatory area which ties the inside to the outside terrace where patrons are served during warm weather. The bar occupies the glass-walled conservatory space with a counter running along the windows where you can sip your beer and watch the world go by, perched on a bar stool. The bar itself is mahogany with two brass rails - one for the feet and one for the elbows. The mosaic tile floor has a turn-of-the-century feel to it, which is repeated in the glass-shaded light fixtures and bentwood furnishings. All contrasted nicely with the contemporary brick walls and solarium structure.

The rectangular bar is a pass-through bar and the other side opens out onto the rose carpeted dining room. The room is furnished in tables with richly stained and highly polished wood tops, and dark bentwood chairs with padded backs and seats that invite you to relax and linger. A magnificent oak and mahogany back bar lines one stretch of wall. Between the round columns capped with carved capitals, and under the gracefully arched opening, sit antique beer casks, a glass carboy, and old beer advertisements.

If you like music with your brew and vittles, R&B, blues and bluegrass groups play Thursday, Friday and Saturday nights. The Vermont Pub and Brewery attracts a broad cross-section of patrons; professionals, business types, tourists and students from the university as well as two other local colleges. The Noonans have created an atmosphere that says welcome, come in and stay a while.

The Brew

Master brewer Greg Noonan and head brewer Glenn Walter are making some pretty incredible beers. One thing they do differently than almost anyone in New England, is a double decoction mash for the lagers, which a portion of the mash is diverted to a second container, where it is heated to a higher temperature and then reintroduced into the main mash. Also, unlike many breweries which have fermenters which are twice the size of their kettles, Vermont Pub and Brewery has a fourteen-barrel kettle and seven-barrel fermenters; so, they are splitting the brews into two fermenters, rather than double batching the brews, like at so many other places. They use a different yeast strain in each fermenter. Then, when they combine the batches in the conditioning tank, the resulting brew has more complexity.

Greg and Glenn are using two-row, Hugh Baird pale and crystal malt from England, which they crush in house. Greg says Hugh Baird is one of the only English maltsters using two-row specialty malts. For hops they are using East Kent Goldings, imported Saaz, and American Cascade, Mt. Hood, and Liberty.

The beers are filtered and dispensed from serving tanks using CO_2 pressure at 46° degrees. The Burley Irish Ale and the Vermont Smoked Porter are pushed with a combination nitrogen CO_2 mix. They normally have seven beers on tap. Beers are available in 12-oz. servings ($2.25), pints ($2.75), and half yards (28 ozs. for $5.50). The Wee Heavy is sold in 8-oz. servings ($2.25). Beer mixology is a big thing at the Vermont Pub and Brewery, and they offer a Black & Tan (half Guinness and half Burley), Snakebite (half cider and half Burly), Shandy (half lime and half Burley), Black Velvet (half cider and half Guinness), and Joe Light (Burley and house-made seltzer). They feature a few imports and a New England guest beer on tap. There are several bottled beers available too, including several Belgians.

Burley Irish Ale - bright; dark amber; nice, tall head; estery aroma; mildly buttery; fruity; lightly hopped; made with rolled oats and raw barley flour, a session beer, low in alcohol

Dogbite Bitter - East Kent Goldings character; not sampled (1.050)

Vermont Smoked Porter - opaque; light brown head; smoky aroma, but not too heavy; very nice, roasted barley hoppy flavor; rich and smoky; fairly bitter; the malt is roasted over a smoky apple, hickory, and maple wood fire; five kinds of malt are used (1.048)

--seasonal - rotating --

Bombay Grab India Pale Ale - bright, medium copper color; hoppy aroma; crisp but sweet too; fairly sweet for an IPA; nice long hoppy bitter finish; bittered and flavored with East Kent Goldings, dry hopped with Cascades; worth a trip to Burlington to try this one; named for the first IPA ever brewed, at the Hodgsen Brewery in London, the pub at this brewery was called the Bombay Grab (1.051)

Betelguise Weiss (also known as Beetle Juice) - an authentic-tasting, clovy, German hefe weizen; hazy gold; nice, banana-clovy taste; made with 50% wheat malt and 50% six-row barley malt; they use a Belgian triple yeast to get the phenolic flavor

Oktoberfest - deep amber color; fairly sweet and malty; a wonderful, fresh and complex Octoberfest; a little hoppier in 1993 than previously

Auld Tartan Wee Heavy - deep amber; full body; sweet and syrupy; caramelized malt; alcoholic; a tad medicinal, but still ambrosial; made with pale malt and 1% roasted barley; they start filling the kettle with wort and stop when it is only one inch deep and then turn the burners on to caramelize the wort, just like making caramel or taffy, it gives a different caramel flavor than you get with the caramel malt; took the gold medal in its category at the 1993 Great American Beer Festival; a Scotch ale or strong ale; 9.5% alcohol by volume (1.093)

O'Fest - amber lager; Vienna style; not sampled

Bohemian Lager - a Pilsner, made with lager yeast; not sampled

Wild Thing - made with a mixture of 85% barley malt and 15% wheat malt; fermented with a Belgian yeast and then matured in a tank with 550 pounds of sour red cherries; their anniversary fruit beer; not sampled (1.042)

Vermont Maple Ale - made with 50% Vermont maple syrup, 35% malted barley, and 15% malted wheat; hopped with Perle; not sampled (1.048)

This is only a partial list, as Greg and Glenn have made more than 40 different kinds of beers since the brewery opened.

Barrel of Miscellany

Address:	144 College Street, Burlington, VT 05401
Telephone:	(802) 865-0500
Hours:	Sunday - Thursday: 11:30 a.m. - 12:30 a.m.; Friday: 11:30 a.m. - 2:00 a.m.; Saturday: 11:30 a.m. - 1:00 a.m.
Music:	live music Thursday (pub sessions); Friday and Saturday (R & B/blues/blue grass)
Credit cards:	American Express, Diners Club, Discover, MasterCard, Visa
	television -- handicapped access -- off-street parking -- non-smoking area -- darts, chess, backgammon -- beer garden

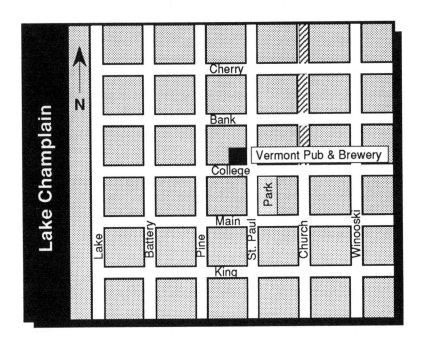

Otter Creek Brewing

Seminar on the Art of Brewing

Middlebury is the quintessential New England village, also widely known for its small, liberal arts college, founded back in 1800. Now, almost two hundred years later Middlebury is also developing a reputation as a source of good beer. This is most appropriate, as no liberal arts education would be complete without a few sessions of beer drinking.

Otter Creek Brewing, the source of Middlebury's newest claim to fame, has already made an impact in Middlebury and across the state. Having sampled some of its beautiful beers, you might be surprised when you arrive at the brewery. It is housed in an ugly, metal warehouse in an industrial park, located on the north edge of town, literally, across the tracks from the college. This is in sharp contrast to the pretty campus and the typical New England town common, with its quaint shops and white, clapboard houses. Since opening, brewery founder Lawrence Miller says faculty, students, shop owners, professionals, tourists, farmers, and blue collar workers alike have been making the trek up Exchange Street to the front door of the brewery, where they buy half-gallon growlers of his fresh beer. Although all the customers have received varying degrees of education, they all have one thing in common: an educated palate.

Lawrence, age 28, a transplant from Princeton, New Jersey, learned about good beer during his years at Reed College in Portland, Oregon. He became intrigued with the new breweries starting up in the area, such as Widmer Brewing, Columbia River Brewing (now Bridgeport), Portland Brewing, as well as Yakima Brewing in Yakima, Washington, and Hart Brewing in nearby Kalama, Washington. He started homebrewing in his apartment with an all-grain set up his friend had left behind when he went off to study brewing at the Weheinstephan Brewery in Germany.

After college, Lawrence made his own trip to Europe, where he spent several months visiting Germany and Belgium. He says it was in these two countries that he "really got turned on to good beer." Upon his return to the States, Lawrence decided to open his own brewery. He found a job working for a landscaping firm in Middlebury. One of his first discoveries was that the water in Middlebury was excellent for brewing ales. Its hard water was influenced by the abundant limestone in the soil (the limestone for the Lincoln Memorial and the Lions in front of the New York Public Library came from near here). Later, he travelled to the West Coast where he took two mini-courses on brewing and brewery operation at UC-Davis and then went back to Portland where Widmer Brewing was in the midst of expanding their operation. He helped them for a few weeks and struck a deal with the owners to purchase their old equipment.

Lawrence started work on his new brewery in the summer of 1990 and produced his first keg of ale the following March. As business grew, he found that many Vermonters enjoyed drinking beer at home--but his beer was only available in restaurants and bars. So, he started pouring fresh, half-gallon growlers right from the tap at the brewery. Business became so brisk, Lawrence began bottling his beer in March of 1993. He has been continuously adding tanks to keep up with the demand.

Lawrence named the brewery after Otter Creek, because it was the reason the town exists. Early settlers harnessed the water power of the creek to create some of the first mechanical textile mills in the country. Middlebury's bridge and falls on Otter Creek are featured on the brewery's logo, followed by the words from William Shakespeare, "For a quart of ale is dish for a king."

The Brew

Lawrence is turning out one all-year product and four seasonals. Demand is so great, he and his staff are making two batches four days a week and four batches three days a week, using a night shift. The closed fermenters are much larger than the ten-barrel mash tun and brew kettle; so, it takes four batches to fill up each fermenter. The ales are made using domestic two-row pale and specialty malts, milled at the brewery. Domestic hops are employed. Aroma hops are added in the whirlpool. All beers are whirlpooled for clarity, filtered, and kegged or bottled under CO_2 pressure. Production for 1993 was about 3,750 barrels (8,000 barrels are forecast for 1994). About 70% of the ales are packaged in 12-oz. bottles. The rest is kegged. Otter Creek ales are available throughout Vermont.

Copper Ale - bright, medium copper; tan, tight head; smooth, bittersweet, caramelized malt finish; made with two-row pale, Munich, two kinds of Caramel, and cara-pils malts and roasted barley; Chinooks for bittering and aroma; a year around product, (1.048)

-- seasonal --

Hickory Switch Smoked Amber Ale - beautiful, tawny, chestnut, deep, reddish brown; delicious, faintly smoky aroma; intriguing, malty-smokey finish; lightly hopped; best smoked beer I've ever had; very drinkable; made with Munich, darker roasted caramel, chocolate, and cara-pils malts; light hopping with Chinook, Willamette, and Cascade; available in the autumn; they do a light smoking of the malt out in the parking lot--it takes four hours to smoke enough malt for a brew, doing 100 pounds at a time (1.050)

Stovepipe Porter - deep brown, almost black, with a reddish tint; deep roasted coffee aroma; deeply roasted malt, sweet and coffeeish; rich and complex; burnt bitterness in the finish; a blend of Munich and some caramel with a preponderance of chocolate malt; hopped with Willamette and Cascade and some Chinook; their winter beer, released at Thanksgiving (1.054)

Mud Bock Spring Ale - made with two-row pale, lots of caramel and a little wheat and Munich malts; domestic Hallertau and Tettnang added near the end of the boil; released in the spring; not sampled (1.059)

Summer Wheat Ale - bright gold; nice hop finish; dry and crisp; a little fruity; very drinkable; clean tasting; made with pale malt and wheat malt (40%); Cascades and Willamette; an American wheat style; released in the summer (1.038)

Barrel of Miscellany

Address: 74 Exchange Street, Unit 1
                   Middlebury, VT 05753-1105

Telephone: (802) 388-0727; (800) 473-0727

Tours: Guided tours at 4:00 and 5:00 p.m. on Friday and 1:00, 3:00 and 5:00
                   p.m. on Saturday; self guided tours from noon - 6:00 p.m., Monday -
                   Saturday; at other times by appointment.

Beer to go: in 64-oz. growlers, kegs, and bottles

Distribution: throughout Vermont in kegs and 12-oz. bottles

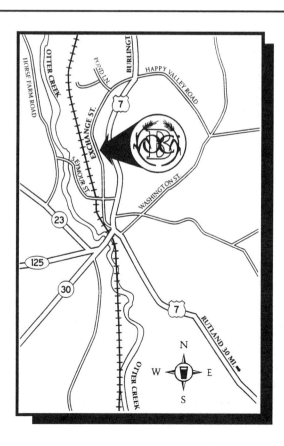

Jasper Murdock's Alehouse at the Norwich Inn

The Haunted Inn

Funny, I could swear I heard footsteps behind me. More than one visitor to the Norwich Inn has said that to him or herself only to find no one behind them as they turned to look. In fact, if you just wait, the sound of footsteps will pass right on by you. And if you don't believe it, just ask Sally Wilson, the innkeeper. She'll tell you that Old Ma Walker, innkeeper at the Norwich during the early part of this century is dead, but definitely not gone.

Perhaps Mrs. Walker is up and out of her cellar haunts more regularly now that beers and ales are being brewed and served legally at the Norwich Inn. It seems that back during Prohibition, Ma Walker bootlegged out of the cellar to the locals, especially the fine young men from nearby Dartmouth College. A photocopy of the guest register for the years 1924-27 is on display (the original is in the local archives) is decorated with lots of little drawings including one notable picture of a gentleman holding a beer stein.

Colonel Jasper Murdock built a huge mansion on this site in 1797 and he must have been a hospitable character, because he took in guests right from the start. Norwich, first settled in 1766 in the beautiful Connecticut River Valley, was situated on a stagecoach route out of Boston. The inn served as a tavern and rest stop for many a thirsty, hungry and tired traveler. When Murdock was gone the property became primarily a tavern and inn and has had dozens of owners and proprietors. Known variously as the Norwich Hotel, Curtis Hotel, The Union House, and the Newton Inn, the little tavern gained quite a reputation over

the years, particularly among tourists and coaching parties destined for the White Mountains.

The Norwich Inn was the first tavern in Vermont to entertain a Chief Executive of the United States. On July 22, 1817, President James Monroe visited the Inn, and while here he addressed the townspeople of Norwich and "partook of a dinner, prepared . . . in handsome style."

In 1889 a fire gutted the inn, the carriage house, and several adjacent buildings. The owners quickly rebuilt, and a year later Main Street had a lovely Victorian inn with a broad porch, gingerbread trim, and a central turret. Much of the Victorian charm has been lost in subsequent "facelifts" by well intentioned, but "architecturally impaired" owners, but all will be restored to its former splendor when Sally and Tim Wilson, the current owners, are finished.

Sally has already done great things on the inside, redecorating the rooms of the fifteen-guestroom inn as well as the carriage house rooms. The parlor is a charming and inviting room with its Victorian settee and side chairs set around ornately carved marble-topped tables. A 1918 Edison phonograph is cranked for the asking and provides crackly music and lots of conversation material. In the cooler months of the year the fireplace welcomes visitors and invites them to sit a spell. There is also a library on the first floor for those who want a quiet place to read and relax.

The dining room is formal with striped paper above the chair rails, mauve carpeting, and fresh flowers on the tables which are set with contrasting tablecloths and starched, fan-folded napkins. A sunroom just off the dining room is a bit more casual in atmosphere and serves as the breakfast room for the inn.

Jasper Murdock's Alehouse, a tiny pub with seating for 30 is a straight shot from the front door. The bar, complete with brass foot rail, seats just seven and is on the right as you enter. The atmosphere here is less Victorian than elsewhere, with ladderback chairs, shutters on the windows, and a marvelous collection of antiques and other interesting things on display. Green walls above a white chair rail show off prints four posters from a 1914 YMCA promoting thrift, framed game boards, two banjos and a rack of maps which once hung in a schoolroom in Central Square, New York. A shelf which runs along the ceiling is loaded with a curious assortment of old bottles.

Downstairs is the Ranger Room, a granite-walled banquet and meeting room where Old Ma Walker used to play hostess to Dartmouth fraternity events. The room is named after Rogers Rangers, a group of highly effective scouts for the British Army during the French and Indian War (1754-1763). The band, led by Robert Rogers, crashed their rafts in a nearby waterfall on the Connecticut River. Ma Walker's bootlegging operation supposedly took place from this room which has access to a sub-cellar via a trap door.

Jasper Murdock's Alehouse attracts the tourists and visitors of Norwich, especially those who are staying at the inn, but its regular crowd comes from the ranks of the local professionals, well-heeled retirees, Dartmouth faculty, and lots of Dartmouth alumni.

The Menu

If a fine dining experience is what you are after than you have come to the right place in Norwich. Sally is a graduate of the Johnson & Wales Culinary Arts Institute and has worked previously at the Kennebunkport Inn in Maine. The lunch and dinner menus change with the seasons and feature a wonderful mix of regional and seasonal ingredients. In the fall the items offered include a smoked salmon plate, Maine crab cakes, pork loin with maple syrup and apples, and Oriental dumplings served with a spicy cider dipping sauce. House brews have been used imaginatively in dishes such as the country pâté, which is made with pork, veal, pistachio, fennel and beer. The venison stew is laced with stout.

The Bill of Fare is shorter in the Jasper Murdock Alehouse, but all of the Inn appetizers are offered here plus the soups and the pub-type entrees such as the chicken pot pie and the beer steamed sausages platters. You can also order a cheeseburger in the pub.

The Brew

Making fifteen-gallon batches in his kitchen, Tim Wilson holds the record for the smallest commercial brewery in the United States. And I guess that would make his ales the rarest in the nation. His entire investment for the brewing equipment and starting inventory was $2,000 (who says you have to have half a million dollars to start a brewery). The equipment was purchased from Pico Brewing Systems in Ypsilanti, Michigan (Tim saw an ad for it one day when he was reading *Zymurgy)*.

Tim is mashing most of his ales, although a few are made from a malt extract, to which he adds specialty grains. He brews in his home, on the stove top. Whole-leaf hops are added to the boil. He then divides each batch into three glass carboys, where it is fermented. The ales are unfiltered, but clarified with gelatin finings. Next Tim racks the ales into Cornelius kegs, to which CO_2 top pressure is added. The brewing process is watched over by the two brewery/inn mascots, Barley, a yellow Labrador retriever and Jasper Murdock, a Welsh corgi.

Tim usually has three ales on tap at any given time.

Old Slippery Skin - malty-hoppy aroma; pronounced hop flavor; a little metalic bitterness in the finish and slightly buttery too; very dry and good; Chinook hops used for bittering; an IPA; Old Slippery Skin is a Vermont legend--he was an old bear that used to roam the woods annoying the Indians and settlers in the 1600s and 1700s, they couldn't hunt him down, so they called him Old Slippery Skin

Whistling Pig Red Ale - bright amber or copper; malty aroma; nutty-woody and dry; some buttery flavor; hopped with Fuggles and Goldings

Short and Stout - opaque black; roasted coffee aroma; lots of coffee and a little chocolate flavor too; sweet front, off dry finish; delicious; made with pale, chocolate, and black malts; hopped with Chinook for bittering and aroma

Other ales, not sampled:

Stackpole Porter, Jasper Murdock's Old Ale, Code Seasod Bild Ale (winter), Dr. Bowles' Amber Elixir (named after the innkeeper who rebuilt the inn in 1890), Fuggle & Barleycorn, and Nonesuch Ale (spiced), Wassail (brewed for the holiday season), Pompanoosuc Wheat Beer (named after a nearby river), Screeching Alt (a Kolsch), Yankee Wit (a Belgian witbier)

Barrel of Miscellany

Address: Main Street, corner of Beaver Meadow Road
Norwich, VT 05055

Telephone: (802) 649-1143

Hours: Jasper Murdock Alehouse -- Tuesday - Sunday: 5:00 p.m. - closing
(ales also available in the dining room with lunch)

dining room -- breakfast: Tuesday - Friday: 7:30 a.m. - 9:30 a.m.
Saturday & Sunday: 8:00 a.m. - 10:00 a.m.

-- lunch: Tuesday - Saturday: 11:30 a.m. - 2:00 p.m.
Sunday brunch: 11:30 - 2:00 p.m.

-- dinner & pub food: Tuesday - Saturday: 5:30 p.m. - 9:00 p.m.
Sunday: 5:30 p.m. - 8:00 p.m.

No meals or ales Monday

Credit cards: American Express, Visa

darts -- handicapped access -- dining room is nonsmoking -- TV -- free off-street parking

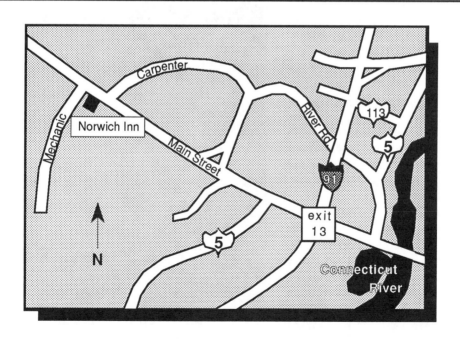

Catamount Brewing

TQM + Zymurgy =

Brewer Stephen Mason believes in total quality. For him, anything less than the best is unacceptable. An example of his enslavement to quality occurred during the start up of the brewery; he spent three months doing practice brews, while investors became apoplectic as they watched their investments literally go down the drain. All this was to ensure that the kinks would be ironed out before the first batch ever hit the market. Steve wanted to make sure the first impression made by Catamount was a good one.

Tuned up and ready to go, the beer hit the market on February 1, 1987, only two months after the first New England craft brewery had opened, Geary's Brewing of Portland, Maine. Catamount was the first to open in Vermont during the 20th century, the last three having closed way back in 1893. Steve gave the Vermonters a double-barreled blast with his Gold and Amber, both packaged in 12-oz. bottles. The Gold was inspired by New England ales from years gone by. The Amber had roots in the English pale ale. The next year the pair was joined by Catamount Porter, originally brewed as a limited edition Christmas beer. It was so popular, Steve made it an all-season beer, and came out with a different Christmas beer in 1989. As Catamount's reputation for quality and consistency grew, other brewing companies approached them to contract their brews. First there was Post Road Ale for the Massachusetts market,

followed by many more, including Frank Jones beers, Newman's Saratoga, Le Garde, Ethan Allen Ale, and Pike's Place Pale Ale.

So, how did all this come about, and why, of all places, in White River Junction? Steve, originally from Detroit, began homebrewing

Stephen Mason

while a college student at the University of Michigan in 1975. He continued to make homebrew for about five years, gradually honing his skills and learning new techniques. He also began to read about beer and how it was made. After graduation he moved to Boston, where he became very interested in the many imported beers which were on the market. In 1979 Steve went to grad school in health and physical education at Norwich University in Northfield, Vermont. After receiving his masters degree, he became a part-time teacher, coach, and fitness instructor at Norwich University and also taught at an elementary school in Montpelier.

By now he had heard about the craft brewing fad and had even sampled some of their beers, which piqued his interest. Then, in 1982 Steve visited the Newman Brewery in Albany, New York, the first craft brewery in the East. This experience convinced him that he could open his own brewery. The next year he started doing research on licensing, equipment, and other factors pertinent to opening a brewery.

In 1983 Steve arranged to do a short apprenticeship at the Swannell Brewery, a craft brewery, outside of London (in Kings Langley, Herts.). It was a mind-awakening experience, and he got his first chance to try cask conditioned ales (his favorite was Brakespear's Ordinary). He also did several day-long brewing sessions with other breweries and brewpubs in the area, sampling hundreds of examples of real ales.

When he returned in the fall of '83, Steve teamed up with Allen Davis to found the brewery. At the time Davis was running an artist-in-residence program in Vermont for the National Endowment for the Arts. Davis is still with Catamount today as a member of the board and a major shareholder, but is no longer involved in the operation of the brewery.

From there it took more than three years to get the brewery going. The pair looked for brewery locations all over the state of Vermont, finally settling on White River Junction because of its central location in terms of markets and transportation facilities, good water supply, and availability of financial assistance from the town. They located an old Swift meat packing plant, built circa 1910, which was the right price and seemed to be ideal for what they wanted to do.

They chose the name Catamount because of its strong regional identity and an interesting bit of trivia: Green Mountain Boys Ethan and Ira Allen used to drink ale at a tavern called the Catamount in nearby Bennington.

They initially raised $425,000 from a small group of Vermont investors, a Small Business Administration loan, and a low-interest community development loan. Unfortunately, the building was not as suited for their brewery as they had initially thought and renovation took more time and money than expected. They patched equipment together from different sources, but decided to buy new fermenters and conditioning tanks from JV Northwest. By the time Steve was doing his test batches, the CBC was running out of money. But, as Steve says, "We managed to rustle up another $185,000."

With the product's reputation for quality and flavor, production increased steadily, and CBC has been adding on and improving equipment constantly. It's sales territory now includes all of New England and beyond.

The Brew

Catamount is running near capacity, brewing double batches four times a week in its 36-barrel mash tun and direct, flame-fired brew kettle. A single step infusion mash is employed. After brewing, the wort is transferred to a 72-barrel, closed fermenter. The malt, primarily American six-row, is milled in house. Only American, whole-leaf hops are used. Steve says the water is very good, coming from an artesian-fed well. Gypsum is added as required. A diatomaceous earth filtration system is employed, followed by a sterile filtration.

During 1993 Catamount produced 13,000 barrels of beer. About three quarters of their output was in bottled beers. Expansion is under way and they plan to increase capacity to 20,000 barrels annually. Steve is planning to release a summer seasonal beer in 1994.

Catamount beers tend to have a hoppy, bitter, dry character with a long finish. Currently there are three regulars and three seasonals.

Catamount Gold - brilliant gold; fresh hop aroma; fairly pronounced hop character; light body; slightly grainy, very dry and crisp; dry maltiness; nice bitter dry finish; very clean taste; generous amounts of whole-leaf Willamette hops are used; a North American style blonde ale (1.046)

Catamount Amber - bright copper; medium body; dry maltiness with nice bitter-hoppy character; very dry, almost astringent; made with pale, Caramel 40, and carapils malt; whole-leaf Galena hops for bittering and Willamettes for aroma; the brewery's best selling beer; it is said to be a traditional British style pale ale, but the brewing method, ingredients and character of the beer suggest an American pale ale to me (1.048)

Catamount Porter - light brown; smooth and malty with a nice roasted barley character to it; dry; made with pale, Caramel 40, carapils, and black malt and roasted barley; whole-leaf Galena and Cascade hops are used (1.042)

-- seasonal --

Catamount Oktoberfest - dark amber; sweet malt entry with some caramelized malt; drying finish; well rounded and smooth; made primarily with two-row malt and a true lager yeast; blend of whole-leaf Hallertau and Tettnang hops used; available in the fall

Catamount Bock - light brown; full bodied; fairly sweet maltiness counterbalanced by a hoppy character; available in late winter and early spring; first appeared in 1993

Catamount Christmas Ale - bright copper; rich, malty, mouth-watering aroma; full bodied; truly delicious finish with an excellent balance of malt and hops; rich and warming; made exclusively with whole-leaf Cascades which are added in the lauter tun; first came out in 1989, an IPA (1.058)

Barrel of Miscellany

Address:	58 South Main Street White River Junction, VT 05001
Telephone:	(802) 296-2248
Tours:	July - October, Monday - Saturday, 11:00 a.m., 1:00 p.m., and 3:00 p.m. Sunday, 1:00 and 3:00 p.m. November - June, Saturday, 11:00 a.m., 1:00 p.m., and 3:00 p.m.
Store Hours:	Monday - Saturday, 9:00 a.m. - 5:00 p.m.; Sunday, 1:00- 5:00 p.m.
Beer to go:	12 oz. bottles, six packs, and cases
Availability:	throughout New England

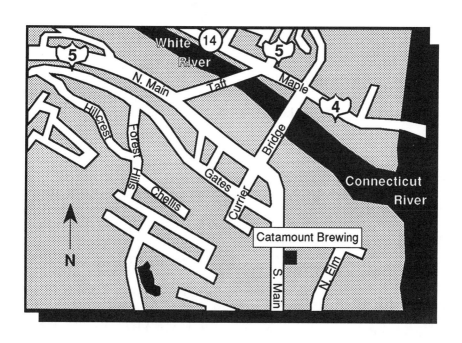

Brewery Index

About the Author

When Steve Johnson lived in Branford, Connecticut, in the 1970s, he didn't even know what good beer was. And with good reason, during that period American beer had sunk to its lowest level in terms of variety and flavor. Since then, beer has become his passion. He discovered good beer in October of 1982, when he visited his first English pub. When he tried an ale, it was love at first taste. Since then he has tried as many brands, learned as much about beer, and collected as much breweriana as possible. During the last seven years, Steve has traveled more than 90,000 miles throughout the United States, Canada, Mexico, England, and Scotland searching for good beer and good places in which to drink it.

Steve quickly learned that the best place to drink beer is at the source, i.e., the brewery. This, in turn, lead to his love of brewpubs. Eager to share his discoveries, in 1987 Steve began writing and publishing the *World Beer Review*, a bi-monthly newsletter devoted to the pursuit of good beer.

Realizing the need for a guidebook to the new breweries, in 1991 Steve published the first edition of *On Tap: the Guide to U.S. Brewpubs*. In 1993 he published an expanded, second edition of *On Tap*, this one including Canadian breweries as well.

In the spring of 1994 the newsletter changed title to *On Tap, the Newsletter*, and became a supplement to the book, aimed at the true fanatic, who wants to keep abreast of the latest developments in the world of brewpubs and craft breweries.

Steve supplements his beer avocation with a library profession; he is a librarian at Clemson University. While living in Connecticut, he worked in the Catalog Department of the Sterling Memorial Library at Yale University. Steve now lives in the town of Clemson, South Carolina, with his wife, Maria, whom he met while serving with the Peace Corps in Costa Rica.

What is Steve's favorite beer? "Well, that is hard to say, there are so many!" Having been weaned from beers which were stale, thin, tasteless, over carbonated, and served too cold; he tends to like those which are fresh, thick, and assertive--and he likes them served warm enough so he can taste them.